African American Eras

Contemporary Times

African American Eras

Contemporary Times

Volume 2:
Communications and Media
Demographics
Education

U·X·L
A part of Gale, Cengage Learning

GALE
CENGAGE Learning™

Detroit • New York • San Francisco • New Haven, Conn • Waterville, Maine • London

GALE
CENGAGE Learning™

African American Eras:
Contemporary Times

Product Managers: Meggin Condino
and Julia Furtaw

Project Editor: Rebecca Parks

Rights Acquisition and Management:
Leitha Etheridge-Sims, Margaret
Abendroth

Composition: Evi Abou-El-Seoud

Manufacturing: Rita Wimberley

Imaging: John Watkins

Product Design: Pamela Galbreath

For product information and technology assistance, contact us at
Gale Customer Support, 1-800-877-4253.
For permission to use material from this text or product,
submit all requests online at **www.cengage.com/permissions.**
Further permissions questions can be emailed to
permissionrequest@cengage.com.

Cover photographs reproduced by permission of Alamy (photo of gospel choir), Getty Images (photo of Tavis Smiley), and Corbis (photo of bell hooks).

While every effort has been made to ensure the reliability of the information presented in this publication, Gale, a part of Cengage Learning, does not guarantee the accuracy of the data contained herein. Gale accepts no payment for listing; and inclusion in the publication of any organization, agency, institution, publication, service, or individual does not imply endorsement of the editors or publisher. Errors brought to the attention of the publisher and verified to the satisfaction of the publisher will be corrected in future editions.

LIBRARY OF CONGRESS CATALOGING-IN-PUBLICATION DATA

African American eras : contemporary times.
    v. ; cm.
    Includes bibliographical references and index.
    ISBN-13: 978-1-4144-3591-6 (set)
    ISBN-10: 1-4144-3591-6 (set)
    ISBN-13: 978-1-4144-3592-3 (vol. 1)
    ISBN-10: 1-4144-3592-4 (vol. 1)
    [etc.]
    1. African Americans--History--1964---Juvenile literature.

E185.615.A5923 2010
973'.0496073--dc22   2009047215

Gale
27500 Drake
Farmington Hills, MI 48331-3535

ISBN-13: 978-1-4144-3591-6 (set)   ISBN-10: 1-4144-3591-6 (set)
ISBN-13: 978-1-4144-3592-3 (Vol. 1)   ISBN-10: 1-4144-3592-4 (Vol. 1)
ISBN-13: 978-1-4144-3593-0 (Vol. 2)   ISBN-10: 1-4144-3593-2 (Vol. 2)
ISBN-13: 978-1-4144-3594-7 (Vol. 3)   ISBN-10: 1-4144-3594-0 (Vol. 3)
ISBN-13: 978-1-4144-3595-4 (Vol. 4)   ISBN-10: 1-4144-3595-9 (Vol. 4)

This title is also available as an e-book.
ISBN-13: 978-1-4144-3704-0 ISBN-10: 1-4144-3704-8
Contact your Gale, a part of Cengage Learning sales representative for ordering information.

Printed in the United States of America
1 2 3 4 5 6 7 14 13 12 11 10

Table of Contents

Reader's Guide . . . . *xix*

Chronology . . . . *xxiii*

Era Overview . . . . *xxix*

VOLUME 1

chapter one *Activism and Reform* *1*

Chronology *2*

Overview *5*

Headline Makers *8*

Mandy Carter *8*

Benjamin Chavis *10*

Eldridge Cleaver *14*

Angela Davis *18*

Marian Wright Edelman *21*

Kweisi Mfume *24*

Al Sharpton *28*

Cornel West *31*

Topics in the News *34*

   Affirmative Action Takes Aim at
     Institutional Racism *34*

   Black Panther Party Is Founded *36*

   Martin Luther King Jr.'s Assassination
     Shocks the Nation *42*

   Jesse Jackson Founds the Rainbow/PUSH
     Coalition *44*

   Womanism Gives Voice to Black
     Women's Struggles *47*

   Support Builds for Slavery Reparations . . . *49*

   The Black Community Reacts to Rodney
     King Verdict *52*

   Louis Farrakhan Organizes the Million
     Man March *54*

   Hurricane Katrina Highlights Racial
     Inequalities *56*

   Jena Six Case Stirs Racial Sentencing
     Debate *59*

   African Americans Fight for Gay and
     Lesbian Rights *61*

Primary Sources *64*

   The Black Panther Party's 10-Point
     Platform and Program (1966) *64*

   Robert F. Kennedy's Speech Announcing
     the Death of Martin Luther
     King Jr. (1968) *66*

   Commission to Study Reparation
     Proposals for African Americans Act (1989) *68*

Research and Activity Ideas *71*

For More Information *72*

chapter two   *The Arts* *75*

Chronology *76*

Overview *78*

Headline Makers *80*

   Maya Angelou *80*

Jean-Michel Basquiat *83*

Octavia Butler *85*

Savion Glover *86*

Bill T. Jones *88*

Wynton Marsalis *89*

Toni Morrison *93*

Suzan-Lori Parks *97*

Faith Ringgold *99*

Ntozake Shange *102*

Alice Walker *104*

Topics in the News *106*

Black Arts Movement Showcases African
American Artistic Expression *106*

Dance Theatre of Harlem Opens Its Doors . . *110*

Black Playwrights Shake Up the World
of Theater *112*

Free Jazz and Traditional Jazz Both Flower . . *116*

Organization of Black American Culture
Inspires Black Visual Artists *118*

Graffiti Becomes a New Kind of Folk Art . . *121*

African American Poets Reach New Heights . . *123*

Black Women Authors Find Mainstream
Success *125*

Opera Opens Up to African Americans . . . *128*

Primary Sources *131*

SAMO Graffiti Messages (1970s) *131*

Nobel Prize Committee Honors Toni
Morrison (1993) *132*

Research and Activity Ideas *134*

For More Information *135*

chapter three *Business and Industry* *137*

Chronology *138*

Overview *141*

Headline Makers *144*

Ursula Burns *144*

Kenneth I. Chenault *145*

Sean Combs *148*

Janice Bryant Howroyd *151*

Daymond John *153*

Robert L. Johnson *155*

Richard Parsons *157*

Russell Simmons *159*

David L. Steward *161*

Oprah Winfrey *162*

Topics in the News *166*

Affirmative Action Programs Rise,
    then Decline *166*

Number of African American CEOs Grows . . *170*

Black Entrepreneurs Introduce
    Traditional Foods to New Fans *173*

Professional Development Organization
    Founded for African American
    Career Women *178*

Wage Gap Persists between African
    Americans and Whites *180*

Collapse of the Automobile Industry
    Devastates African Americans *183*

Modern Economy Challenges African
    Americans *186*

Primary Sources *189*

The First Federal Affirmative Action
    Policy (1965) *189*

Supreme Court's *Bakke* Decision (1978)   . . . *191*

Research and Activity Ideas *195*

For More Information *196*

VOLUME 2

chapter four   *Communications and Media*   . *199*

Chronology *200*

Overview *202*

Headline Makers 205

    Mara Brock Akil 205

    Jayson Blair 206

    Ed Bradley 207

    Farai Chideya 208

    Don Cornelius 210

    Bill Cosby 211

    Earl G. Graves Sr. 213

    Gwen Ifill 215

    Tom Joyner 216

    Spike Lee 218

    Robert C. Maynard 220

    Michele Norris 221

    Shonda Rhimes 222

    Bernard Shaw 224

    Tavis Smiley 225

    Will Smith 227

    Susan L. Taylor 228

    Denzel Washington 229

Topics in the News 232

    African American Media Challenged
       by Modern Times 232

    Studios Turn to "Blaxploitation" Films . . .239

    Black Musicians Cross Over
       to Film 242

    Black Comedians Thrive in Film in the
       1970s and 1980s 243

    A New Generation of Black Filmmakers
       Finds Success 245

    Television Opens Up to Black Stories
       and Characters 250

    Cable Networks Target African
       Americans 254

Primary Sources 258

    Do The Right Thing Movie Review
       (1989) 258

Testimony on the Impact of the 1996
    Telecommunications Act on Black
    Radio (2006) *260*

Research and Activity Ideas *263*

For More Information *264*

chapter five   *Demographics* *267*

Chronology *268*

Overview *271*

Headline Makers *274*

    Roland G. Fryer *274*

    bell hooks *276*

    Mildred Loving *280*

Topics in the News *284*

    The 2000 Census Provides a Snapshot
       of African American Demographics . . .*284*

    Drugs and Gangs Plague African
       American Communities *285*

    African American Family Life
       Undergoes Changes *291*

    A Black Middle Class Emerges *297*

    Great Migrations Change the
       Demographics of U.S. Cities *300*

Primary Sources *304*

    Supreme Court's *Loving v. Virginia*
       Decision (1967) *304*

    Ten Places of 100,000 or More
       Population with the Highest Percentage
       of Blacks or African Americans: 2000 . .*306*

Research and Activity Ideas *308*

For More Information *309*

chapter six   *Education* *311*

Chronology *312*

Overview *315*

Headline Makers *318*

   Joe Clark *318*

   Johnnetta B. Cole *321*

   Michael Eric Dyson *326*

   Harry Edwards *330*

   Henry Louis Gates Jr. *333*

   Rod Paige *338*

Topics in the News *343*

   Black Studies Programs Are Established
     in Higher Education *343*

   Courts Order School Busing to Achieve
     Integration *346*

   School Administrators Propose Ebonics
     to Aid Black Students *352*

   Charter Schools Provide an Alternative
     to Minority Students *354*

   States Take Over Failing Inner-City
     Schools *358*

   Historically Black Colleges and
     Universities Face Challenges *363*

Primary Sources *369*

   Supreme Court's *Green v. County
     School Board of Kent County*
     Decision (1968) *369*

   The No Child Left Behind Act Statement
     of Purpose (2001) *371*

   Impact of the No Child Left Behind Act
     (2004) *373*

Research and Activity Ideas *375*

For More Information *376*

VOLUME 3

chapter seven   *Government and Politics* *379*

Chronology *380*

Overview *383*

Headline Makers *385*

    Shirley Chisholm *385*

    Keith M. Ellison *387*

    Barbara Jordan *390*

    Cynthia McKinney *392*

    Carol Moseley-Braun *395*

    Barack Obama *397*

    Condoleezza Rice *399*

    J. C. Watts Jr. *402*

    L. Douglas Wilder *404*

Topics in the News *407*

    Black Voters Play Important Role
        in Elections *407*

    Walter Washington Becomes "Father
        of Modern Washington" *409*

    Congressional Black Caucus Increases
        Politicians' Clout *411*

    Detroit's Mayors Face a City in Crisis *414*

    Black Leadership Forum Exerts
        Influence *418*

    Martin Luther King Day Declared a
        Federal Holiday *419*

    Harold Washington Tries to Reform
        Chicago Politics *420*

    Barack Obama Becomes First Black
        President *422*

Primary Sources *428*

    Barbara Jordan's Opening Statement to
        the House Judiciary Committee,
        Proceedings on the Impeachment
        of Richard Nixon (1974) *428*

    President-Elect Barack Obama's Victory
        Speech (2008) *430*

Research and Activity Ideas *433*

For More Information *434*

chapter eight **Health and Medicine** *435*

Chronology *436*

Overview *439*

Headline Makers *442*

    Patricia Bath *442*

    Keith L. Black *448*

    Clive Callender *450*

    Benjamin Carson *454*

    Joycelyn Elders *460*

    Levi Watkins Jr. *467*

Topics in the News *472*

    Tuskegee Syphilis Study Outrages Black
        Community *472*

    African American Poverty Leads to
        Health Disparities *474*

    Breast Cancer Hits African American
        Women Harder *478*

    HIV/AIDS Disproportionately Harms
        African Americans *482*

    Obesity Epidemic Impacts African Americans .*486*

    African Americans Hope for Sickle Cell
        Anemia Cure *488*

    National Black Women's Health Imperative
        Advocates for Health Reform *492*

Primary Sources *494*

    Tuskegee Syphilis Study Apology (1997) . *494*

    Sally Satel's Congressional Testimony on
        Minority Healthcare Reform (2008) . . .*496*

Research and Activity Ideas *500*

For More Information *501*

chapter nine **Law and Justice** *503*

Chronology *504*

Overview *507*

Headline Makers *510*

Janice Rogers Brown *510*

Lani Guinier *512*

Anita Hill *515*

Eric Holder *517*

Thurgood Marshall *519*

Charles Moose *524*

Constance Baker Motley *526*

Charles J. Ogletree Jr. *528*

Clarence Thomas *531*

Topics in the News *536*

The Voting Rights Act of 1965 Ends
  Racial Discrimination in Voting *536*

Major Court Cases Define Affirmative
  Action *540*

Major Civil Rights Legislation Promotes
  Equality *544*

Police Brutality Sparks Public Outcry *546*

Controversy Erupts at Clarence
  Thomas's Confirmation Hearing . . . *549*

High-Profile Cases Spark Debate About
  Hate Crime Laws *553*

Racial Profiling Generates Controversy . . . *556*

Crime Emerges as a Major Issue for
  African American Communities *558*

Primary Sources *562*

Bakke Dissenting Opinion (1978) *562*

Grutter v. Bollinger Dissenting
  Opinion (2003) *564*

Research and Activity Ideas *568*

For More Information *569*

VOLUME 4

chapter ten *Military* 571

Chronology *572*

Overview *575*

Headline Makers . . . . *.577*

    Clifford Alexander . . . . *.577*

    Daniel "Chappie" James Jr. . . . . *.580*

    Hazel Johnson . . . . *.586*

    Colin Powell . . . . *.588*

    J. Paul Reason . . . . *.595*

Topics in the News . . . . *.600*

    Vietnam War Disillusions Black Soldiers . *.600*

    Boxer Muhammad Ali Refuses the Draft . . *.602*

    Racial Tensions Prompt Changes in the
        Military . . . . *.606*

    The Gesell Committee Addresses
        Discrimination in the Military . . . . *.610*

    Colin Powell Oversees Gulf War . . . . . *.612*

    African American Participation in the
        Military Rises and Falls . . . . *.613*

Primary Sources . . . . *.617*

    Colin Powell Makes the Case for War
        in Iraq to the United Nations (2003) . *.617*

    Clifford Alexander Defends the Rights
        of Gays in the Military (2009) . . . . *.620*

Research and Activity Ideas . . . . *.624*

For More Information . . . . *.625*

chapter eleven   *Popular Culture* 627

Chronology . . . . *.628*

Overview . . . . *.631*

Headline Makers . . . . *.633*

    Arthur Ashe . . . . *.633*

    Barry Bonds . . . . *.634*

    James Brown . . . . *.636*

    Aretha Franklin . . . . *.638*

    Jimi Hendrix . . . . *.639*

    Michael Jackson . . . . *.643*

    Michael Jordan . . . . *.648*

    Kimora Lee Simmons . . . . *.650*

Venus and Serena Williams *652*

Stevie Wonder *653*

Tiger Woods *656*

Topics in the News *658*

African Americans Break through in
Golf and Tennis *658*

African American Music Goes
Mainstream *659*

Black Power Salute Causes Stir at
Olympics *662*

The Afro Hairstyle Makes Bold Statement . *665*

Hank Aaron Breaks Home Run Record . . *667*

Funk and Soul Give Way to Disco *669*

The Pop Music Color Barrier Comes
Down *672*

African American Culture Influences
Fashion *676*

Rap and Hip Hop Become Cultural
Phenomena *680*

Black Coaches Make Progress in Sports . . *684*

Primary Sources *687*

"Say It Loud—I'm Black and I'm Proud"
by James Brown (1968) *687*

Muhammad Ali's Pre-Fight
Comments (1974) *688*

"Ladies First" by Queen Latifah (1989) . . *688*

Tommie Smith Reflects on His Black
Power Salute at the 1968 Olympics
(2007) *690*

Research and Activity Ideas *692*

For More Information *693*

chapter twelve **Religion** 695

Chronology *696*

Overview *699*

Headline Makers *702*

Juanita Bynum *702*

James H. Cone 704

Louis Farrakhan 706

Wilton Gregory 709

T. D. Jakes 712

Bernice A. King 714

Vashti Murphy McKenzie 715

Anna Pauline Murray 718

Iyanla Vanzant 720

Jeremiah Wright 722

Topics in the News 725

African American Religious Leaders
Impact Politics 725

Black Judaism Remains Diverse 728

Nation of Islam Offers Different
Approach to Equality 733

The Civil Rights Movement Sparks
Black Theology 735

The Womanist Theology Emerges 739

Black Women Take Leadership Roles
in the Church 740

African Americans Challenge the
Catholic Church 742

The Issue of Gay Rights Strains Black
Churches 744

Contemporary Times See Changes in
the Black Church 746

Primary Sources 748

"Go Down, Moses" Lyrics
(Date Unknown) 748

The Nation of Islam Responds to the
September 11th Terrorist
Attacks (2001) 749

Research and Activity Ideas 754

For More Information 755

chapter thirteen   *Science and Technology* 757

Chronology *758*

Overview *761*

Headline Makers *763*

Guion "Guy" Bluford *763*

George R. Carruthers *767*

Christine Darden *771*

Philip Emeagwali *775*

Shirley Ann Jackson *778*

Mae Jemison *784*

Topics in the News *788*

Airline Industry Employs African
Americans *788*

NASA Is Integrated *790*

Inventions by African Americans
Improve Lives *797*

African Americans Suffer Knowledge
Gap in Information Age *800*

Black Scientists Promote Science
Education for Minorities *803*

African Americans Shape the Age of
Information Technology *806*

Primary Sources *813*

Senate Testimony of William H. Gray
on the Digital Divide and
Minority-Serving Institutions
(2002) *813*

Charles Bolden's Confirmation
Hearing Testimony for NASA
Appointment (2009) *815*

Research and Activity Ideas *819*

For More Information *820*

Where to Learn More . . . . *xxxiii*

Index . . . . *xxxv*

Reader's Guide

U•X•L *African American Eras: Contemporary Times* provides a broad overview of African American history and culture from 1965 through the first decade of the twenty-first century. The four-volume set is broken into thirteen chapters. Each chapter covers a major subject area as it relates to the African American community. Readers have the opportunity to engage with history in multiple ways within the chapter, beginning with a chronology of major events related to that subject area and a chapter-specific overview of developments in African American history. They are next introduced to the men and women who shaped that history through biographies of prominent African Americans, as well as topical entries on major events related to the chapter's subject area. Primary sources provide a firsthand perspective of the people and events discussed in the chapter, and readers have the opportunity to engage with the content further in a research and activity ideas section.

The complete list of chapters is as follows:

- Activism and Reform
- The Arts
- Business and Industry
- Communications and Media
- Demographics
- Education

- Government and Politics

- Health and Medicine

- Law and Justice

- Military

- Popular Culture

- Religion

- Science and Technology

These chapters are then divided into seven sections:

Chronology: A timeline of significant events in the African American community within the scope of the chapter's subject matter.

Overview: A summary of major developments and trends in the African American community as they relate to the subject matter of the chapter.

★ **Headline Makers:** Biographies of key African Americans and their achievements within the scope of the chapter's subject matter.

❖ **Topics in the News:** A series of topical essays describing significant events and developments important to the African American community within the scope of the chapter's subject matter.

◉ **Primary Sources:** Historical documents that provide a firsthand perspective on African American history as it relates to the content of the chapter.

Research and Activity Ideas: Brief suggestions for activities and research opportunities that will further engage the reader with the subject matter.

☛ **For More Information:** A section that lists books, periodicals, and Web sites directing the reader to further information about the events and people covered in the chapter.

OTHER FEATURES

The content of U•X•L *African American Eras: Contemporary Times* is illustrated with 240 black-and-white images that bring the events and people discussed to life. Sidebar boxes also expand on items of high-interest to readers. Concluding each volume is a general bibliography of books and Web sites, and a thorough subject index that allows readers to easily locate the events, people, and places discussed throughout the set.

COMMENTS AND SUGGESTIONS

We welcome your comments on U•X•L *African American Eras: Contemporary Times* and suggestions for other history topics to consider. Please write: Editor, U•X•L *African American Eras: Contemporary Times*, 27500 Drake Rd., Farmington Hills, MI 48331-3535; call toll-free: 1-800-877-4253; or send e-mail via http://www.galegroup.com.

Chronology

1965 **February 21** Black nationalist Malcolm X is killed in New York by a member of the Nation of Islam, a religious and political faction he had recently left.

1965 **March 21** African Americans begin a four-day march from Selma, Alabama, to the state capital of Montgomery, Alabama, to protest the government's interference with voting rights.

1965 **April 9** Congress enacts the Elementary and Secondary Education Act of 1965 (ESEA), a landmark legislative act intended to close the achievement gap between students from low-income families— a large percentage of whom are minorities—and those from privileged families.

1965 **July 2** The federal government establishes the Equal Employment Opportunity Commission (EEOC) to investigate discrimination complaints in the workplace and prevent retaliation for reporting workplace discrimination.

1965 **August 6** President Lyndon B. Johnson signs the Voting Rights Act into law. The act outlaws many practices common in southern voting precincts that were designed to keep African Americans from exercising their right to vote.

1965 **August 11** Riots begin in the largely African American Watts neighborhood in Los Angeles and end six days later with thirty-four people dead.

1966 Huey Newton and Bobby Seale found the Black Panther Party for Self-Defense in Oakland, California.

1967 **June 12** In *Loving v. Virginia,* the Supreme Court unanimously rules that a Virginia state law banning marriages between people of different races is unconstitutional.

1967 **October 2** Thurgood Marshall is confirmed as the first African American justice on the U.S. Supreme Court.

1968 President Lyndon B. Johnson signs the Civil Rights Act of 1968, making it illegal to discriminate against African Americans and other minorities in the sale, rental, or financing of housing.

1968 **April 4** Prominent African American minister and civil rights leader Martin Luther King Jr. is assassinated.

1968 **November 5** Shirley Chisholm becomes the first African American woman elected to the U.S. Congress. She represents New York's Twelfth District as a Democrat.

1969 Alfred Day Hershey becomes the first African American to win a Nobel Prize in Physiology or Medicine (which he shares with two other researchers) for his research on the structure of viruses and how they reproduce themselves.

1969 Arthur Mitchell and Karel Shook found the Dance Theatre of Harlem, which is credited with bringing ballet to African American audiences and with bringing African American performers to ballet.

1970 Maya Angelou publishes her landmark autobiography *I Know Why the Caged Bird Sings.*

1970 **May** *Essence* magazine becomes the first monthly magazine for African American women.

1970 **September 17** Flip Wilson becomes the first African American comedian to host his own television program *The Flip Wilson Show.*

1971 **February** The Congressional Black Caucus is founded, consisting of thirteen members.

1971 **April 20** In *Swann v. Charlotte-Mecklenburg Board of Education,* the Supreme Court rules that school districts in the South can be required to bus children to schools in different neighborhoods in order to achieve racial integration.

1972 Willie Hobbs Moore is the first African American woman ever to receive a doctorate in physics when she graduates from the University of Michigan.

1972 Shirley Chisholm becomes the first black woman to run for president of the United States from one of the major parties.

1972 **April 21** Astrophysicist George E. Carruthers invents the ultraviolet camera/spectrograph. The device is placed on the surface of the moon and records more than two hundred ultraviolet pictures of Earth's atmosphere, newly discovered stars, and the Milky Way galaxy.

1972 **July 25** Associated Press reporter Jean Heller exposes the Tuskegee Syphilis Study, an unethical government study on the effects of untreated syphilis on poor black men through the Tuskegee Institute. Doctors never told the men they had syphilis, and withheld treatment that would have cured them.

1974 **April 8** Baseball player Hank Aaron beats Babe Ruth's record for most career home runs—a record once thought unbreakable—when he hits home run number 715.

1975 **July 5** Arthur Ashe becomes the first African American man to win the Wimbledon singles tennis championship, defeating Jimmy Connors.

1975 **September 1** Upon his promotion to four-star general, the Air Force's Daniel "Chappie" James becomes the first African American to achieve the rank.

1977 **February 14** Clifford Alexander Jr. becomes the first African American to serve as secretary of the Army.

1978 Louis Farrakhan reestablishes the Nation of Islam under the teachings of Elijah Muhammad.

1978 The Supreme Court decides in *Regents of the University of California v. Bakke* that university admissions programs cannot set aside a certain number of slots for minority students.

1979 **September 1** Hazel Johnson becomes the first African American woman to attain the rank of general in the U.S. Army.

1980 **January 25** Black Entertainment Television (BET) becomes the first television cable network for African Americans.

1982 **November 30** Michael Jackson releases the album *Thriller*. The album is the number-one seller in the nation for thirty-seven consecutive weeks.

1983   African Americans make up 20 percent of all new enlisted personnel in the armed forces despite making up just over 10 percent of the civilian population in the United States.

1984   Trumpeter Wynton Marsalis becomes the first recording artist to win Grammy Awards for best classical soloist and best jazz soloist in the same year.

1984   African American civil rights activist Jesse Jackson runs for president of the United States for the first time, but does not ultimately win the Democratic nomination. He would run for president, and again fail to secure the nomination, in 1988.

1984   **September 20**   *The Cosby Show* debuts. The program about an affluent African American family living in Brooklyn becomes one of the most successful television shows of the 1980s.

1984   **October 26**   Michael Jordan makes his professional basketball debut with the Chicago Bulls. Within a month, he makes the cover of *Sports Illustrated*. He goes on to win the NBA Rookie of the Year award for the 1984–1985 season.

1985   **April 29**   Astronaut Frederick D. Gregory becomes the first African American to pilot a space shuttle.

1985   **September 9**   African American inventor Mark Dean collaborates with Dennis Moeller to create a microcomputer system that paves the way for devices such as keyboards, monitors, and printers to be plugged into the computer and work together at high speeds.

1986   **January 7**   *The Oprah Winfrey Show* debuts. Featuring African American host Oprah Winfrey, it becomes the most popular daytime talk show in the history of American television.

1987   **June 4**   Mae C. Jemison becomes the first African American woman ever admitted into NASA's astronaut training program.

1988   Toni Morrison wins the Pulitzer Prize for her novel *Beloved*.

1989   Democratic representative John Conyers introduces Resolution 40 in Congress, calling for an investigation into the legacy of slavery in America and a consideration of whether reparations, or payments, are warranted for descendants of slaves.

1989   **September 24**   The Reverend Barbara C. Harris becomes the first African American female bishop in the Episcopal Church.

1989   **November 7**   L. Douglas Wilder of Virginia becomes the first African American governor.

1992 Hip-hop promoter Russell Simmons founds Phat Farm, a line of urban-inspired clothing. The same year, the clothing company FUBU begins operations in Queens, New York.

1992 **April 29** The four white police officers charged with police brutality for beating African American motorist Rodney King are acquitted of all charges, sparking a violent uprising in protest in Los Angeles.

1992 **November 3** Carol Moseley-Braun becomes the first African American woman to be elected to the U.S. Senate.

1993 Toni Morrison is awarded the Nobel Prize for Literature, becoming the first African American woman to win the prize.

1993 **September 8** Joycelyn Elders is named the U.S. surgeon general, becoming the first African American and the second female to hold that position.

1995 **February** Physician and astronaut Bernard Harris becomes the first African American to walk in space.

1995 **October 16** Louis Farrakhan and the Nation of Islam host the Million Man March in Washington, D.C. This event demonstrates solidarity among African American men and encourages black men to cultivate responsibility and self-respect.

1996 **December** J. Paul Reason becomes the first African American ever to attain the rank of four-star admiral in the U.S. Navy.

2000 **July 8** Tennis player Venus Williams wins her first Wimbledon title, becoming the first African American female to do so since Althea Gibson in 1958.

2002 A U.S. Census Bureau report reveals that between 1997 and 2002 the number of black-owned businesses in the United States rose by 45 percent to 1.2 million.

2002 **March 24** Halle Berry becomes the first African American woman to win an Academy Award for Best Actress. Berry wins the award for her performance in *Monster's Ball*.

2002 **April 8** Suzan-Lori Parks wins the Pulitzer Prize for Drama for her play, *Topdog/Underdog*. She is the first African American woman to win the award.

2003 **January 8** Representative Charles Rangel (D–NY) introduces a bill in Congress to reinstate the military draft, arguing that the makeup of the military's combat forces should reflect the makeup of American society.

2004 **July** A CBS News poll shows that 84 percent of African Americans oppose the war in Iraq. The same poll shows that only 57 percent of white Americans oppose the war.

2005 **August 29** Hurricane Katrina makes landfall in southeastern Louisiana, eventually causing massive flooding and catastrophic damage to the city of New Orleans and other parts of the Gulf coast. The hurricane causes the most damage in poor, predominantly African American neighborhoods in New Orleans. More than 90 percent of New Orleanians needing evacuation assistance after the hurricane are African American.

2007 According to the U.S. Census, nineteen percent of the African American population has completed four or more years of college, as opposed to thirty-two percent of the white population.

2007 **August 7** Surrounded by questions and controversy regarding alleged steroid use, Barry Bonds hits career home run 756, passing Hank Aaron's record.

2008 **November 4** Barack Obama is elected the 44th president of the United States.

2009 Eric Holder becomes the first African American to serve as the U.S. attorney general.

2009 **July 1** Ursula Burns becomes the first African American woman to run a Fortune 500 company when she becomes the CEO of Xerox.

2009 **July 27** Major General Charles Frank Bolden Jr., a veteran of four shuttle missions, becomes the first African American administrator of NASA.

Era Overview

The African American community has gone through enormous changes since 1965, thanks in large part to the tireless work of civil rights activists. The civil rights movement, which began in the 1950s, came to a climax in the second half of the 1960s as leaders of various parts of this diverse movement pushed urgently for change. Martin Luther King Jr., who had promoted a peaceful approach to change for more than a decade, was increasingly critical of the U.S. government and its treatment of African Americans. Frustrated by the slow rate of progress in their fight for equal rights, some African American civil rights activists veered away from King's nonviolent philosophy and took a more radial position. These leaders, often called "black nationalists," argued that African Americans should cut ties with the white community and work on fostering their own unique culture. Finally, after a tumultuous end to a troubled decade, African Americans began to see some real change.

This transformation is most obvious in the area of politics and government. In 1945, just three percent of voting-age blacks in the South were registered to vote. The registration of black voters became a major goal of the civil rights movement. But despite the brave efforts of voter registration volunteers who faced violence and harassment in the South, by 1964 only about 40 percent of eligible black voters were registered. In 1965, President Lyndon B. Johnson signed the historic Voting Rights Act into law. The Voting Rights Act banned many of the practices (such as literacy tests and poll taxes) that had prevented blacks from voting for so long. The results were dramatic. African American voter registration shot up to nearly the same level as white voter registration. African American politicians at the local, state, and federal levels saw new opportunities open up for them. By the early 1970s, major cities across the country elected their first black mayors. The number of African Americans holding office in state legislature and the U.S. Congress grew dramatically. And in 2008, forty years after Martin Luther King Jr. was assassinated because of his pursuit of equal rights for African Americans, the people of the United States elected Barack Obama, the nation's first black president.

A stronger African American presence in the public sphere was complemented by a growing African American presence in the private sector. In 1965, President Johnson established the Equal Employment Opportunity Commission (EEOC) and issued executive orders meant to ensure that African Americans, who had faced generations of employment discrimination, would get fair consideration for jobs, promotions, and government contracts. The wage gap between blacks and whites shrunk (though it did not disappear). By the 1990s, several African Americans had worked their way to the very top of the corporate ladder. Some, including Franklin Delano Raines and Lloyd Ward, became chief executives of Fortune 500 companies. Other African Americans found enormous success as entrepreneurs. Influential talk-show host Oprah Winfrey, for example, built a fortune worth billions of dollars on the success of her publishing and media business. Still, while African Americans in the business world reached the highest levels of success, African Americans as a population still earned only about two-thirds of what whites earned.

Success in business sprang from new educational opportunities for African Americans. Though the U.S. Supreme Court decision *Brown vs. the Board of Education of Topeka, Kansas* (1954) had made racial segregation in public schools illegal, the process of desegregation in education took many years. In 1970, only around 40 percent of African Americans had finished high school. The number rose to nearly 80 percent by 2000. According to the American Council on Education, black enrollment in college surged 122 percent between 1984 and 2004.

These higher achievement rates were evident in humanities as well as science and technological fields. In 1969, Clarence Ellis became the first African American to earn a doctorate in computer science. In 1972, Willie Hobbs Moore became the first African American woman to earn a doctorate in physics. African Americans played key roles in the growth of the U.S. space program starting in the 1970s, both as engineers and astronauts. In the early 1970s, astrophysicist George E. Carruthers developed a spectrograph that recorded important images of Earth, stars, and the Milky Way galaxy. In 1983, Guion "Guy" S. Bluford became the first African American astronaut in space. He was followed by the first African American female astronaut, Mae Jemison, in 1987.

On college campuses, in community centers, and in theaters and art spaces across the country, African Americans began eagerly exploring their unique cultural heritage with confidence and creativity. Students protesting at San Francisco State University prompted the establishment of the country's first black studies program in 1968. Several prominent universities followed suit. This interest in black identity, black collective power, and black culture gave rise to the black arts movement in the late 1960s and early 1970s. The leaders of the black arts movement took their cues from black nationalist activists who called for African Americans to establish a culture independent of the majority white culture. Black arts movement writers and artists, such as poet Amiri Baraka (born LeRoi Jones) and visual artist Haki Madhubuti (formerly Don Lee), rejected white artistic traditions and created openly political art based on African and African American models. The black arts movement boomed through the mid-1970s, at which point its influence faded and gave way to a wider range of African American artistic voices. Many black female artists and writers, including visual artist Faith Ringgold and writer Toni Morrison, found success in the late 1970s and early 1980s.

African Americans grabbed the spotlight in sports and entertainment in the last decades of the twentieth century and into the twenty-first, as performers and athletes, but also as coaches, managers, directors, and producers. Many of the biggest sports stars of that time period were black, including Michael Jordan, Hank Aaron, Venus and Serena Williams, and Tiger Woods. African American actors won acclaim for a wide variety of challenging roles. African American music, especially hip hop, became a mainstream cultural phenomenon.

American society became significantly more integrated in the latter half of the twentieth century. Interracial marriage became fully legal in the United States in 1967. The Fair Housing Act of 1968 made racial discrimination in the rental, sale, or financing of homes illegal. African Americans made up 14.5 percent of the U.S. military and almost 10 percent of the U.S. Congress at the beginning of the twenty-first century. Despite this progress, African Americans still suffered disproportionately from certain health and social problems. The life expectancy for African Americans was six years less than the life expectancy for whites, and young African American men were imprisoned at ten times the rate of young white men. African Americans were also more severely affected by economic downturns than whites. During the global recession of 2008 and 2009, unemployment for white Americans reached 10 percent, but it topped 15 percent for African Americans. While change has been dramatic since 1965, and successes by African Americans in all areas have been numerous, it is clear that some of the goals of the civil rights era have yet to be achieved.

chapter four **Communications and Media**

Chronology *200*

Overview *202*

Headline Makers *205*
Mara Brock Akil. *205*
Jayson Blair. *206*
Ed Bradley *207*
Farai Chideya. *208*
Don Cornelius *210*
Bill Cosby *211*
Earl G. Graves Sr. *213*
Gwen Ifill *215*
Tom Joyner. *216*
Spike Lee. *218*
Robert C. Maynard. *220*
Michele Norris *221*
Shonda Rhimes *222*
Bernard Shaw *224*
Tavis Smiley *225*
Will Smith *227*
Susan L. Taylor *228*
Denzel Washington *229*

Topics in the News *232*
African American Media
    Challenged by Modern
    Times *232*
Studios Turn to
    "Blaxploitation" Films . . .*239*
Black Musicians Cross Over
    to Film. *242*
Black Comedians Thrive in
    Film in the 1970s and
    1980s *243*
A New Generation of Black
    Filmmakers Finds
    Success. *245*
Television Opens Up to Black
    Stories and Characters . . .*250*
Cable Networks Target
    African Americans *254*

Primary Sources *258*

Research and Activity Ideas . .*263*

For More Information *264*

1965 September 15 Bill Cosby becomes the first African American to star in a television drama as *I Spy* debuts on NBC.

1966 Belva Davis becomes the West Coast's first African American news anchor.

1969 Max Robinson becomes the first African American to work as a television news anchor in Washington, D.C.

1970 March 13 Gordon Parks's *The Learning Tree* is the first film directed by an African American to be released by a major studio.

1970 May *Essence* magazine becomes the first monthly magazine targeted to African American women.

1970 August Earl G. Graves Sr. publishes the first issue of *Black Enterprise* magazine.

1970 September 12 Animated series *Josie and the Pussycats* debuts. Valerie is the first African American character on an animated television series.

1970 September 17 Flip Wilson becomes the first African American comedian to host his own television program: *The Flip Wilson Show.*

1971 July 2 *Shaft* is released, beginning the era of blaxploitation films.

1971 October 2 *Soul Train,* the first dance show focused on music made by African Americans, debuts.

1972 Percy Sutton becomes the first African American radio-station owner when he purchases WLIB in New York City.

1978 July Max Robinson becomes the first African American news anchor on a major television network when he co-hosts ABC's *World News Tonight.*

1980 January 25 Black Entertainment Television (BET) becomes the first television cable network for African Americans.

1983 April 30 Robert C. Maynard purchases the *Oakland Tribune,* becoming the first African American owner of a major newspaper.

1984 September 20 *The Cosby Show* debuts. The program about an affluent African American family living in Brooklyn became one of the most successful television shows of the 1980s and helped to revive NBC's sinking ratings.

1986 January 7 *The Oprah Winfrey Show* debuts. Featuring African American host Oprah Winfrey, it went on to become the most popular daytime talk show in the history of American television.

1989 June 30 African American director Spike Lee's controversial film *Do the Right Thing* is released. The film makes Lee one of the hottest young directors in America.

1990 Former basketball player Robin Robert becomes ESPN's first African American anchor and co-host of the network's popular *Sports Center* show.

1990 April 15 *In Living Color* debuts on the FOX network, becoming the first sketch comedy program created by African Americans with a largely African American cast.

1991 December 27 Julie Dash's *Daughters of the Dust* is the first feature film by an African American woman to be nationally distributed.

1995 September 23 San Diego BLAACK Pages becomes the first African American Web site to focus on a local community.

1996 William Kennard is named the first African American chairman of the Federal Communications Commission.

1996 June 19 African American journalist Farai Chideya founds one of the first pop-culture blogs, Pop+Politics.

1997 December 18 Former blaxploitation actress Pam Grier is nominated for her first Golden Globe Award for her role in *Jackie Brown*.

2000 September 11 *Girlfriends* debuts, becoming one of the most popular sitcoms among African American women for eight seasons.

2002 January 7 Tavis Smiley becomes the first African American to host his own show on National Public Radio with *The Tavis Smiley Show*.

2002 March 24 Halle Berry becomes the first African American woman to win an Academy Award for Best Actress. Berry won the award for her performance in *Monster's Ball*.

2004 October 2 Gwen Ifill becomes the first African American to moderate a vice-presidential debate on national television.

2005 Dean Baquet becomes the editor of the *Los Angeles Times*. This publication is the largest newspaper on the West Coast.

2005 Robin Roberts becomes co-anchor of ABC's successful morning news and talk show, *Good Morning America*.

2006 May 8 America Online (AOL) names Neal Scarbrough as the company's new general manager and editor of sports. Scarbrough had previously been the vice president and news editor for ESPN.

2007 April 4 Jesse Jackson and Al Sharpton call for the firing of white radio talk-show host Don Imus after he refers to African American female basketball players with racial slurs. *Imus in the Morning* is dropped by radio stations across the nation.

2009 Actresses Viola Davis and Taraji P. Henson receive Best Supporting Actress Oscar nominations. Davis plays the mother of a boy who may have been sexually molested by a priest in *Doubt* (2008). In *The Curious Case of Benjamin Button* (2008) Henson plays the nursemaid of a man who is aging backwards.

Overview

African Americans have long had to fight to gain control over the way they are depicted (represented or portrayed) in the media. Early twentieth-century movies made by white filmmakers tended to portray African Americans as lazy and ignorant. In some cases, they were played by white actors in black makeup. These conditions also existed in radio comedy shows. Groups such as the NAACP (National Association for the Advancement of Colored People) spoke out against the negative way blacks were depicted in the media. More progressive attitudes slowly began to emerge.

The movement away from stereotype-based humor and drama continued gradually through the first half of the twentieth century. However, it was not until the late 1940s and the 1950s that genuine change first became noticeable. African American actors managed to get strong, relatively dignified roles in Hollywood films. At the same time, black disc jockeys (DJs) were beginning to find work on radio. In 1950, J. B. Blayton Jr. became the first black radio station owner. Six years later, singer Nat "King" Cole became the first African American to host his own television show. In print media, black newspapers were struggling for survival, but magazines were thriving.

In the 1960s, the civil rights movement paved the way for greater acceptance of African Americans in the media. In 1963, Sidney Poitier became the first African American to win the Academy Award for best actor. Comedian Bill Cosby achieved similar success on the television drama *I Spy*. He won the Emmy Award for Best Actor in a Dramatic Series in 1968. That same year *Essence* became the first magazine for African American women, even as black newspapers continued to disappear. On radio, DJs such as future music star Sly Stone spun soul and R&B records. Ex-convict Ralph "Petey" Greene hosted his own challenging talk show called *Rapping with Petey Greene*.

The 1970s saw an explosion of African American influence in the media. Ed Bradley began reporting for CBS TV. He was fast on his way to becoming one of the most respected journalists on television. Susan L. Taylor made history as the first African American woman to become editor-in-chief of a major magazine when she took over *Essence*. Earl G. Graves Sr. launched *Black Enterprise*, the first black business magazine. An increased black presence on the radio included the formation of the first two all-black radio networks: the Mutual Black Network and the National Black Network. The formation of the National Association of Black Journalists in 1975 worked to strengthen the black journalistic community. It also furthered the positive portrayal of African Americans in the news. In the cinema, blaxploitation films rescued Hollywood from a commercial slump and provided numerous jobs for black filmmakers, actors, and actresses. Yet they also stirred up a storm of controversy for their use of negative stereotypes. Similar issues were affecting television. TV shows such as *Good Times* and *Sanford and Son* were achieving great popularity even as they provoked cries of racism. In sum, the decade of the 1970s was a somewhat awkward time of growth for African Americans in the media.

By contrast, the 1980s became an era of real change. In 1983, Robert C. Maynard purchased the *Oakland Tribune*. He became the first African American owner of a major metropolitan newspaper. Newspaper journalists fought for equal rights, successfully suing *New York Daily News* in 1987 to receive salaries and assignments comparable to those of white journalists. Black Entertainment Television (BET) became the first all-black cable channel. Increased sensitivity toward the portrayal of African Americans resulted in fewer stereotype-based television programs and films. *The Cosby Show* triumphed over its initially weak ratings and the lack of confidence of executives at NBC TV to become the most popular television program of the decade. On the talk show circuit, *The Oprah Winfrey Show* debuted. Winfrey was on her way to building a media empire that would eventually include her own magazine and a successful Internet Web site. Director Spike Lee revived black cinema, which had been inactive since the end of the blaxploitation era in the mid-1970s. Lee's films, such as *She's Gotta Have It* (1986) and *Do the Right Thing* (1989), were complex, realistic, and vividly entertaining explorations of the modern African American experience.

Lee's film career continued to flourish in the 1990s as he created thoughtful yet entertaining films such as *Jungle Fever* (1991), *Malcolm X* (1992), and *Clockers* (1995). Black filmmakers such as Mario Van Peebles and John Singleton followed Lee's lead. Black actors and actresses—including Denzel Washington, Halle Berry, Angela Bassett, and Morgan Freeman—were among the most respected stars in Hollywood. Hollywood was also discovering that rappers such as Will Smith, Ice T, and Ice Cube possessed genuine acting talent. Meanwhile a wealth of black programs, including *The Fresh Prince of Bel-Air*, *Martin*, *Living Single*, and *The Steve Harvey Show*, flooded onto television. In 1996, publisher Earl G. Graves Sr. continued to expand his business with the debut of a black history and culture magazine called *American Legacy*. Long-running black newspapers, such as *Carolina Peacemaker*, *Baltimore Afro-American*, and the *Chicago Defender*, remained alive despite overwhelming competition from white-owned papers. At the same time, a new crop of black journalists, including Gwen Ifill, Michele Norris, and Farai Chideya, achieved success in print, radio, and on television news programs.

Black radio stations ran into trouble following the 1996 Telecommunications Act, which relaxed ownership restrictions on radio and television stations and led to a massive consolidation of ownership of radio stations serving black, urban areas. Many critics of the Telecommunications Act say it squashes musical diversity and discourages controversial content. However, during this time black magazines, television shows, and films grew stronger and more diverse than ever.

The first decade of the twenty-first century was a time of new technology and new opportunities in the media for African Americans. Following an uncertain relationship with the Internet during the early 1990s, African Americans began to launch black-oriented Web sites, blogs, search engines, and social networking sites. Farai Chideya's site Pop+Politics, launched in 1996, was one of the first political/popular culture blogs to focus on issues of African American interest. After the turn of the century, black-oriented resources on the Internet expanded significantly. For example, the social networking site blackplanet.com drew seventeen million members as of 2007. Launched in 2009, BlackPlanet Rising (blackplanetrising.com) offers users information on volunteer opportunities in African American communities. Recent statistics show that African Americans are eager and sophisticated Internet users, so online offerings for the black community will likely continue to multiply.

★ MARA BROCK AKIL
(1970–)

Television writer and producer Mara Brock Akil is one of few African American women to produce more than one television program airing at the same time. During the 2007–2008 television season, Akil produced the long-running situation comedy *Girlfriends* and its spin-off series *The Game*.

Akil was born in Los Angeles, but she lived most of her childhood in Kansas City, Missouri. She later attended Northwestern University in Chicago. She received a bachelor's degree in journalism. Following college, Akil sought a career in writing. Her first television writing job was for *South Central* (1994), a half-hour comedy-drama about an African American family in south-central Los Angeles. Only ten episodes of the series aired. Akil spent the next few years taking occasional writing and acting work on the hit series *Moesha*. She also served as supervising producer on *The Jamie Foxx Show*.

In 2000, Akil created a comedy titled *Girlfriends* that would become her first major success. The show was produced by Akil and Kelsey Grammer (star of television's *Frasier*). *Girlfriends* followed the close friendship between four African American women in Los Angeles. Akil based the tight-knit quartet of pals on *Girlfriends* on her own circle of friends. That circle of friends includes fellow television-show creator Felicia D. Henderson and film director Gina Prince-Bythewood. *Girlfriends* aired for a total of eight seasons between 2000 and 2008. It aired for six seasons on UPN and an additional two seasons on The CW. It collected NAACP Image Award nominations for Outstanding Comedy Series in 2002 and 2003.

In 2006, Akil's second series debuted. *The Game* follows medical student Melanie Barnett, a character originally introduced on an episode of *Girlfriends*. Barnett must choose between her own career and supporting that of her boyfriend, a rising pro-football star. *The Game* became the

Television writer and producer Mara Brock Akil. *Amanda Edwards/Getty Images*

top-rated comedy program on The CW during its second season. In 2009, The CW announced it would be moving away from half-hour comedies, ending production of *The Game*.

★ JAYSON BLAIR
(1976–)

Jayson Blair is a controversial figure in journalism. Formerly a writer for the *New York Times*, he was revealed to have plagiarized—stolen someone else's work and attempted to pass it off as his own—and lied in numerous articles. The scandal dealt a blow to the respected newspaper. Blair was forced to resign.

As a boy growing up in Centreville, Virginia, Jayson Blair displayed a true passion for journalism. He wrote for his high school newspaper. In 1995, he began studying journalism at the University of Maryland. Professors remember him as ambitious and charming. He was soon working as the editor-in-chief of the school's student newspaper, *The Diamondback*. He held that position from 1996 to 1997. Blair was already attracting controversy during his time at *The Diamondback*. He often

Journalist Jayson Blair. *New York Times/Getty Images*

missed deadlines, which cost the paper money. He also tended to make up quotations in his articles. In some cases, he stole quotations from articles that had already been published in other papers. Blair's poor management at *The Diamondback* forced him to give up his editorial position less than a year after taking it. But before he left the paper, he edited an article claiming that a basketball player and fellow student had died of a cocaine overdose. In reality, the student had died of a heart problem. The false story ignited the outrage of Blair's peers at the newspaper. His successor as editor-in-chief, Danielle Newman, published a letter of apology for Blair's deliberate falsehoods.

Blair generated a lot of controversy while he was at the University of Maryland. He also never graduated from the university. Nonetheless, in 1998 the *New York Times* offered Blair an internship. Blair took a full-time position at the *New York Times* in 2001. However, controversy continued to follow him.

In April 2003, an editor at the *San Antonio Express-News* accused Blair of plagiarizing an article written by one of the paper's reporters. Before long, the *New York Times* revealed that the article was just one of many that Blair had either plagiarized or padded with lies. As a result, two top editors at the *Times* resigned. They were ashamed they had not noticed or controlled Blair's unethical tendencies. Blair was also out of a job, but he managed to score a book deal worth 150,000 dollars out of the scandal. In 2004, he published *Burning Down My Master's House: My Life at the New York Times*. The book told his side of the story. It began with the confession, "I lied and I lied—and then I lied some more." Throughout *Burning Down My Master's House*, Blair blamed his behavior on drug and alcohol abuse and mental illness.

★ ED BRADLEY
(1941–2006)

Ed Bradley was one of the most honored journalists of the later part of the twentieth century. Bradley is best known as a reporter on the long-running television news program *60 Minutes*. His work earned him numerous awards and the respect of the public and the journalistic community alike.

Bradley grew up in Philadelphia, Pennsylvania. He was largely raised by his mother after his parents' divorce. He studied to become a teacher at Cheyney State College in his home state. However, it was his time at the school's radio station that most sparked his interest. After a disc-jockey friend allowed Bradley to read the news on air, he fell in love with radio. Following graduation, Bradley taught sixth-grade classes for several years, but he still loved radio. When he was not teaching, Bradley worked without pay at radio station WDAS-FM out of Philadelphia. He played jazz records and announced basketball games.

During the mid-1960s, a series of race riots occurred in Philadelphia. Bradley was there to report on the violence. He did such an impressive job that the station finally gave him a paying position as a reporter. Shortly afterward, Bradley gave up his teaching position for good to further explore the world of radio

Journalist Ed Bradley in 2006. *Ray Tamarra/Getty Images*

journalism. He left Philadelphia for New York City. In New York, he got a reporting job on WCBS Radio in 1967. The job led to an on-screen position as a news reporter for CBS TV. Bradley reported on location from Saigon during the Vietnam War. He was even injured by mortar shrapnel (sharp metal fragments produced by an explosion) while on the air. Back in the United States following his injury, he worked in Washington, D.C. He reported on Jimmy Carter's presidential campaign and presidency.

Bradley missed the nonstop action that came along with reporting abroad (from a different country). Soon enough, Bradley found himself back in Vietnam. He arrived just in time for the fall of Saigon in 1975. This event brought the war to a dramatic end. In 1979, Bradley once again shipped off to Vietnam. This time he covered the flight of Vietnamese refugees from Saigon, which had been ravaged—destroyed by violence and chaos—by the war. While in Vietnam, Bradley crossed the line from news reporter to newsmaker when he plunged into Malaysian waters to help rescue refugees from their sinking boat. Bradley's act of heroism and his inspiring journalism won him his first Emmy Award. It also led to a job on *60 Minutes* two years later.

For the next twenty-five years, Bradley was a fixture in American households every Sunday night. He reported on such major stories as the AIDS epidemic, the September 11th terrorist attack on the World Trade Center in 2001, and the Catholic Church's sexual abuse scandal. He also conducted challenging interviews with public figures and celebrities, including Michael Jackson (1958–2009) and Muhammad Ali (1942–). He was regarded for the humanity he brought to any story he covered. As busy as *60 Minutes* kept Bradley, he still found time to devote to his undying love of jazz music. He hosted a Peabody Award-winning radio show called *Jazz at Lincoln Center* every week. Ed Bradley continued his work on television and radio until two weeks before chronic lymphocytic leukemia, a form of cancer, took his life on November 9, 2006.

★ FARAI CHIDEYA
(1969–)

Farai Chideya is a media Renaissance woman, which means she has interests and expertise in numerous aspects of media. She has written novels, hosted her own radio show, and has distinguished herself as an expressive and insightful journalist. Chideya has made it her personal goal to change the way African Americans are perceived in journalism and the world as a whole.

Chideya grew up in Baltimore, Maryland. She was exposed to numerous cultures as a young girl. Her father was a businessman from

Zimbabwe. Her mother was an American journalist and high school teacher. She and her parents traveled to Kenya and her father's home country. Chideya's parents divorced when she was still a young child. Her father moved back to Zimbabwe, and Chideya stayed with her mother in Baltimore. Chideya's mother encouraged her to develop a fascination with politics and a thirst for education. She taught Chideya to read at the age of three. That love of reading would last a lifetime. It was a major influence on Chideya's career decisions.

Chideya considered pursuing a career in medicine. Eventually, her interest in reading and writing drew her to journalism. While attending Harvard University, Chideya was offered an internship by *Newsweek* magazine. She brought a passion for government, social issues, music, and multiculturalism to the magazine. Soon Chideya was writing for other major magazines, such as *Essence, Time, Spin,* and *Mademoiselle.* During this time, she often focused on encouraging young African Americans to vote and get involved in politics. Her concerns about race inspired her first book. *Don't Believe the Hype: Fighting Cultural Misinformation About African-Americans* (1995) criticized the "liberal" media for being inept in its portrayals of African Americans. Chideya used the book to expose numerous racial stereotypes she discovered in various newspapers. She argued that such journalism is often more the result of laziness than racism.

In an effort to further reach a young audience, Chideya left her position at *Newsweek* in the mid-1990s for a job as an assignment editor at MTV News. There, she was not able to tackle the kinds of sophisticated news stories she wrote for *Newsweek.* However, MTV News provided her the opportunity to reach teenagers and college students and educate them about politics and music. Chideya enjoyed her experience at MTV News. Still, she aspired to cover more hard-hitting news stories. While working at MTV, Chideya made regular appearances on *Inside Politics,* a political discussion show on CNN. The program allowed her a means of debating the most pressing political issues of her day. Before long, CNN offered her a full-time position on *Inside Politics.*

Chideya took advantage of her high-profile position by launching Pop+Politics in 1996. The Web site was one of the first blogs to focus on both politics and pop culture. It afforded Chideya a forum to discuss everything from hip hop to her own personal dating stories. Pop + Politics won a MOBE IT Innovator Award in 2001. Chideya has also continued to publish nonfiction books. Her books include *The Color of the Future* (1999) and *Trust: Reaching the 100 Million Missing Voters* (2004). In 2009, Chideya published her first fictional novel, *Kiss the Sky,* proving once again that she is adept (highly skilled) at working in all forms of media.

★ DON CORNELIUS
(1936–)

When the dance show *Soul Train* first aired in 1971, music made by African American artists reached a wider audience than it ever had before. Every Saturday, viewers would tune in to watch a crowd of young people dancing along to the latest soul, disco, and rhythm and blues records. The deep-voiced, well-dressed man who hosted *Soul Train* from the year it debuted until 1993 was also its creator: Don Cornelius.

Cornelius grew up on the south side of Chicago. As a child, Cornelius displayed a flair (an instinctive ability or talent) for art. He later studied art as a student at DuSable High School. Following a tour in the U.S. Marines Corps, Cornelius wanted to attend college, but he had little money and a new family to support. He resigned himself to working as a salesman. Cornelius earned a decent living selling cars and insurance. Still, he longed to explore his creative side. Cornelius received much attention for his rich voice, so in 1966 he decided to spend four hundred dollars on a broadcasting class. That very same year he landed his first job on the radio. He worked as an announcer for the Chicago-based station WVON. The pay did not compare to what he earned as a salesman, but the work was infinitely more satisfying. At the station, Cornelius did a little bit of everything. He read the news, substituted for disc jockeys, read advertisements, and hosted talk shows.

Soul Train creator and host Don Cornelius in 2003. *Frederick M. Brown/Getty Images*

Cornelius was grateful to be working in radio. His schedule was tiring because it constantly changed, and he often had to work late-night shifts. So, when his boss at WVON left the station to take a position at a small local television station called WCIU-TV, Cornelius followed. At WCIU-TV, he created a program based on Dick Clark's long-running *American Bandstand,* a show that featured teenagers dancing to the latest pop hits. Cornelius's program focused on music made by African American artists. It primarily featured African American dancers. *Soul Train* debuted on August 17, 1970. Cornelius produced, hosted, and even sold advertising for the show. At first, it was very difficult to convince major companies to purchase commercial time on a program directed at African Americans. However, the show's high ratings eventually tempted major companies like Sears and Coca-Cola to buy advertising time on *Soul Train*.

The local success of *Soul Train* inspired Cornelius to bring his program to a wider audience. Cornelius struck a deal with the African-American-owned Johnson Products Company to sponsor the program. As a result, *Soul Train* could be watched in living rooms across the country beginning October 2, 1971. *Soul Train* attracted an impressive array of musical acts. It became even more popular than *American Bandstand,* the show that inspired it. By 1974, *Soul Train* was aired on ninety-five stations across the country. As the ever-popular host of his program, Cornelius became a nationally recognized celebrity.

In 1982, Cornelius experienced a life-threatening setback when he was hospitalized after suffering a brain hemorrhage (a large, rapid loss of blood from blood vessels in his brain). He took six months to recover from the operation to stop the bleeding. As soon as he was well enough, he was back on the show he loved. By 1992, *Soul Train* had become the longest-running music program in the history of syndicated television. The following year, Cornelius hosted his final episode of *Soul Train*. He sold the program to MadVision Entertainment in 2008.

★ **BILL COSBY**
(1937–)

For more than four decades, Bill Cosby has been one of the most beloved entertainers in America. His comic observations on family have fueled his stand-up comedy act, numerous comedy albums, much of his writing, and his tremendously popular sitcom *The Cosby Show* that ran from 1984 to 1992.

Bill Cosby grew up in an all-black housing project in North Philadelphia, Pennsylvania. As a child, he spent hours listening to the comedic radio shows of Jack Benny (1894–1974), Jimmy Durante (1893–1980), and Burns &

Actor and comedian Bill Cosby. *George De Sota/ Newsmakers/Getty Images*

Allen. Inspired by his heroes, he strove to become a funny man himself. When he was not performing comedy routines for his classmates and teachers, Cosby played a variety of sports. Although he was quite intelligent, his athletic activities often got in the way of his studies. As a result, he was faced with the prospect of having to repeat the tenth grade. Instead, he decided to drop out of school and join the Navy.

Cosby soon realized he had made a mistake in ending his education prematurely (earlier than scheduled). So, he planned to earn his diploma through correspondence classes while still in the Navy. In 1961, he won a scholarship to Temple University in Philadelphia. At Temple, he studied physical education. While attending the university, he earned pocket money by tending bar and performing comedy shows at a coffeehouse. The money was not great. However, the thrill of making an audience laugh was enough to convince Cosby that he had a future in comedy.

Every night on stage, Cosby perfected his funny stories, silly faces, and crazy characters. The Gaslight, a café in Greenwich Village, New York City, offered him a room and sixty dollars per week to perform his standup routine. During his time at the Gaslight, he was signed to a contract by the William Morris Agency. The deal resulted in Cosby's comedy albums, national standup tours, and an appearance on the popular talk show *The Tonight Show with Johnny Carson*. Cosby's appearance on *The Tonight Show* led to him being cast in a weekly one-hour drama series called *I Spy*. Cosby became the first African American actor to star in a television drama. He won three Emmy Awards for his work as the tough but witty CIA agent Alex Scott during the show's run from 1965 to 1968.

Cosby was on more familiar comedic ground when he starred in his first television comedy in 1969. *The Bill Cosby Show* found him playing a physical education teacher in a poor Los Angeles neighborhood. Unfortunately, *The Bill Cosby Show* was not the hit that *I Spy* had been. The show only lasted two seasons. Cosby next found a more unusual outlet for his comedic talents. In 1972, he created and hosted a Saturday morning cartoon called *Fat Albert and the Cosby Kids*. The show was based on Cosby's own boyhood friends. Each episode conveyed an educational message to its young viewers. Meanwhile, Cosby continued to pursue his own education. He earned two degrees from the University of Massachusetts at Amherst. In 1977, he received a doctorate of education. His dissertation (a very long paper that a student must write to earn a doctoral degree) was about his own *Fat Albert* program.

Bill Cosby had enjoyed great popularity ever since he starred in *I Spy*. However, he would achieve superstardom during the 1980s as a result of a sitcom called *The Cosby Show*. When the program debuted in 1984, the television network NBC had been suffering from poor ratings. The half-hour sitcom format was growing stale. *The Cosby Show* brought new life to both NBC and the sitcom format. The show starred Cosby as Dr. Heathcliff Huxtable. It also starred Phylicia Rashad (1948–) as his wife Clair, a lawyer. *The Cosby Show* became the number-one television show from 1985 to 1989. It was also notable as the first television program to focus on a professional African American couple. It was hailed as a major break from the stereotypes that were usually presented on television.

While continuing work on his show, Cosby penned a series of bestselling humor books. The books focused on marriage and parenting, including *Fatherhood* (1986) and *Time Flies* (1987). Meanwhile, *The Cosby Show* remained incredibly popular until it ended its decade-long run in 1992. Bill Cosby attempted to return to television several times after the end of *The Cosby Show*, but he never again matched its success.

In 1997, Cosby suffered his greatest personal tragedy. That year, his son Ennis was robbed and murdered while fixing a flat tire on a Los Angeles highway. In the wake of his son's death, Cosby started the Hello Friend/Ennis William Cosby Foundation. The foundation promotes the detection and treatment of dyslexia, a condition from which Ennis had suffered.

Bill Cosby remained active. He wrote the *Little Bill* series of books about children with learning disabilities. He also created a *Little Bill* animated series for Nickelodeon. In 2004, Cosby stirred up a storm of controversy when he blamed the problems of African Americans on African Americans themselves. He accused many African Americans of choosing violence over education and failing as parents. His speech inspired critics and supporters alike. Bill Cosby likely will continue to be a forceful public figure for many more years to come.

★ EARL G. GRAVES SR.
(1935–)

Earl G. Graves Sr. is one of America's premier entrepreneurs. He is a respected writer, humanitarian, and businessman. He is also the founder and publisher of *Black Enterprise* magazine.

Publisher Earl G. Graves in 1983. *Bachrach/Getty Images*

Graves was born in Brooklyn, New York. Graves looked up to his father as a boy. The elder Graves, who came from a poor background, valued education greatly. He had been the only African American in his high school graduating class. Following in his father's footsteps, the younger Graves was one of only two African Americans to graduate in his class. The Graves children were raised to be ambitious and business-minded. Earl was hard-working, focused, and goal-oriented. After high school, he attended Morgan State University in Baltimore, Maryland. He earned excellent grades and enthusiastically participated in school activities, including a number of campus businesses.

After graduating from college with a degree in economics, Graves enlisted in the U.S. Army. In the army, his achievements were just as impressive as they had been at school. He achieved the rank of captain in the Green Berets. Later, he worked for the U.S. Treasury Department as a narcotics agent. He then returned to Brooklyn. Back home, he bought and sold real estate until an extraordinary opportunity arose in 1966. Senator Robert F. Kennedy (1925–68) hired Graves to work on his staff as an administrative assistant. Graves organized and supervised events for Kennedy until the senator's tragic assassination in 1968. Graves was devastated by the death of his mentor. However, he was also inspired by Kennedy's "never give up" attitude. Later that year, he established Earl G. Graves Associates. His new company consulted with corporations regarding economic development and urban affairs. The company served a large number of clients. By all standards, it was a tremendous success.

In the late 1960s, Graves took a trip to Fayette, Mississippi, to work on Charles Evers's mayoral campaign. The trip inspired Graves to contribute much of his own money to the improvement of Fayette's African American community. At the time, African American economic development was becoming a major social issue. Graves decided to provide a resource for those who wanted to get involved. In 1970, he started *Black Enterprise,* the first business magazine for African Americans. The magazine provided business advice and profiled leaders in the African American business community. By the tenth issue of *Black Enterprise,* Graves had made back his investment in the magazine. He was already turning a profit.

Near the end of the first decade of the twenty-first century, *Black Enterprise* had 4.3 million readers. The Web site Black Enterprise.com attracted 450,000 visitors per month. The Earl G. Graves Publishing Company has become a true family business. Graves's wife, Barbara, is vice-president of the publishing company. Their son Earl Jr. is the company's president and chief executive officer (CEO). Their son John leads Black Enterprise Unlimited. Along with his numerous business ventures, Graves Sr. continues to give back to communities around the world. He volunteered on the board of TransAfrica Forum, a nonprofit organization focused on improving human rights and economic conditions in Africa, the Caribbean, and Latin America. Graves contributed one million dollars to the business school at Morgan State University. The university in turn honored him in 1995 by renaming the school the Earl G. Graves School of Business and Management.

★ GWEN IFILL
(1955–)

Gwen Ifill is one of the most respected political moderators working in the early 2000s. As the first African American woman to moderate a political talk show, she is also a media pioneer. Ifill was one of five children. Her father was an African Methodist Episcopal minister. He raised her and her siblings to respect their religious background and to be aware of current events. When Gwen was growing up, her father's position in the church required the family to move around constantly throughout New England and the East Coast. The church and her family were the only two constants in young Gwen Ifill's life.

Political moderator Gwen Ifill in 2007. *Alex Wong/ Getty Images for Meet the Press*

No matter where the family was living, her father made sure they tuned in to a television program called *The Huntley-Brinkley Report* every night. *The Huntley-Brinkley Report* kept the Ifills informed about the main news stories of the day. Gwen Ifill developed a keen interest in current events. She went on to study communications at Simmons College in Boston, Massachusetts. She earned her bachelor's degree in 1977. She pursued a career in journalism as soon as she graduated.

Ifill's first job was an internship at the *Boston Herald*. Although she had ambitions of covering major news stories, the only available position was food writer. The *Herald* gave Ifill a full-time position to apologize after a co-worker left a racist note on her desk. However, she did not remain at the paper for long. In 1981, she moved on to the *Baltimore Evening Sun*. Shortly afterward, she was offered the opportunity to appear on a news program for PBS called *Maryland Newswrap*. Ifill was an on-screen natural. She displayed both a sharp eye for important stories and a lucid (clear and easy to understand) manner of explaining them to her audience.

Three years after taking her position at the *Baltimore Evening Sun*, Ifill went to work for the *Washington Post* newspaper. She moved up the ranks rapidly at the *Post*. By 1988, she was covering the presidential campaign. Three years later, she was working as a reporter for the *New York Times*. She covered the White House and also spent more time on television as a panelist on the news program *Washington Week*. Ifill's skill and presence on the show resulted in job offers from all three major television networks. She finally took a job at *NBC News*. There, she continued to cover the White House. However, she missed the action and personal interaction of print journalism. Luckily for Ifill, PBS soon made a twin offer she could not refuse. PBS wanted to give her a position as a reporter *and* her very own television program.

Gwen Ifill debuted as host of *Washington Week in Review* in 1999. As the first African American and the first woman to host such a program, she became a welcome role model for others interested in pursuing journalism as a career. She broke further ground in 2004 when she became the first African American woman to moderate a vice-presidential debate. She performed that task again in 2008. In 2009, she published her first book, *The Breakthrough: Politics and Race in the Age of Obama*. The book was published on the day Barack Obama (1961–) was sworn in as president. The book commemorated the political achievements of other groundbreaking African Americans like herself.

★ TOM JOYNER
(1949–)

Since 1994, radio listeners across America have started their days laughing along with Tom Joyner. On the nationally-syndicated *Tom Joyner Morning Show*, he plays music, presents the news, and performs his special brand of humor. Tom Joyner was born in Tuskegee, Alabama. He was a creative young man who enjoyed performing. While going to school at the Tuskegee Institute, Joyner and classmate Lionel Richie (1949–) formed a singing group called the Commodores. Richie and the group would go on to international fame, but Joyner left before they achieved stardom. He later joked that leaving the Commodores was his greatest mistake, but Joyner would be no stranger to fame and success.

Joyner's relationship with radio began when he attended a protest against the only radio station in Tuskegee. The station refused to play records by African American artists. After the protest proved successful, Joyner took a volunteer position at the station. He had no previous experience in radio. Nonetheless, he soon developed a genuine love for it. He took an on-air job at his school's radio station to help pay his tuition. He also continued his unpaid position at the local station.

Joyner spent the 1970s working at radio stations across the South. He collected valuable experience and developed his broadcasting skills. He finally ended up in Chicago in the early 1980s. In Chicago, he found work at several local stations. When KDKA in Dallas, Texas, offered him his own morning radio show in 1983, he returned to the South. Two years later, WGCI, a former employer in Chicago, asked him to return to take on an afternoon program. Unable to turn down a good deal, Joyner accepted the second job while keeping his position in Dallas. Every day he would perform his morning job in Dallas, fly to Chicago for his afternoon show, and then fly back to Dallas to spend the evening with his family. Joyner's exhausting schedule earned him the nicknames "The Hardest Working Man in Radio" and "The Fly Jock." Joyner continued his demanding commute for eight years. During that time, both his morning show and his afternoon show were number-one in their respective markets.

Radio personality Tom Joyner in 2008. *Frederick M. Brown/Getty Images*

In 1993, an offer from ABC Radio Networks finally brought an end to Joyner's commute. Having his own syndicated show would allow him to broadcast from a single location. What's more, it would give him the opportunity to reach more listeners than ever before. *The Tom Joyner Morning Show* debuted in January 1994. On the show, Joyner played music, conducted interviews with celebrities, performed comedy routines, broadcasted news, and played host to a live band. By the end of the decade, *The Tom Joyner Morning Show* was airing on almost one hundred stations and attracting eight million listeners per day.

Joyner knew that his ability to speak to such a large number of people was a valuable power. He used his position to benefit the African American community. He began the Tom Joyner Foundation in 1996. The foundation contributes to African American universities. He also partnered with other established organizations, such as the United Negro College Fund and the NAACP, to further benefit society.

In 2005, Joyner published his book, *I'm Just a DJ but … It Makes Sense to Me*. The book chronicled his rise to success. That same year he hosted a one-hour comedy variety program called *The Tom Joyner Show*. The show aired for a single season in syndication. Meanwhile, he continues to host his wildly successful radio program and to work with various charity organizations.

★ SPIKE LEE
(1957–)

If there is one filmmaker who could be credited with completely revolutionizing the face of African American cinema, that filmmaker is Spike Lee. From independent favorites like *She's Gotta Have It* to breakthroughs like *Do the Right Thing* to epics like *Malcolm X*, Lee has created works that are thought-provoking, energetic, and controversial.

Shelton Jackson "Spike" Lee was born in Atlanta, Georgia. He is the son of an art teacher and a jazz musician. When he was two years old, his family moved to Brooklyn, New York. Lee's parents emphasized the importance of racial pride. They also emphasized art, music, and humor. All of these elements would influence the films Lee would make as an adult.

Film director Spike Lee in 1998. *Touchstone/The Kobal Collection/Clairborne, Barron*

Spike Lee first took an interest in film while attending Morehouse College in Atlanta. After graduating from Morehouse in 1979, he attended the New York University (NYU) Graduate Film School. Lee was already stirring up controversy during his graduate school days. He wrote a short screenplay titled *The Answer*. The script focused on an African American rewriting of *The Birth of a Nation*, a silent movie famed as much for its pioneering film techniques as for its extreme racism. The script nearly got Lee kicked out of school, but he was able to complete his studies at NYU. He even won a Student Academy Award for a short film about a Brooklyn barber shop. *Joe's Bed-Stuy Barber Shop: We Cut Heads* went on to film festival screenings, but it failed to get Lee work on a feature film.

Eventually, Lee scored a 20,000-dollar grant from the American Film Institute in 1984. Although the amount of money was not enough to produce *Messenger*, a script he had written about a New York bike messenger, Lee believed it was enough to begin work on another one of his screenplays. *She's Gotta Have It* (1986) is the story of Nola Darling, an independent young woman choosing between romance and freedom. The American Film Institute was not willing to back the new film, as it was still too costly. So Lee and a small group of backers worked hard to raise the 175,000 dollars needed to make the movie. *She's Gotta Have It* was filmed in just twelve days with Lee himself playing one of Nola's potential boyfriends.

She's Gotta Have It was widely praised for its fresh portrayal of urban African Americans. It won an award at the Cannes Film Festival. It also earned Lee a contract to make two more films. He followed *She's Gotta Have It* with *School Daze* (1988), a vibrant musical about rival gangs at a fictional college. *School Daze* was another hit on the independent circuit.

Lee's true breakthrough arrived in 1989 with *Do the Right Thing*. Films had been made about racism before, but none approached the subject quite like *Do the Right Thing*. Lee's story of pizza deliverer Mookie (played by Lee), his white employer Sal, Sal's racist son, and a host of other characters in the Bed-Stuy (Bedford-Stuyvesant) area of Brooklyn offered no easy solutions to racial issues. The film ends with conflicting quotes about violence from two slain African American leaders: Martin Luther King Jr. (1929–68) and Malcolm X (1925–65). *Do the Right Thing* is a complex, mature film that deals with sensitive issues. It is also funny, brilliantly entertaining, and bursting with music. It became a huge box office hit. It has since been hailed as one of the greatest American movies in film history by the American Film Institute, the very foundation that decided not to fund *She's Gotta Have It*.

With the success of *Do the Right Thing*, Spike Lee became one of cinema's most celebrated and debated filmmakers. He continued to make challenging films, including *Mo' Better Blues* (1990) and *Jungle Fever* (1991). In 1992, Lee made *Malcolm X*, a nearly three-and-one-half-hour biography about the assassinated African American activist Malcolm X. Actor Denzel Washington (1954–) received an Academy Award nomination for portraying the title role. Lee worked with Washington again in 2006 on the feature film *Inside Man* in which Washington played a hostage negotiator trying to secure the release of fifty hostages taken prisoner by bank robbers.

In the twenty-first century, Spike Lee produced more television work than feature films. Most notably, his 2006 television documentary *When the Levees Broke: A Requiem in Four Acts,* earned him three Emmy Awards. The documentary, first aired on HBO, explores the devastation and loss caused by Hurricane Katrina in 2005.

★ ROBERT C. MAYNARD
(1937–1993)

Journalist Robert Clyve Maynard was a passionate writer, publisher, and humanitarian. He was born in Brooklyn, New York. His parents were immigrants from Barbados. His father, Samuel Maynard, was a preacher and a businessman. He owned a trucking company. Robert Maynard would eventually become a businessman himself as an adult, but he spent his childhood infatuated with writing. Young Maynard would cut classes from Boys' High School to hang around a local African American-owned newspaper called *New York Age.* At the age of sixteen, he dropped out of high school to write for the paper.

During his time at *New York Age*, Maynard developed his writing craft. He also received encouragement from such major African American writers as Langston Hughes (1902–67) and James Baldwin (1924–87). He received less encouragement when he went looking for a full-time job. Maynard was repeatedly refused work because of his race. He finally landed a position writing about police and urban affairs at the *York Gazette and Daily*, a Pennsylvania-based paper, in 1961. A series of pieces he wrote about the southern civil rights movement earned him a fellowship from Harvard University.

Newspaper owner and editor Robert C. Maynard in 1983. *Christopher Springmann/Time & Life Pictures/Getty Images*

In 1967, Maynard made history as the first African American national correspondent to write for the *Washington Post*. At the *Post*, he covered pressing news items such as racial unrest and the Watergate scandal involving President Richard Nixon (1913–94). Maynard split his time between reporting at the *Washington Post* and working as a senior editor for a monthly magazine called *Encore*. In 1974, the *Post* made Maynard an associate editor. He remained at the paper for the following decade.

In 1977, Maynard and his wife, Nancy, founded the Institute for Journalism Education at the University of California. Since its founding, the organization has placed more nonwhite journalists in jobs than any other organization in America. Two years later, Maynard took a job as the editor of the *Oakland Tribune*, making him the first African American director of editorial operations for a major daily newspaper. Maynard took advantage of his position by hiring a number of nonwhite journalists. He also hired an openly gay writer. Maynard bought the *Oakland Tribune* in 1983. He thus became the first African American to own a major newspaper.

Maynard juggled his multiple roles as president, publisher, and editor of the *Oakland Tribune* for nearly ten years. In 1992, he decided to sell the paper. He continued his work with the Institute for Journalism Education. He also composed his autobiography, *Letters to My Children*. The book was published in 1995, two years after he died from prostate cancer. Today, the institute he helped found has been renamed the Robert C. Maynard Institute for Journalism Education in his honor.

★ MICHELE NORRIS
(1961–)

Multi-media journalist Michele Norris is best known as the host of the evening news show *All Things Considered* on National Public Radio. She has also distinguished herself in print and on television. Norris was born to Belvin and Elizabeth Norris in Minneapolis, Minnesota. Her parents stressed the importance of watching the evening news and reading newspapers. Their encouragement created a lifelong fascination in their daughter. Norris majored in electrical engineering at the University of Wisconsin-Madison for three years. She eventually returned to her home state to study at the University of Minnesota School of Journalism and Mass Communications. During her time at the school, she wrote for the *Minnesota Daily* and earned the distinction of minority scholar. In 1985, she received her journalism degree.

Following graduation, Norris found work at the *Chicago Tribune*. The job led to further work with major papers, such as the *Los Angeles Times* and the *Washington Post*. At the *Post*,

Radio host Michele Norris in 2008. *Alex Wong/Getty Images for Meet the Press*

Norris wrote a powerful story detailing the life of Dooney Waters. Waters was the six-year-old son of a crack-addicted mother. The story won Norris the Livingston Award—an honor given to journalists under the age of thirty-five—in 1990. Four years later, it was reprinted in the book *Ourselves Among Others: Cross-Cultural Readings for Writers*.

In 1993, Norris made her television debut on *ABC News*. She was a correspondent on *World News Tonight with Peter Jennings*. As a correspondent, she tackled issue-oriented stories about poverty, education, and the drug problem. Norris worked on *ABC News* for nine years. She won a Peabody Award for her coverage of the 9/11 terrorist attacks. She also won an Emmy Award in 2002, her final year on the program.

Following her run with *ABC News*, Norris further expanded her experience by taking a job in radio. *All Things Considered* is the longest running news program on National Public Radio. Norris became host of the program on December 9, 2002.

Television executive producer Shonda Rhimes in 2007. *Frederick M. Brown/ Getty Images*

Norris is highly regarded for her perceptive and insightful understanding of social issues. She has been nominated for the esteemed Pulitzer Prize four times. She has also been honored by the National Association of Black Journalists and *Ebony* magazine. In 2006, she received the University of Minnesota's Outstanding Achievement Award.

★ SHONDA RHIMES (1970–)

Award-winning television and film writer Shonda Rhimes is the creator of the popular nighttime drama *Grey's Anatomy*. The show has aired on ABC since Rhimes was thirty-five years old. However, she has been creating stories since she was a four-year-old girl living in Chicago. Young Rhimes spent hours telling her stories to a tape recorder. When she was finished, she would pass along the tape she had made to her mother. Her mother would write the stories down for her creative daughter.

When Rhimes was in high school, she volunteered at a local hospital, where she worked as a "candy striper." The nickname "candy striper" comes from the red-and-white striped uniforms, which resembled peppermints, that female volunteers used to wear. Rhimes loved listening to the stories of the patients with whom she worked. The concept of a hospital as a place where tales unfold would play a major role in Rhimes's adult life.

Toward the end of the 1980s, Rhimes enrolled at Dartmouth College in Hanover, New Hampshire. She indulged her passion for reading and writing as an English major. After graduating in 1991, she dreamed of a creative writing job. Her parents, however, encouraged her to take a more "practical" position. On her parents' advice, Rhimes briefly worked as an advertising copywriter in San Francisco, California. She hated writing commercials, so she decided to further her education at the University of California School of Cinema-Television. Rhimes graduated with a master's degree in 1994. Two years later she sold a script to Disney. Unfortunately, the script was never produced. In 1998, she managed to get *Blossoms and Veils*, a romance starring Jada Pinkett Smith (1971–) and Omar Epps (1973–), produced, but it was not very successful. *Introducing Dorothy Dandridge* (1999), a film for HBO television, was a different story. The film was about an African American actress from the mid-twentieth century, and it was a critical hit. Rhimes won the NAACP Image Award for outstanding television movie for her script.

The success of *Introducing Dorothy Dandridge* led to more work. Rhimes wrote a movie script for pop singer Britney Spears (1981–) called *Crossroads* (2002). She also wrote the sequel to the popular *Princess Diaries* movie, which came out in 2004. During this time, Rhimes realized she also had ambitions of motherhood. In 2002, she adopted a baby girl. She named the girl after Harper Lee (1926–), the author of the famous book *To Kill a Mockingbird*. After she would put Harper to bed in the evening, Rhimes enjoyed curling up in front of her television. She developed an appreciation for the stories that could unfold gradually on television because, unlike movies, they were free of the limitations of a two-hour running time. She also noticed that there were few substantial roles for female and nonwhite actors on TV. Rhimes was inspired to begin developing *Grey's Anatomy*.

Grey's Anatomy recalls Rhimes's teenage years as a hospital worker. The program is set at Seattle Grace Memorial Hospital. It focuses on the personal and professional lives of the doctors there. ABC purchased *Grey's Anatomy* in 2005. It quickly became one of the network's biggest hits. It won acclaim for its multicultural cast. It also won multiple awards. Rhimes next created *Private Practice*, a spin-off of *Grey's Anatomy* that debuted in 2007. She also signed a deal with Disney to develop more feature films.

★ **BERNARD SHAW**
(1940–)

As an anchor on CNN for twenty years, Bernard Shaw made sure that his personal views never slanted the news stories he reported. Shaw's unemotional and impersonal manner made him one of the most widely recognized journalists on television. Despite his cool personality, Shaw had a passion for the news ever since he was a boy growing up in Chicago. As a teenager, he would trek to a bookstore near the University of Chicago to hunt down the Sunday edition of the *New York Times*. He would then take a seat in a local coffee shop and read the sizable paper from cover to cover.

Shaw's fascination with the news led to local opportunities. He was allowed to make informative announcements over the loudspeaker at his high school. He also took part in radio shows. Many of his peers were watching the sitcoms and game shows popular in the 1950s, but Shaw favored news-oriented television programs. In 1961, Shaw met famed TV journalist Walter Cronkite (1916–2009). He so impressed the elder newsman that Cronkite helped him get a job on CBS ten years later.

Anchorman Bernard Shaw in 2002. *Mark Mainz/Getty Images*

Shaw spent the ten years prior to his position on CBS sharpening his journalistic skills. He took jobs at an all-news Chicago radio station and as an anchor and reporter for the Westinghouse Broadcasting Company. In 1971, he began working as a reporter for the Washington bureau of *CBS News*. Shaw's desire to explore the world outside of Washington, D.C., led him to accept a job offer from *ABC News* as the Latin American correspondent. It was not as high-profile as his position at CBS, but Shaw knew it would be an opportunity to gain experience. From 1977 to 1979, he covered major international news stories such as the bizarre mass suicide in Jonestown, Guyana, and the civil war brewing in Nicaragua. Shaw's ability to present edgy stories with his trademark professional composure led to a position covering the tense hostage crisis at the American embassy in Tehran, Iran, in 1979.

As Shaw's career was on the rise at ABC, he received a job offer from the brand new Cable News Network (CNN). Shaw had no idea whether the twenty-four-hour news network

Breaking the Story of the Gulf War

In 1991, Bernard Shaw was in Baghdad waiting to interview the Iraqi dictator Saddam Hussein. While he was waiting, the United States began the bombing attacks that would spark the Gulf War. Shaw was one of the very first journalists to report on the war from its center. His harrowing experiences in Iraq elevated him to star status by the time he returned to the United States. He never allowed any of the attention to go to his head. He remained as professional and composed as ever.

would be a success, but the idea sparked his curiosity and interest. He decided to take a gamble on his career and accepted the job. He would stay in that job for twenty years.

In 1988, Shaw moderated the second presidential debate between George H. W. Bush (1924–) and Michael Dukakis (1933–). He was stern with the audience and tough with the presidential candidates. In 1991, he broke the story of the U.S. bombing attacks that would spark the Gulf War, one of the biggest news stories of the decade.

In 2000, Bernard Shaw announced that he would be bringing his long career as a television news journalist to an end. He still planned to take the occasional assignment, but he wanted to focus more on writing and spend more time with his family. Shaw made his final broadcast as the top anchor on CNN on February 28, 2001.

★ TAVIS SMILEY
(1964–)

Tavis Smiley has taken his political and social commentary to television, radio, and print. He is particularly concerned with issues affecting his fellow African Americans. Smiley has been an inspiring force in the media.

Tavis Smiley was one of ten children. The Smiley family was poor. Even so, their father was a hard worker who always provided for his wife and children. When Smiley was thirteen, he saw a campaign speech by Senator Birch Bayh (1928–) that inspired him to pursue a political path. Impressed by the influence Bayh had on his audience, Smiley ran for class president and won. As a student at Indiana University, he continued his work in student government. He also excelled on the debate team. Later

Talk show host Tavis Smiley in 2007. *Alex Wong/ Getty Images for Meet the Press*

he took an internship working for Los Angeles mayor Tom Bradley (1917–98).

At this point in his life, Smiley had ambitions of becoming a politician rather than reporting on politics. He ran for city council in Los Angeles in 1991. He lost the election but was not discouraged. He planned to run again in the next election. In the meantime, Smiley was determined to remain in the public spotlight. He started his own radio program called *The Smiley Report* as a means of speaking about political and social issues to potential voters. Each episode was only one minute long. The show became so popular that it was soon syndicated throughout America, which means it was broadcast simultaneously by many radio stations. In 1993, Smiley collected some of his favorite commentaries in a book titled *Just a Thought: The Smiley Report*.

In 1996, Smiley published his second book. *Hard Left: Straight Talk About the Wrongs of the Right* was a strong criticism of political conservatives and an argument in favor of liberalism that won wide critical praise. That same year, he began contributing radio commentaries to *The Tom Joyner Morning Show*. He also began hosting *BET Tonight*, a news program on Black Entertainment Television. Five years later, Smiley lost his job on BET after the channel was sold to Viacom. Viacom wanted to steer *BET Tonight* away from potentially controversial content. Smiley did not miss a beat. He seemed to be more present in the media than ever in 2001. He took jobs as a commentator on National Public Radio, CNN, and ABC News. He also published his next book, *How to Make America Better*.

In 1999, Smiley launched a program called the Tavis Smiley Foundation that contributes to the development of leaders in the African American community. In 2004, The Tavis Smiley School of Communications and The Tavis Smiley Center for Professional Media Studies opened at Texas Southern University. Smiley had become the youngest African American to have a university's professional school named after him. Toward the end of the first decade of the twenty-first century, Smiley hosted *Tavis Smiley*, a late night talk show on PBS television. He also hosted a radio show on Public Radio International and wrote articles for the online news source the Huffington Post. For his tireless work, Tavis Smiley has received the NAACP Image Award and the Du Bois Medal from Harvard University.

★ WILL SMITH
(1968–)

Ever since his song "Parents Just Don't Understand" became a smash hit in 1988, Will Smith has been one of the most popular entertainers in America. Smith has conquered the music industry, television, and film. It seems there is nothing he cannot do.

Will Smith grew up in Philadelphia, Pennsylvania. As a boy he played the piano and was learning to rap by the age of twelve. In 1981, he met Jeffrey Townes (1965–) at a party. Townes shared Smith's love of rap music. The two boys began working on an act together. In his role as record spinner, Townes took the name DJ Jazzy Jeff. Smith's teachers had nicknamed him Prince (as in "Prince Charming"). So, Smith became the Fresh Prince. The duo released their first album *Rock This House* in 1987. Their breakthrough arrived the following year. *He's the DJ, I'm the Rapper* contained the big hits "Parents Just Don't Understand," "Girls Ain't Nothing But Trouble," and "Nightmare on My Street,"

Actor Will Smith in 2009. *Florian Seefried/Getty Images*

which was inspired by the popular 1984 horror film *A Nightmare on Elm Street*. The duo released the album at a time when rap lyrics often contained profanity and references to graphic sex and violence. DJ Jazzy Jeff & the Fresh Prince made wholesome records that could be enjoyed by people of all ages.

Now that he was a genuine music star, Will Smith turned his sights to television. NBC offered him his very own sitcom titled *The Fresh Prince of Bel-Air*. The show ran from 1990 to 1996. The show starred Smith as a teen from the streets of Philadelphia who is sent to live with rich relatives in Bel-Air, California. Much like Smith's records, *The Fresh Prince of Bel-Air* was a hit. His sense of humor and charisma won him many new fans. The show won the best comedy series honor at the NAACP Awards in 1992.

Smith would next try out his oversized personality on the big screen. In 1992, Smith made his feature film debut as Manny in *Where the*

Day Takes You. The following year he received critical praise for his daring portrayal of a gay street-kid in *Six Degrees of Separation.* Smith's success in such small independent films led to starring roles in big-budget blockbusters like *Independence Day* (1996) and *Men in Black* (1997). In 1997, he released his first solo record. *Big Willie Style* proved that Smith could deliver the goods on his own. The dance track "Gettin' Jiggy Wit It," as well as the more personal "Just the Two of Us," a tribute to his son, were ubiquitous (seemingly everywhere at the same time) on the radio. *Big Willie Style* sold eight million copies. Smith quickly returned to the studio to record its follow-up, *Willennium,* which was released in 1999.

Will Smith's ever increasing popularity allowed him to take more serious acting roles alongside parts in big action-adventure and science-fiction movies. He played legendary boxer Muhammad Ali in the 2001 film *Ali.* He was nominated for an Academy Award for his performance. Smith has continued to star in films, including *Hitch* (2005) and *The Pursuit of Happyness* (2006). He has also maintained his music career. Will Smith is one of the most beloved and widely recognized entertainers in America.

Magazine editor Susan L. Taylor in 2009. *Jemai Countess/WireImage*

★ SUSAN L. TAYLOR
(1946–)

Ever since *Essence* magazine first hit newsstands in 1970, Susan L. Taylor's main goal has been the emphasis of inner beauty as well as outer beauty. As the publisher of the first magazine specifically aimed at young African American women, she had an irreversible effect on contemporary culture.

The child of Caribbean parents, Susan L. Taylor grew up in Harlem and Queens in New York City. A number of the women in the Taylor family had run businesses. Inspired by her heritage and encouraged by her business-minded parents, Taylor developed such ambitions as well. Early in her career, she took a job as a receptionist in Manhattan. At the same time, she was taking a typing class so she could increase her salary. Taylor continued to pursue a career even after she married at the age of twenty. She briefly tried her hand at acting, but she felt discouraged by the limited roles available to African American women. She next focused on starting her own line of cosmetics. Taylor attended cosmetology school while she was pregnant. She then took a job at the makeup counter in a department store. She took the job not only to earn money but also to learn more about what women wanted from their makeup. Taylor and her husband launched Nequai Cosmetics. The company was named after their daughter Shana-Nequai. The business was short-lived, however. Nequai Cosmetics failed as Taylor's marriage fell apart.

Despite the challenges of being a single mother in her early twenties, Taylor never lost sight of her career goals. In 1971, she was hired as a freelance beauty writer at a new magazine called *Essence*. The magazine provided beauty advice and inspirational tips to African American women, targeting women aged eighteen to forty-nine. Before long, Taylor was promoted to beauty editor. Later, she was promoted again to fashion editor.

In 1981, the editor-in-chief of *Essence* departed. Taylor recognized this as a great opportunity. She presented a fresh business plan for the magazine to its owner, Ed Lewis. Many people told Lewis he should not hand *Essence* over to an editor without a college degree, but he was impressed with Taylor's abilities. Taylor got the job.

With Susan Taylor at its helm, *Essence* attracted four hundred thousand new subscribers. To her credit, she has resisted pressure to cover scandalous topics. She has regularly emphasized the value of positive thinking. During the 1990s, she expanded her influence to television, hosting a program named after her magazine. Her first book, *In the Spirit: The Inspirational Writings of Susan L. Taylor*, was published in 1993. Incredibly, Taylor was attending college courses while juggling her magazine, her television show, and her blooming book-writing career. She retired from *Essence* in 2008 after nineteen years as its editor-in-chief. Taylor devoted herself to the national CARES mentoring movement. The program is an African American community mentoring program she founded in 2006 as Essence Cares.

★ DENZEL WASHINGTON
(1954–)

Denzel Washington is one of the most critically acclaimed actors of his generation. He is known for selecting quality roles and playing them with trademark intensity and intelligence. Washington is a multiple award winner and was listed among America's ten favorite actors by *USA Weekend* in 1998.

Washington was born the son of a Pentecostal minister and a barbershop owner in Mount Vernon, New York. He grew up in an integrated

Actor Denzel Washington in 2009. *Michael Kappeler/ AFP/Getty Images*

neighborhood near the Bronx. His parents encouraged him and his two siblings to be active in their community. Washington was a member of the Boys Club and the YMCA. After school, he worked in his mother's barbershop and at a local dry cleaner. When Washington was fourteen, he began to develop behavioral problems. His parents' divorce was devastating for him, and he responded by causing trouble. Washington's mother sent him to Oakland Academy, a wealthy, primarily white private school in upstate New York, in an attempt to get him under control. Washington's time at Oakland Academy instilled a renewed seriousness in him. While at the school he excelled at a number of sports and developed an interest in music.

Washington enrolled at Fordham University in 1972. He studied pre-medicine, but his grades were not strong. After a single semester, he dropped out of Fordham. He worked various jobs, including postal worker, trash collector, and summer camp counselor. A successful onstage recitation at Camp Sloane led him to consider a career in acting.

With new enthusiasm for his education, Washington reenrolled at Fordham. He switched his major to journalism and began participating in a theater workshop. At school, he starred in productions of *The Emperor Jones* and *Othello*. His stellar performances resulted in an offer to act in a television movie about track star Wilma Rudolph (1940–94) called *Wilma*. Washington made his onscreen debut while completing his degree in journalism and drama. Journalism soon fell by the wayside, and he settled on acting full-time.

Washington next studied acting at the American Conservatory Theater in San Francisco. Praise for his performances in the plays *Man and Superman* and *Moonchildren* inspired him to leave the conservatory after a year and travel to Los Angeles to look for acting work. The move did not pay off with jobs, so Washington returned home to Mount Vernon. There, he reconnected with *Wilma* actress Pauletta Pearson. The two developed a relationship that resulted in marriage. Pauletta's support kept him grounded during this unsuccessful stretch of his career. Just as Washington was about to begin a job teaching acting and sports to children, he was offered the role of African American activist Malcolm X in a play called *When the Chickens Come Home to Roost*. The play led to more acting work. It also would not be the last time Washington played Malcolm X.

In 1982, Washington won the Outer Circle's Critic Award and the Obie Award for his performance in *A Soldier's Play*. He also began getting supporting roles in feature films such as *A Soldier's Story* (1984; based on the play in which he starred) and *Power* (1986). He also took on television work. A recurring role as Dr. Philip Chandler on the popular medical drama *St. Elsewhere* grew into a full-time job that would last until 1988. In 1987, his performance as South African activist Steve Biko (1946–77) in *Cry Freedom* scored him an NAACP Image Award and an Academy Award nomination. Two years later, he won an Academy Award for best supporting actor for his performance as an American Civil War soldier in *Glory*.

In 1990, Denzel Washington began one of the most successful professional relationships in his career when he starred in director Spike Lee's *Mo' Better Blues*. Two years later, he and Lee collaborated again on a film about a man that was already quite familiar to Washington. *Malcolm X* was a vibrant, epic-length film about the assassinated activist. Washington delivered one of his most powerful performances as Malcolm X. He won a number of major awards and nominations for his work. He was now officially one of Hollywood's most sought-after stars.

Denzel Washington has continued to create consistently excellent work throughout his career. He has had the courage to turn down roles that do not represent African Americans well. Starring roles in *Courage Under Fire* (1996) and Spike Lee's *He Got Game* (1998) brought him further acclaim. In 2002, Washington won his second Academy Award for his role in *Training Day*. He was only the second African American to win the Oscar for best actor. Washington continues to star in successful films. In 2006 he starred in *Inside Man*, a film directed by Spike Lee. In 2007, he teamed up with Academy Award–winner Russell Crowe (1964–) in *American Gangster*. In addition to his work as a world-renowned actor, Denzel Washington works with the Boys & Girls Clubs of America and has donated large sums of money to charitable organizations.

◆◆
◆◆ *Topics in the News*
••

❖ AFRICAN AMERICAN MEDIA CHALLENGED BY MODERN TIMES

African American informational media faced considerable changes and challenges at the end of the twentieth century and beginning of the twenty-first century. A majority of challenges have been the result of diminishing audiences due to alternate sources of news and entertainment. A downturn in the U.S. economy from 2008 to 2009 also contributed to a decline in the number of black media sources in operation. Newspapers, for instance, have been hit particularly hard by Internet-provided news sources. Magazines, on the whole, have maintained a stronger readership than newspapers, in part because they are more entertainment-focused. A large portion of the market for African American media in the future will likely rely on the Internet as a source of information and entertainment.

Black Newspapers Face Many Challenges

Once-successful African American newspapers suffered from a loss of readership during the 1960s due to the civil rights movement. These included such papers as the *Baltimore Afro-American* and the *Chicago Defender*, which was the first black newspaper to have a mass readership. The civil rights marches of the 1960s were major news, but African American-owned newspapers did not have the resources to cover them as completely as white-owned papers did. Black readers began looking to white-owned papers to learn about the civil rights movement that would become such an important part of their history.

In 1968, a government report criticized the white press for misleading the public about a series of urban riots. It said that this coverage, or media reporting, threatened to damage the public image of African Americans. The report was written by a commission established by President Lyndon B. Johnson (1908–73). It explained that the riots were the result of poor economic conditions for African Americans and white racism. Responding to the report by Johnson's Kerner Commission, white newspapers began hiring black journalists in large numbers. African American journalists were hired in the hundreds during the 1970s. Roughly

A member of the Nation of Islam sells the group's official newspaper, *The Final Call*, on the streets of Chicago in 1995. © Ralf-Finn Hestoft/Corbis

four thousand African American journalists worked for daily newspapers by the 1990s. The mass hiring of African American journalists by white-owned papers led to the downfall of the black newspaper industry because there were fewer trained African American journalists available to work at black newspapers. Furthermore, the African American readership found itself better represented in mainstream newspapers that employed black journalists.

Despite the greater presence of African American journalists in the media, critics still recognized that the representation of blacks in mainstream newspapers was often negative and misinformed. There may have been more black writers, but they had little to no control over how their work was presented in the newspaper by white editors. This situation resulted in a number of reactions from the black journalism community. The National Association of Black Journalists was formed in 1975 to strengthen the black journalism community. The association worked to achieve a more realistic and less subjective (biased) portrayal of African Americans in the news. Another goal was to increase the number of jobs for black journalists.

Four African American journalists successfully sued the *New York Daily News* for discrimination, or negative employment action based on prejudice, in 1987. The journalists charged that they did not receive salaries or work assignments comparable to those of white journalists employed by the paper. At least one African American, Robert C. Maynard (1937–93), achieved diversity in the newsroom by actually buying the newspaper company. He purchased the *Oakland Tribune* in 1983 and added many black journalists to its staff.

Black journalists have certainly made headway in the newspaper industry since the 1960s. However, the relative lack of African American-owned papers means that they continued not to have the voice in the news media that white journalists have. In spite of everything, black newspapers such as the *Carolina Peacemaker, Ink Newspaper,* the *Baltimore Afro-American,* and the *Chicago Defender* continued to publish. Furthermore, a number of black journalists, including Nancy Maynard (1937–2008), Gwen Ifill (1955–), and Michele Norris (1961–), came to be ranked among the top newspaper journalists in America.

In the 2000s, black-owned newspapers have suffered a decrease in circulation as more people turn to the Internet for their news. The Black Press of America reported that the average weekly circulation of its papers in 2008 had decreased by half since 2000. Some daily newspapers have adopted a weekly schedule. Many African American newspapers, such as the *Afro-American, St. Louis American,* and *Philadelphia Tribune,* have begun to dedicate more resources to online news databases. Some small newspapers got out of the print business completely and moved online.

Black Magazines Hold Steady

The modern history of black magazines can be mainly attributed to one man: John H. Johnson (1918–2005). Johnson founded the Johnson Publishing Company in 1945. His company premiered *Ebony* and *Jet*, two magazines that have remained enormously popular since they debuted in the late 1950s. In 1965, Johnson launched *Black World.* This was around the time that black newspapers were losing their readership as African Americans began seeking the coverage of issues such as the civil rights movement in white-owned newspapers. *Black World* drew some African American readers back to black media sources by reporting on current events and issues relevant specifically to the African American community.

Former Ebony *and* Jet *magazine model Joanna LaShane poses with a cover of* Ebony *magazine in 2006.* Ebony *magazine became one of the premiere black magazines following its debut in 1945. © Noak K. Murray/Star Ledger/Corbis*

The continuing success of John H. Johnson's publishing empire inspired other African American entrepreneurs to launch their own magazines. *Essence,* the first magazine specifically marketed to African American women, debuted in 1968. The magazine featured articles about fashion and beauty along with news and entertainment stories. In 1970, Susan L. Taylor (1946–) made history as the first black woman to become editor-in-chief of a major magazine when she took over *Essence. Essence* would eventually have a readership of more than 8 million readers. That same year, Earl G. Graves Sr. (1935–) established *Black Enterprise,* the first magazine for African American businesspeople. *Black Enterprise* went on to reach 4.3 million readers. Graves next published *American Legacy,* a black history and culture magazine, which debuted in 1996. As of 2010 there were dozens of successful African American magazines, including *about . . . time, Black Beat,* and *African Voices.*

In 2000, multimedia star Oprah Winfrey (1954–) launched her own magazine. *O, The Oprah Magazine* covers a wide variety of topics, including fashion, books, fitness, food, business, and self-improvement. Oprah herself appears on the cover of every issue. (She had shared the cover only twice as of 2009: once with First Lady Michelle Obama and once with fellow talk-show host Ellen DeGeneres.) *O, The Oprah Magazine* is unique in the world of African American magazine publishing because it is geared towards all women, not just blacks. As of 2009, it had a readership of over 300,000.

Black magazines had fared much better than black newspapers in the early 2000s. In 2008, three of the four biggest African American magazines had a growth in circulation: *Ebony,* up 3 percent; *Jet,* up 2 percent; and *Black Enterprise*, also up 2 percent. These increases reflect the result of the magazines' extensive coverage of Barack Obama's rise to the presidency. *RiseUp,* a weekly national magazine dealing with racial issues, was introduced in June 2008 as an insert in mainstream newspapers. The magazine was targeted for readers of all ages but was printed for only a few months.

Black Radio Shows Go Nationwide

During the 1960s, the popularity of black soul and rhythm & blues music led to the creation of several "top forty" soul stations. Although these stations were white-owned, they did employ black DJs. However, the music these disc jockeys played was heavily controlled by the white station owners. DJs such as Sid McCoy, Herb Kent, Skipper Lee Frazier, and future funk legend Sly Stone found great success during the 1960s. They inspired their audiences in unexpected ways. Los Angeles DJ "Magnificent Montague" introduced hit records with the catch phrase "burn, baby, burn." During the racially charged Watts rebellion of 1965, a large-scale uprising in Los Angeles, protesters adopted Montague's words as a rallying cry. The previous year, former convict Ralph "Petey" Greene (1931–84) became a sensation as the host of the pioneering black talk show *Rapping with Petey Greene.* Ten years later, Greene starred in a television talk show of the same name. In 2007, he became the subject of the major motion picture *Talk to Me.*

Although black-oriented radio stations remained popular at the dawn of the 1970s, only sixteen of the three hundred such stations were owned by African Americans. Over the course of the decade, an increasing number of stations and networks were purchased by black owners. These networks were more news- and talk-oriented than most black stations had been. In 1972, the Mutual Black Network debuted. This network specifically targeted African Americans. It aired an hourly 5-minute newscast, as well as sports broadcasts and a 15-minute daily soap opera, *Sounds of the City.* The Mutual Black Network also produced programming that included African American history specials. The following year, the National Black Network was launched. It was the first network entirely under African American ownership to have a coast-to-coast audience. Like the Mutual Black Network, the National Black Network had 5-minute newscasts every hour

African American country-blues singer Rufus Thomas, shown in 1973, became one of the first black DJs at a white radio station in the late 1940s. © David Reed/Corbis

and sportscasts several times a day. It also aired an overnight talk show hosted by Bob Law, who would become a radio legend.

In the mid-1970s, major music stars such as Stevie Wonder (1950–) and James Brown (1933–2006) bought their own radio stations. The birth of the "urban contemporary" radio style in the early 1970s contributed to the growth of black radio. Frankie Crocker (1937–2000) of WBLS-FM switched the formerly jazz-oriented station to a pop-soul format that included white soul artists. He scored a number of new listeners. Several other stations followed Crocker's urban contemporary lead, including WHUR-FM in Washington, D.C.

In the 1980s, 88 out of 450 black-oriented stations were owned by African Americans. The decade saw the appearance of black sports shows and the increasing popularity of talk programs. The National Black Network was now drawing 4 million listeners per week. The Sheridan Broadcasting Network (formerly the Mutual Black Network) had 6.2 million listeners. Sheridan Broadcasting merged with the National Black Network in 1991 to form the American Urban Radio Networks (AURN). In the first decade of the twenty-first century AURN produced more urban programming than all other broadcasting companies—including television, cable, and national radio—combined. It was responsible for broadcasting more than three hundred shows every week, reaching about 25 million listeners.

Despite the growth of major African American stations, smaller independent stations have been disappearing. In 1996, the Telecommunications Act allowed conglomerates, or large companies consisting of multiple sub-companies, to purchase as many stations as they wanted. Black independent stations were being bought up by largely white-owned conglomerates. Their African American-centered formats were lost. By 2009, black-owned radio was fighting to survive. The small networks and companies were not the only ones to struggle. As of 2008, Radio One, the largest black-owned broadcasting company, owned 53 stations in 16 urban markets. During the first three quarters of 2008, the company posted a net loss of 296.6 million dollars. It appears that the future of African American radio will depend on factors outside its control: the business decisions made by conglomerates.

The Internet Creates New Opportunities

The personal computer developed into the most widely used and important new technology in America during the 1990s. Despite the widespread use of the Internet in the 1990s, it did not have a major impact on certain cultural groups, including African Americans. The U.S. National Telecommunications and Information Administration (NTIA) issued a report titled *Falling Through the Net: A Survey of the "Have Nots" in Rural and Urban America* in July 1995. This report coined the term "digital divide" to describe the gap between white Internet users and lower-income African

Americans without Internet resources. The personal computer became increasingly common in white households and schools, but the cost of computers kept them out of the reach of many African Americans. Some local governments acquired computers for use in community centers in low-income neighborhoods and schools. A number of critics, though, felt that this effort still did not provide enough Internet access to African American users. There was also a lack of resources specifically targeted at African Americans on the Internet. However, sites targeted to African Americans began to appear by the late 1990s. These were inspired by journalists such as Alondra Nelson, Anna Everett, and Lisa Nakamura. These women had written of the importance of an increased multicultural presence on the Internet.

In 1996, Farai Chideya (1969–) unveiled Pop+Politics, one of the first political/popular culture blogs. The blog often focused on issues of African American interest. Today there are a number of African American-oriented Web sites, news sources, and search engines throughout the Internet. These include blackfacts.com, blackrefer.com, and everythingblack.com. The social networking site blackplanet.com drew seventeen million members as of 2007, when future president Barack Obama (1961–) joined the site. Several organizations and for-profit companies have used their presence on the Internet to promote education and social causes in the African American community. These include the Black Women's Health Network and Black Entertainment Television. In August 2009, Interactive One, LLC,

African Americans as a group lag behind whites in computer ownership and usage, a phenomenon known as the "digital divide." © Bill Bachmann/ Alamy

the Digital Connection for Black America and the digital division of Radio One, Inc. launched BlackPlanet Rising (blackplanetrising.com). This site provides tools and information to connect African Americans with opportunities for volunteer service in their communities.

❖ STUDIOS TURN TO "BLAXPLOITATION" FILMS

At the beginning of the 1960s, African Americans were beginning to experience greater acceptance in the American film industry. Two decades earlier, the NAACP (National Association for the Advancement of Colored People) made a deal with several major studios. They wanted the studios to offer more jobs to African Americans. In the 1950s, black actors such as Sidney Poitier (1927–), Harry Belafonte (1927–), and Dorothy Dandridge (1922–65) were approaching stardom in Hollywood. Despite the success of such actors in major studio productions, black audiences craved films that focused on issues to which they could relate. They wanted movies featuring casts with more than one or two African American actors.

The slow progress of African Americans in the film industry continued through the 1960s. During this time, new stars like Al Freeman Jr. (1934–), Ossie Davis (1917–2005), Ruby Dee (1924–), and James Earl Jones (1931–) emerged. By the end of the 1960s, a financial crisis in Hollywood helped pave the way for an increased African American presence in film. Movies faced serious competition from television and foreign films. American films produced in Hollywood were selling fewer tickets at the box office in the late 1960s. Meanwhile, middle-class whites were relocating from cities to the suburbs. This left urban cinemas with more empty seats. African Americans made up 30 percent of movie audiences in cities, so it became clear to Hollywood that there might be a big demand for movies that catered to African American audiences.

Sweetback Starts a Trend

In 1971, black director Melvin Van Peebles (1932–) made a low-budget, experimental, and highly controversial film titled *Sweet Sweetback's Baadasssss Song*. The film starred the director as Sweetback, a black man who revolts against white society. It contained scenes of graphic violence and sex. One such scene involved Van Peebles's thirteen-year-old son, Mario, who would grow up to be a successful actor and director himself. *Sweetback* became tremendously popular among young, male, urban African Americans, but it appealed less to white audiences. Furthermore, the emphasis on Sweetback's sexual abilities and the film's poor treatment of women were heavily criticized. Despite such comments, Van Peebles's film earned ten million dollars over the course of its run. It had only cost five hundred thousand dollars to make. Hollywood quickly looked to *Sweet Sweetback's Baadasssss Song* as the kind of film black audiences wanted to see.

With *Sweetback*, the era of blaxploitation was born. "Blaxploitation" is the name given to the types of movies directors made, starting in the 1970s, to appeal to black urban audiences. Most film critics argue that *Sweet Sweetback's Baadasssss Song* was too experimental to qualify as a true blaxploitation film. Whether the movie fit the label or not, its gritty depiction of inner-city street life became a standard feature of blaxploitation films.

In the first half of the 1970s, blaxploitation films created even more parts for black actors. Nevertheless, the violent and highly sexual nature of these movies caused many critics to regard such films as a major step backward for the public image of black people. These films often showed African Americans as pimps, prostitutes, drug dealers, and gang members. Still, they did provide starting points for the successful non-blaxploitation careers of such actors and actresses as Richard Roundtree (1942–), Fred Williamson (1938–), and Pam Grier (1949–).

Shaft Sets the Standard

Shaft (1971) is usually regarded as the first true blaxploitation film. It was co-directed by father-and-son team Gordon Parks Sr. (1912–2006) and Gordon Parks Jr. (1934–79). Race did not factor into the original concept of *Shaft*. The tough-but-charming detective John Shaft was written to be played by a white actor, but studio executives had the film rewritten to take

The 1971 movie *Shaft* is one of the best known of the blaxploitation movies. *The Kobal Collection/The Picture Desk, Inc.*

advantage of the demand for black films, and Richard Roundree was cast in the role. John Shaft was now an African American determined to clean up his Harlem neighborhood. Both the film and its funky theme song became huge hits. Singer/songwriter/producer Isaac Hayes (1942–2008) won an Academy Award for "Theme from Shaft." Two sequels followed: *Shaft's Big Score* in 1972 and *Shaft in Africa* in 1973.

In 1972, Gordon Parks Jr. directed a film that was more controversial than *Shaft* had been. The main character in *Super Fly* is no civic-minded detective like John Shaft. Instead, Priest is a Harlem drug dealer who wants to leave his life of crime after completing one last big drug deal. Throughout the film, Priest's lifestyle of crime is glamorized. The film was well written and well acted. Its soundtrack by soul legend Curtis Mayfield (1942–99) was hailed for its frank assessment of life in the urban ghettoes. After being released as a single, the film's title song earned more money than the film itself. In 2003, *Rolling Stone* magazine rated the *Super Fly* soundtrack as the sixty-ninth greatest album of all time.

The Women of Blaxploitation

While blaxploitation was launched as a genre, or category of movie, directed at young men, its success led to more substantial roles for African American women. In 1973, Tamara Dobson (1944–2006) and Pam Grier both starred in their own blaxploitation movies. Dobson played the title role in *Cleopatra Jones* (1973) as a secret agent bent on wiping out the drug trade. Grier starred in *Coffy* (1973) and would go on to become one of the most popular actresses in the genre. Like the blaxploitation films featuring male stars, the ones with female leads also raised debate. Some critics felt that characters like Cleopatra Jones and Coffy supported negative stereotypes, or prejudicial mental images, of black women. Others praised them for their portrayals of strong, independent women.

With the massive success of blaxploitation films came both a degree of expansion and a great number of limitations. On the one hand, films such as Rudy Ray Moore's *Dolemite* (1975) expanded blaxploitation into comedy. Others, such as *Blacula* (1972) and *Blackenstein* (1973), became the first blaxploitation horror films. On the other hand, Hollywood pushed the stars of blaxploitation further away from the radical nature of the characters of Sweetback and Priest and more toward traditional ideals. Some critics claim that this was a deliberate move by Hollywood to belittle black empowerment. As critics further denounced the genre, studios basically stopped producing such films by the mid-1970s. They were able to do this in part because blaxploitation movies had helped Hollywood solve its financial problems, and in part because black actors began to play more prominent roles in big-budget Hollywood movies, which helped boost their appeal to black audiences.

❖ BLACK MUSICIANS CROSS OVER TO FILM

Throughout the history of cinema, a number of musicians have successfully made the jump from the concert stage to the big screen. In many cases, those musicians played themselves or some versions of themselves in pop musicals. Some examples are *A Hard Day's Night* (1964), starring the Beatles, and *Performance* (1970), starring Rolling Stones singer Mick Jagger (1943–). In other cases, these musicians-turned-actors have displayed great acting ability in roles quite different from their musical personas, or characters.

Calypso singer Harry Belafonte (1927–) was one of the first African American musicians to achieve film stardom. The charisma, or magnetic charm, and expression seen in his music translated nicely to roles in films. Examples are the musical *Carmen Jones* (1954) and the serious drama *Islands in the Sun* (1957), in which Belafonte played an up-and-coming politician facing racism. Even in that film he briefly broke character to sing a song.

During Belafonte's time, few other African American musicians pursued film acting with great success. Diana Ross (1944–), formerly of the pop-soul group the Supremes, was one of the few who managed to find substantial acting roles during the 1970s. Her daring role as troubled blues singer Billie Holiday in *Lady Sings the Blues* (1972) won much critical praise. She was nominated for an Academy Award for her work in the film. She also starred in *Mahogany* (1975) as a poor woman who rises to success as a fashion designer. This movie received poor reviews compared to *Lady Sings the Blues,* but was a hit at the box office. Then, in 1978, a movie adaptation, or remake, of the Broadway musical *The Wiz* was made. *The Wiz* was based on *The Wizard of Oz.* The movie provided large roles for a number of popular African American singers, including Ross, Michael Jackson (1958–2009), and Lena Horne (1917–). Although the film had limited success at the box office, it was nominated for four Academy Awards.

Few quality roles for African American musicians emerged during the 1980s. *Purple Rain* (1984), the semi-autobiographical story of multi-talented musician Prince, was tremendously successful. The movie's popularity may have had more to do with the film's spectacular, Oscar-winning soundtrack than it did with Prince's acting or the quality of the script. His starring roles in *Under the Cherry Moon* (1986) and *Graffiti Bridge* (1990) (both of which he also directed) were far less popular.

In the early 1990s, a number of rappers achieved a great degree of success as actors. With its emphasis on expressive spoken words, rap already had quite a bit in common with acting. On television, Will Smith (1968–) of DJ Jazzy Jeff & the Fresh Prince was on his way to stardom. He starred in the popular show *The Fresh Prince of Bel-Air* (1990–96), and translated that success into one of the most successful careers in Hollywood. Smith has starred in numerous dramatic, action, and comedic roles in such hits as *Independence Day* (1996), *Men in Black* (1997), *Ali* (2001, for which he received an Academy Award nomination for Best Actor), and *I Am Legend* (2007). During the 1990s, Kid 'n Play were also bringing in moviegoers in *House Party* (1990). Their roles in that movie had originally been written for Smith and DJ Jazzy Jeff. In 1991, rappers Ice-T (*New Jack City*) and Ice Cube (*Boyz n the Hood*) displayed great dramatic skill. Their roles in these movies were serious and demanding. Both of these men went on to have acting careers as successful as their musical ones. Suddenly, Hollywood viewed rappers as potential movie stars.

The phenomenon of the rapper-turned-actor has continued consistently since the early 1990s. Mos Def (1973–), Queen Latifah (1970–), DMX, Bow Wow, and Ludacris are just a few of the rappers who have carved out thriving acting careers for themselves. Latifah was nominated for the Best Actress in a Supporting Role Academy Award for her performance in the musical *Chicago* (2002). Several soul singers have also found success in cinema. In 2006, former *American Idol* contestant Jennifer Hudson (1981–) won an Academy Award for her supporting role in *Dreamgirls*. Two years later, Hudson's *Dreamgirls* co-star and Destiny's Child lead singer Beyoncé Knowles (1981–) received multiple award nominations and much critical praise for her portrayal of legendary singer Etta James in *Cadillac Records* (2008).

Jennifer Hudson (center) and Beyoncé Knowles (right), shown here in their roles for the 2006 movie *Dreamgirls*, are two African American singers who crossed over into acting. *Dreamworks/The Kobal Collection*

❖ BLACK COMEDIANS THRIVE IN FILM IN THE 1970S AND 1980S

By the 1950s and 1960s, the popularity of African American comedians was on the rise. Redd Foxx, Bill Cosby, and Jackie "Moms" Mabley (1894–1975) all made hit comedy records. Foxx and Cosby both had hits on television— Foxx with *Sanford and Son* (1972–77) and Cosby with the children's show *Fat Albert and the Cosby Kids* (1972–79). In 1970, Flip Wilson broke new ground as the first African American to host his own television comedy variety program.

Black comedians did not have the same opportunities in film, however. Cosby's first starring role was a dramatic one in *Man and Boy* in 1972. Later that year he starred in a crime action film titled *Hickey & Boggs*. Cosby's first pure comedy role arrived in 1974 when he costarred with Harry Belafonte and Sidney Poitier (who also directed) in *Uptown Saturday Night*. Roles in such comedies as *Mother, Jugs & Speed* (1976) and *The Devil and Max Devlin* (1981) followed. None of Cosby's film work was as commercially or artistically successful as his television and standup comedy work.

Richard Pryor Breaks Barriers

The first black comedian to have a major impact on the big screen was Richard Pryor (1940–2005). Perhaps the most important and innovative comedian of the 1970s, Pryor was a fearless performer. There was no subject too controversial for him, no taboo too untouchable. His unpredictability made him an exciting comedian. The personal nature of his act often made it quite moving. Pryor's larger-than-life, yet completely human persona made him a natural for film. He had a few minor roles in the late 1960s and early 1970s. He also had larger parts in the 1973 blaxploitation films *The Mack* and *Hit!* Pryor made his first major impact in film not on screen but as a screenwriter. In 1974, he co-wrote a Western parody titled *Blazing Saddles* for famed funny filmmaker Mel Brooks (1926–). Comedic actor Cleavon Little (1939–92) played the leading role of Black Bart. Like Pryor's standup comedy routines, *Blazing Saddles* was filled with manic energy and edgy attacks on racism. In 2000, the American Film Institute named *Blazing Saddles* the sixth funniest American film ever made.

Richard Pryor was known for his controversial stand-up comedy act in the 1970s before he broke into movies as an actor. *Michael Ochs Archives/Getty Images*

Pryor finally got his chance to make a splash as an actor on the big screen in 1976 when he starred in *Silver Streak*. He essentially played Gene Wilder's (1933–) sidekick in the film. Pryor's comedic acting is one of the most memorable aspects of the film. The success of *Silver Streak* led to three more Pryor-Wilder pairings in *Stir Crazy* (1980), *See No Evil, Hear No Evil* (1989), and *Another You* (1991). His 1979 concert film *Richard Pryor: Live in Concert* has been described as the best of its genre. Sadly, Richard Pryor died after a long battle with multiple sclerosis in 2005. His final role was a cameo in David Lynch's surreal thriller *Lost Highway* (1997). Although Pryor needed to use a wheelchair by that point in his life, he still displayed his comedic gifts in the film.

Murphy Builds on Pryor's Success

Pryor enjoyed only occasional success in his various film roles, but a comedy star emerged in the 1980s who would be highly successful. Eddie Murphy (1961–) first found fame as a cast member on the late-night comedy-sketch show *Saturday Night Live*. He was adored just as much for his original characters, such as inner-city dweller Mr. Robinson (a spoof of children's show host Fred Rogers), as he was for impersonations of celebrities, including Stevie Wonder and James Brown. Murphy made his film debut in 1982 as Reggie Hammond in *48 Hours*. This action-comedy became a smash success and made Murphy an instant movie star. The following year he had similar success in *Trading Places*, a satire about racism and Wall Street greed. Huge hits like *Beverly Hills Cop* (1987) and *Coming to America* (1988) followed. In 1989, Murphy directed his first film, *Harlem Nights*. The film co-starred Richard Pryor, but it was a commercial and critical disappointment. Murphy continued to make films in the twenty-first century, but none of them have been as successful as his hits from the 1980s.

In 1982, another African American comedian crossed over from the stage to the screen. Comedian Whoopi Goldberg (1955–) starred in *Citizen*, but it was not quite the success that Murphy's *48 Hours* had been. She would have to wait a few more years to achieve stardom. As a standup comic, Goldberg became wildly popular for playing multiple characters in her insightful routines. Though she was a comedian, her first major film role was in Steven Spielberg's drama *The Color Purple* (1985). In that movie, she starred as Celie, a girl growing up during the early 1900s who suffered problems with men. The role was not a showcase for Goldberg's comedic talent, but it did earn her a nomination for an Academy Award for her dramatic work. Soon afterward, she was finally given the opportunity to star in comedies. Her first few efforts, including *Jumpin' Jack Flash* (1986) and *Burglar* (1987), were fairly unsuccessful. A comedic supporting role as a psychic in the otherwise serious romance *Ghost* (1990) scored Goldberg her first Academy Award. She never quite achieved the success in her film comedies that she did in her dramas and standup performances, with the exception of her one major comedy hit, *Sister Act*, in 1992. Goldberg continued to make films in the twenty-first century, and in 2007 became one of the hosts of the popular television program *The View*.

❖ A NEW GENERATION OF BLACK FILMMAKERS FINDS SUCCESS

The opportunities for African American filmmakers that arose during the early 1970s came to a halt following the end of the blaxploitation era. The American film industry had used blaxploitation films (low-budget films featuring mainly black characters as well as violent and sexual content) to help it recover from its financial crisis. Once the studios started making profits, they relied less on that particular type of movie. African American groups like the Coalition Against Blaxploitation and Jesse Jackson's Operation PUSH (People United to Save/Serve Humanity) were devoted to battling the negative stereotypes shown in blaxploitation films and helped end their production. As a result, few black filmmakers emerged during the late 1970s and much of the 1980s. Then, in 1986, a determined young writer/director/actor named Spike Lee (1957–) ushered in a new era of African American cinema.

Spike Lee's Success Opens Doors for Others

Spike Lee had received some fame for his short film "Joe's Bed-Stuy Barbershop: We Cut Heads" (1983). This success did not initially help him get financing to make a feature film. In 1986, he finally raised enough money to make his first feature. *She's Gotta Have It* became an independent movie success. Independent movies are movies that are not produced by a major film studio. *She's Gotta Have It* won an award at the Cannes Film Festival in France. The film portrayed an independent, intelligent, career-minded African American woman. The character was a refreshing change from some of the violent, sex-obsessed characters seen in blaxploitation films. Lee had another low-budget hit called *School Daze* (1988). After that, Lee made a huge splash with *Do the Right Thing* (1989). The movie had a vibrant energy, sharp comedy, and challenging racial politics. *Do the Right Thing* became one of the biggest hits of 1989, earning more than thirty-seven million dollars throughout the world. It also won numerous awards, and sparked serious debate about its themes. The film demonstrated that African American movies could tackle complex and serious issues. It also showed that a movie featuring African American characters and themes could be successful in the mainstream market.

African American filmmaker Warrington Hudlin (1952–) proved this to be the case when he teamed with his brother Reginald to make the teen comedy *House Party* in 1990. Hudlin had first started in the movie business back in the 1970s when he created two short documentaries: *Black at Yale* (1974) and *Streetcorner Stories* (1977). Because few opportunities were available to African American filmmakers during that period, Hudlin's career did not take off until *House Party*. The movie about a black teenager trying to get to a party starred rappers Kid 'n Play. The film became popular with audiences and critics alike. Three sequels followed. In 1987, former standup comedian Robert Townsend (1957–) also achieved success with his *Hollywood Shuffle*. The movie was satire, or comedy meant to criticize real life, based on his own experiences as a struggling African American actor in Hollywood. The low-budget feature won a Critics Award and was

nominated for an Independent Spirit Award. These awards are presented annually by Film Independent, a nonprofit organization dedicated to independent films and their makers.

The groundbreaking work of film director Spike Lee ushered in a new era of African American filmmaking after the end of the blaxploitation era. *Columbia TriStar/The Kobal Collection*

Black Directors Focus on Gangs and Poverty

Do the Right Thing, House Party, and *Hollywood Shuffle* were great successes. This led Hollywood to acknowledge the demand for intelligent films made by African Americans. In 1991, a number of important films by black directors were released. Though not a Hollywood movie, Matty Rich's (1971–) *Straight Out of Brooklyn* made 2.7 million dollars at the box office. This was impressive, considering it was a low-budget film made for 450,000 dollars. Of that, 77,000 dollars was raised by Rich following a plea for funding on a Brooklyn radio show. Rich was only nineteen years old at the time. From inside the Hollywood system came John Singleton's (1968–) *Boyz n the Hood*. It was made by the major studio Columbia Pictures, but it had the gritty feel of the independent films by Spike Lee and Matty Rich. *Boyz n the Hood* was the story of a young black man's attempt to survive in a poor, violent neighborhood. It led to a new category of movies: "hood" films. The son of *Sweet Sweetback's Baadasssss Song* filmmaker Melvin Van Peebles also spawned a genre. Mario

African Americans Win Top Acting Award

W hen director Spike Lee made the smash hit *Do the Right Thing* in 1989, opportunities for black actors and actresses increased significantly. They received work from African American filmmakers such as Lee, Mario Van Peebles, John Singleton, and Kasi Lemmons. They also began receiving more roles from white directors and producers such as Tony Scott and Bill Condon. The roles African Americans were given to play were often complex and demanding. With better parts, African American actors and actresses received greater acclaim and more prestigious awards. Their breakthroughs have not brought a permanent end to negative stereotypes of African Americans in Hollywood films. Even so, they have signified the acceptance of African American actors in Hollywood and the rest of the society.

Denzel Washington and Halle Berry pose with the Academy Awards they won for Best Actor and Actress in 2002. *Frederick M. Brown/Getty Images*

The following is a list of African Americans who have won an Academy Award, the most prestigious award in movies.

1939, Hattie McDaniel: Best Supporting Actress for *Gone With the Wind.*

1963, Sidney Poitier: Best Actor for *Lilies of the Field.*

1982, Louis Gossett Jr.: Best Supporting Actor for *An Officer and a Gentleman*

1989, Denzel Washington: Best Supporting Actor for *Glory*

1991, Whoopi Goldberg: Best Supporting Actress for *Ghost*

1996, Cuba Gooding, Jr.: Best Supporting Actor for *Jerry Maguire*

2001, Halle Berry: Best Actress for *Monster's Ball*

2001, Denzel Washington: Best Actor for *Training Day*

2004, Morgan Freeman: Best Supporting Actor for *Million Dollar Baby*

2005, Jamie Foxx: Best Actor for *Ray*

2006, Forest Whitaker: Best Actor for *The Last King of Scotland*

2006, Jennifer Hudson: Best Supporting Actress for *Dreamgirls*

Van Peebles's (1957–) *New Jack City* sparked "New Jack cinema" with its tale of Harlem gangsters.

In the early 1990s, this new era of black filmmaking sometimes had an emphasis on sensationalistic gang violence. Some examples of this are Ernest Dickerson's *Juice* (1992), Allen and Albert Hughes's *Menace II Society*, and F. Gary Gray's *Set It Off* (1996). *Set It Off* is notable because it focused on a young woman rather than a young man. Soon, satires of the "hood" films were being produced. Some examples are Tamra Davis's *CB4* (1993) and Paris Barclay's *Don't Be a Menace to South Central While Drinking Your Juice in the Hood* (1996).

A number of filmmakers created works that stood apart from gang-oriented films of the time. Female African American filmmakers, such as Julie Dash (*Daughters of the Dust*, 1993), Cheryl Dunye (*The Watermelon Woman*, 1996), and Kasi Lemmons (*Eve's Bayou*, 1997) examined the varying experiences of black women in America and abroad. Lee also continued to make thought-provoking movies about the black experience during the 1990s, including *Mo' Better Blues* (1990) about a jazz musician, *Jungle Fever* (1991) about an interracial relationship, the epic biography *Malcolm X* (1992) about the slain civil rights leader, and *Crooklyn* (1994) about an African American family living in Brooklyn.

African American Filmmakers Branch Out

By the beginning of the twenty-first century, the cinematic work of African Americans was increasingly viewed as part of mainstream culture. Lee, in particular, proved that African American filmmakers do not have to limit themselves to making films only about African Americans. In 1999, Lee made *Summer of Sam,* his first film with a primarily white cast. Three years later he made *25th Hour,* starring white actor Edward Norton (1969–) as a drug dealer preparing to serve a seven-year jail sentence. In 2006 he made *Inside Man,* a thriller about a negotiator trying to resolve a hostage situation during a bank robbery. Lee did not neglect works with African American themes during this time, criticizing the portrayal of African Americans on television in the 2000 movie *Bamboozled.* He also made several television documentaries about prominent African Americans, including Black Panther leader Huey Newton, football star Jim Brown, and basketball legend Kobe Bryant. His best-known documentary is *When the Levees Broke: A Requiem in Four Acts* (2006), which explored the devastation and loss caused by Hurricane Katrina in 2005. It was first aired on HBO, and won three Emmy Awards.

The original stars of black cinema expanded their ranges as well. Mario Van Peebles made a black western called *Posse* (1993) as well as the horror film *From Hell* (2003). John Singleton made action films like the blaxploitation remake *Shaft* (2000) and *2 Fast 2 Furious* (2003).

❖ TELEVISION OPENS UP TO BLACK STORIES AND CHARACTERS

In television as in radio, African Americans have had to fight for both creative equality and the right to a dignified image. The first African American to achieve lasting success on television was Bill Cosby. In 1965, he debuted as secret agent Alexander Scott in the one-hour drama *I Spy*. Cosby was the first African American performer to win an Emmy Award. He paved the way for an increased black presence on television in the 1970s.

Black Comedies in the 1970s

One of the most important creators of black-themed television shows of the 1970s was a white writer/producer named Norman Lear (1922–). Lear's goal was to bring socially conscious situation comedies, or "sitcoms" to television. In 1971, he introduced the world to *All in the Family* (1971–79). It was based on a British program called *Til Death Us Do Part*. The main character in *All in the Family* was Archie Bunker, a white racist living in Queens, New York, played by Carroll O'Connor (1924–2001). The show brought issues of race, gender, homosexuality, and the Vietnam War to American living rooms. While Archie Bunker was depicted as somewhat lovable, the show held his racist remarks and opinions up to ridicule. In 1975, Bunker's African American neighbors, the Jeffersons, received their own sitcom. *The Jeffersons* (1975–85) broke with stereotypes by presenting a professional black man, George Jefferson, who owned a chain of dry cleaners. The sitcom featured an interracial married couple, something not seen on a mainstream television series before. Like Bunker, Jefferson, played by Sherman Hemsley (1938–), was also a racist. He often referred to white characters in offensive terms. *The Jeffersons* was a comedy that dealt with controversial subject matter, including gun control and suicide, not typically aired on television during those times.

A year before *The Jeffersons* debuted, Lear brought *Good Times* (1974–79) to television. *Good Times* was a spinoff of another successful Lear show, *Maude* (1972–78), which was itself another spin-off of *All in the Family*. Unlike *The Jeffersons, Good Times* focused on a poor black family living in a low-income housing project in Chicago. The comedy originally generated praise as the first television show to focus on black poverty. The show received criticism as well, because the character of J. J. Evans, played by comedian Jimmy Walker (c. 1947–), was seen as the kind of clownish

stereotype from the comedies of the pre-1960s era. Lear's *Sanford and Son* (1972–77), which starred comedian Red Foxx as a junk dealer, received similar criticism.

While Norman Lear was receiving mixed responses to his programs, Bill Cosby was pushing black television into new areas. His *Fat Albert and the Cosby Kids* (1972–85) became the first weekly cartoon featuring African American characters. The show also tackled social issues, including drug use, racism, and child abuse. *Fat Albert and the Cosby Kids* was a major success. It continued for years in syndication, meaning that other networks played reruns of the show. As a live-action TV star, Cosby had only modest success in the 1970s. *The Bill Cosby Show*, on which the comedian played a physical education instructor, ended its two-year run in 1971. *The New Bill Cosby Show,* a variety program featuring comedy sketches, was a ratings failure. It lasted just one season, from 1972 to 1973. A far more successful variety program was *The Flip Wilson Show* (1970–74), starring African American comedian Flip Wilson. Wilson played a number of different comic characters. He also hosted such legendary black musicians as James

Sherman Hemsley (center) played the main character George Jefferson in the 1970s television hit *The Jeffersons*. The show was the first to feature well-to-do African Americans. *CBS-TV/The Kobal Collection*

Brown, Aretha Franklin (1942–), Stevie Wonder, and Ray Charles (1930–2004). During its first two seasons, *The Flip Wilson Show* was the second-most-watched show in America.

Although African American-oriented comedies thrived in the 1970s, black dramas were rare. Two exceptions were *The Autobiography of Miss Jane Pittman* (1974), a television movie version of the novel by Ernest J. Gaines (1933–), and the miniseries *Roots* (1977). Based on a novel by Alex Haley (1921–92), *Roots* told the story of Haley's own family history, beginning with the abduction of African Kunta Kinte into slavery. The program provided numerous high-quality dramatic roles for African American actors and became a tremendous success among critics and viewers. In 1978, *Roots* won an impressive nine Emmy Awards.

Many of the new black television programs aired in the mid- to late 1970s continued in the comedic footsteps of *The Jeffersons* and *Good Times*. Most of these programs, however, were criticized for leaning on old-fashioned stereotypes, such as *What's Happening!!* (1976–79) and *Grady* (1975–76). Despite the flaws of these programs, their very existence meant that African Americans now had a foothold in television that would grow more secure in the 1980s.

The Cosby Show Breaks New Ground

The stereotypes and unrealistic situations that had crept back into African American sitcoms toward the end of the 1970s continued into the beginning of the 1980s. *Diff'rent Strokes* (1978–85) and *Webster* (1983–87) were two of the more popular programs with black characters. Both shows featured African American children adopted by wealthy white parents. But comedian Bill Cosby hoped to break with these stereotypes with his idea for a new program about an upper-middle-class black family living in Brooklyn, New York.

At first, the NBC network was not convinced Cosby's program would be a success. However, a screening of the first episode of *The Cosby Show* in 1984 was a major hit with television editors. They were delighted by the sophisticated humor of the program. On the show, Cosby starred as Dr. Heathcliff "Cliff" Huxtable. Cliff and his lawyer wife Clair (played by former Broadway musical actress Phylicia Rashad) lived in a Brooklyn brownstone, or row house, with their four children. The children were Denise (Lisa Bonet), Theo (Malcolm-Jamal Warner), Vanessa (Tempest Bledsoe), and Rudy (Keshia Knight-Pulliam). Daughter Sondra (Sabrina LaBeauf, added to the show in 1985) was away from home at Princeton University. *The Cosby Show* was unlike other family-oriented sitcoms such as *All in the Family, The Jeffersons,* and *Mama's Family* (1983–84; 1986–90). The humor on *The Cosby Show* centered on loving relationships rather than family fighting. Although Cliff's children could baffle him, he and Clair loved and nurtured their kids.

The Cosby Show was a hit with critics when it debuted on September 20, 1984. It was not an instant ratings success, however. NBC was worried. The network was already behind the other two major TV networks in the ratings race. Network executives tried to convince Cosby to add an adopted white child to the show, a reverse of the formula that had made hits of *Diff'rent Strokes* and *Webster*. Cosby refused. Executives then suggested that the Huxtables hire a white housekeeper. Cosby rejected this idea as well. Some critics complained that race was not enough of an issue in the show's storylines. Others grumbled that the marriage of a black doctor to a black lawyer was unrealistic. Cosby ignored the critics and continued to create quality comedy according to his own rules. He was rewarded when the show became a hit, finishing its first season as the third-most-watched program on television. From 1985 to 1990, *The Cosby Show* was the number-one show on TV, single-handedly reviving the sitcom genre and the NBC network. With the massive success of *The Cosby Show*, viewers began tuning in to NBC again. The network went from a distant third to CBS and ABC to the number-one network on television.

The Cosby Show, featuring an upper-class African American family, was one of the most popular television shows in the 1980s. *The Kobal Collection/The Picture Desk, Inc*

African American-oriented programs slowly received new life following *The Cosby Show*. One of the first such shows was the *Cosby* spin-off *A Different World* (1987–93). *A Different World* followed Denise Huxtable to college. Unlike *The Cosby Show*, *A Different World* was more likely to tackle issues of race, class, and equal rights. The program enjoyed a successful run for four seasons from 1987 to 1991 before its cancellation in 1993. Other successful African American sitcoms, including *227* (1985–90) and *Amen* (1986–91)—both starring former cast members of *The Jeffersons*—appeared in the mid-1980s.

African Americans Go Beyond Sitcoms

In 1986, a show debuted that became the most successful afternoon talk show ever to appear on television: *The Oprah Winfrey Show*. Winfrey (1954–) became one of the most important figures in media,

African American or otherwise. Since her talk show debuted, she has also distinguished herself in film, publishing, and on the Internet. The first network late-night talk show with a black host appeared in 1989 with the launch of *The Arsenio Hall Show* (1989–94). The debut of the first comedy-sketch show with a mostly black cast was in 1990. Keenen Ivory Wayans's *In Living Color* (1990–94) became one of the first big hit shows on the new FOX network. The show launched the careers of such future stars as Oscar-winner Jamie Foxx (1967–), singer Jennifer Lopez (1970–), comedian David Alan Grier (c. 1955–), and movie star Jim Carrey (1962–), who was one of only two white members of the cast. Wayans (1958–) moved on to a successful career as a filmmaker. The same year that *In Living Color* debuted on FOX, *The Fresh Prince of Bel-Air* (1990–96) premiered on NBC. Rapper Will "Fresh Prince" Smith (1968–) starred as a kid from inner-city Philadelphia sent to live with his wealthy relatives in Bel-Air, California. The show became a major ratings hit and set in motion Smith's tremendously successful acting career.

African American comedy shows continued to thrive through the 1990s with shows such as *Family Matters* (1989–98). The sitcom introduced the nerdy character of Steve Urkel (Jaleel White), who became the show's most recognizable star. Other African American sitcoms were successful during this time as well. These include *Martin* (1992–97), *Living Single* (1993–98), *The Steve Harvey Show* (1996–2002), *Malcolm & Eddie* (1996–2000), and *Hangin' with Mr. Cooper* (1992–97). The program that started it all, *The Cosby Show,* ended its wildly successful run in 1992. During its final season, the show experienced its lowest ratings but was still among the top twenty most-watched TV programs. In 2002, *TV Guide* ranked *The Cosby Show* as the twenty-eighth greatest television program of all time.

African Americans on TV in the 21st Century

Black shows that debuted in the twenty-first century still tended to be comedies. *Girlfriends* (2000–08), *My Wife and Kids* (2001–05), *The Bernie Mac Show* (2001–06), *Eve* (2003–06), *All of Us* (2003–07), *Everybody Hates Chris* (2005–09), and *The Game* (2006–09) all enjoyed great success in mainstream media in the 2000s. A notable exception to the black comedy genre has been ABC's *Grey's Anatomy* (2005–), a one-hour drama created by African American writer Shonda Rhimes (1970–). While the cast is too multicultural for it to be considered a "black" program, it has featured prominent African American characters during its run.

❖ CABLE NETWORKS TARGET AFRICAN AMERICANS

As black television programs flourished on network television in the 1980s, a desire for black programming grew in cable television as well.

A 2007 Nielsen report revealed that African Americans spend ten hours and forty-eight minutes watching television every day. This figure is significantly higher than that of any other race in America. Despite this fact, there were only three black channels on television: BET, TV One, and the Africa Channel. At the same time, however, there was more of an African American presence on cable and broadcast television than ever before.

African American-oriented entertainment flourished on cable television. Although the technology had existed since the 1950s, cable television did not come into common use until 1972. In 1972, the Federal Communications Commission (FCC) allowed cable television operators to use satellite transmissions. In November of that year, Home Box Office (HBO) began broadcasting movies. In 1976, HBO became widely available to paying subscribers who wanted to watch uncut, uninterrupted feature films on their televisions. With the success of HBO, other cable channels, such as Showtime and The Movie Channel, appeared. The first network created exclusively for African Americans came to cable TV with the debut of Black Entertainment Television (BET) in 1980.

BET was the creation of Robert L. Johnson (c. 1946–). Johnson recognized black television viewers as a 75-billion-dollar consumer market, and he aimed for his channel to cater to them. He saw BET as an alternative to white-owned stations. He planned to air programs that commercial television would not. He knew black viewers wanted to see programming with black actors and actresses. He also knew that African Americans did not want to be limited to the caricatures and stereotypes seen on popular shows such as *Good Times* and *What's Happening!!*

In the beginning, BET aired only two hours a week. By 1982, it aired for six hours per day to 3.8 million households. Two years later, BET finally made the transition to a 24-hour channel. It offered a wide variety of entertainment, including, movies, news, specials, and music programs. At first, BET featured gospel, soul, funk, and jazz music only. By the middle of the 1980s, it started featuring rap and hip hop as well. The program *Rap City,* which debuted in 1989 and ran for ten years, was only the second rap-oriented show on cable television. The first was *Yo! MTV Raps,* (1988–) which aired on the MTV channel.

BET spawned two other cable channels: the jazz channel BET J and BET Movies: Starz! BET has been criticized because it has not been owned by African Americans since it was sold to the media giant Viacom in 2000. In addition, several high-profile celebrities and organizations have condemned BET for airing programs that support stereotypes and focus on violence. This controversy gave rise to channels that sought to provide alternatives to such programming. Some, such as New Urban Entertainment

Black Entertainment Television (BET), the first cable channel to specifically target African American viewers, celebrates its 25th anniversary at the Shrine Auditorium in Los Angeles on October 26, 2005. *Vince Bucci/Getty Images*

Television (2000–02) did not last long. TV One (2004–), which focuses on family programming, has been highly successful. The network posted a pretax profit around 90 million dollars in 2008. The Africa Channel was launched in 2005 and expanded in 2006 to reach viewers from coast to coast. This channel is unique in that it offers the African continent's best English-language television programs, a format that includes biographies, business news, travel features, reality shows, music and soap operas. The Africa Channel, BET, and TV One all extended their markets to reach more households in 2008. This expansion meant that these networks were potentially able to expand their audiences and their advertising revenues. In 2008, rapper Master P announced that he planned to launch Better Black Television (BBT), the first all-hip-hop music channel in 2009.

There have been many African American programs on cable television, several of them hits with both black and white audiences, even though channels such as BET and TV One continue to draw viewers. In 1997, *The Chris Rock Show* debuted on HBO. Comedian and former *Saturday Night Live* cast member Chris Rock (1965–) interviewed various guests and performed humorous, issue-oriented monologues. The program ran for three seasons, ending in 2000, and won an Emmy Award for its writing.

Comedian Dave Chappelle's comedy-sketch program *Chappelle's Show* became a sensation when it first appeared on Comedy Central in 2003. Chappelle (1973–) broke new ground with characters like blind white supremacist Clayton Bigsby, who does not realize he is black, and crack addict Tyrone Biggums. It was one of the most popular shows in the history of Comedy Central, but ended in 2006 when Chappelle abruptly left during the making of the third season.

Not all African American cable programs achieved the success of *The Chris Rock Show* and *Chappelle's Show*. In 2006, Wanda Sykes starred in an offbeat show called *Wanda Does It* (2006). On the show, the comedian tried her hand at a new job every week. The program aired just six episodes on Comedy Central. *Chocolate News* (2008), starring *In Living Color* veteran David Alan Grier, had a similarly short run. It was an attempt to put an African American spin on the successful news satire programs *The Daily Show with Jon Stewart* (1999–) and *The Colbert Report* (2005–). Grier's show aired for ten episodes in 2008. Programs such as Showtime's *Soul Food* (2000–04), Nickelodeon's *That's So Raven* (2003–07), and TBS's *The Boondocks* (2005–07) have enjoyed longer runs. No matter how long an African American–oriented program remains on air, it is obvious that African Americans are more represented than ever on both cable and network television.

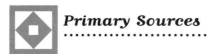

◆ *DO THE RIGHT THING* MOVIE REVIEW (1989)

Spike Lee's *Do the Right Thing* was the most controversial film of the year when it was released in 1989, according to movie critic Roger Ebert. The movie was controversial because it provided a realistic look at inner-city racial tension and violence without suggesting solutions or assigning blame. Some criticized the movie and said it promoted violence. Roger Ebert gave the movie four stars, his highest possible rating. Part of Ebert's review appears below. In this passage, he takes on some of these criticisms of Lee's movie.

● ●

Spike Lee's *Do the Right Thing* is the most controversial film of the year.... [E]verywhere I go, people are discussing it. Some of them are bothered by it; they think it will cause trouble. Others feel the message is confused. Some find it too militant, others find it the work of a middle-class director who is trying to play street-smart. All of those reactions, I think, simply are different ways of avoiding the central fact of this film, which is that it comes closer to reflecting the current state of race relations in America than any other movie of our time.

Of course it is confused. Of course it wavers between middle-class values and street values. Of course it is not sure whether it believes in liberal **pieties** or militancy. Of course some of the characters are sympathetic and others are hateful. And of course some of the likable characters do bad things. Isn't that the way it is in America today? Anyone who walks into this film expecting answers is a dreamer or a fool. But anyone who leaves the movie with more intolerance than they walked in with wasn't paying attention.

Piety
Dutiful devotion

The movie takes place during one long, hot day in the Bedford-Stuyvesant neighborhood of Brooklyn. But this is not the typical urban cityscape we've seen in countless action movies about violence and guns and drugs. People live here. It's a neighborhood like those city neighborhoods in the urban movies of the Depression: People know one another and accept one another, and although there are problems, there also is a sense of community.

The neighborhood is black, but two of the businesses aren't. Sal's Famous Pizzeria has been on the same corner since before the neighborhood changed, and Sal (Danny Aiello) boasts that "these people have grown up on my pizza." And in a nearby storefront that had been boarded up for years, a Korean family has opened a fruit and vegetable stand. Nobody seems to quite know the Koreans, but Sal and his sons are neighborhood fixtures: They know everybody, and everybody knows them.

It's the hottest day of the summer.
You can do nothing,
you can do something,
or you can...

DO THE
Right
Thing

Bed-Stuy

A
SPIKE LEE
JOINT

A 40 ACRES AND A MULE FILMWORKS PRODUCTION
A SPIKE LEE JOINT "DO THE RIGHT THING" DANNY AIELLO
OSSIE DAVIS · RUBY DEE · RICHARD EDSON · GIANCARLO ESPOSITO
SPIKE LEE · BILL NUNN · JOHN TURTURRO and JOHN SAVAGE as Clifton Casting ROBI REED
Production Design WYNN THOMAS Original Music Score BILL LEE Editor BARRY ALEXANDER BROWN Photographed by ERNEST DICKERSON

Movie poster from the
1989 Spike Lee movie *Do
the Right Thing. Universal/
The Kobal Collection/The
Picture Desk, Inc.*

Sal is a tough, no-nonsense guy who basically wants to get along and tend to
business. One of his sons is a vocal racist—in private, of course. The other is more open
toward blacks. Sal's ambassador to the community is a likable local youth named
Mookie (Spike Lee), who delivers pizzas and also acts as a messenger of news and
gossip. Mookie is good at his job, but his heart isn't in it; he knows there's no future in
delivering pizzas.

We meet other people in the neighborhood. There are Da Mayor (Ossie Davis), a kind of everyman who knows everybody; Buggin Out (Giancarlo Esposito), a vocal militant; Radio Raheem (Bill Nunn), whose boom box defines his life and provides a musical cocoon to insulate him from the world; Mother Sister (Ruby Dee), who is sort of the neighborhood witch. There are the local disk jockey, whose program provides a running commentary, and a retarded street person who wanders around selling photos of Martin Luther King Jr. and Malcolm X. And then there are three old guys on the corner who comment on developments, slowly and at length. . . .

But things are happening under the surface. Tensions are building. Old hurts are being remembered. And finally the movie explodes in racial violence.

The exact nature of that violence has been described in many of the articles about the film . . . but in this review I think I will not outline the actual events. . . . Since Lee does not tell you what to think about it, and deliberately provides surprising twists for some of the characters, this movie is more open-ended than most. It requires you to decide what you think about it.

Do the Right Thing is not filled with brotherly love, but it is not filled with hate, either. It comes out of a weary, urban cynicism that has settled down around us in recent years. The good feelings and many of the hopes of the 1960s have evaporated, and today it no longer would be accurate to make a movie about how the races in America are all going to love one another. I wish we could see such love, but instead we have deepening class divisions in which the middle classes of all races flee from what's happening in the inner city, while a series of national administrations provides no hope for the poor. *Do the Right Thing* tells an honest, unsentimental story about those who are left behind. . . .

Incitement
Encouragement;
provocation

Some of the advance articles about this movie have suggested that it is an **incitement** to racial violence. Those articles say more about their authors than about the movie. I believe that any good-hearted person, white or black, will come out of this movie with sympathy for all of the characters. Lee does not ask us to forgive them, or even to understand everything they do, but he wants us to identify with their fears and frustrations. *Do the Right Thing* doesn't ask its audiences to choose sides; it is scrupulously fair to both sides, in a story where it is our society itself that is not fair.

◆ TESTIMONY ON THE IMPACT OF THE 1996 TELECOMMUNICATIONS ACT ON BLACK RADIO (2006)

In December 2006, St. John's University law professor Akila N. Folami testified before the Federal Communications Commission (FCC) to describe the damaging effects of the 1996 Telecommunications Act on black radio. Because the act relaxed media ownership restrictions, it led to mass consolidation of media outlets, meaning large companies bought and managed multiple radio and television stations. This meant that the programming on these stations had less diversity. Folami argues that the Telecommunications Act stifled the freedom of expression many young, urban blacks had enjoyed through the radio. Folami explains that hip-hop music, often politically focused, was played on local black radio stations and performed almost like a "Black CNN," spreading information about issues of importance to the black community. Further, Folami argues, the musical genre of hip hop was also stifled and twisted because only a certain kind of rap and hip hop were played on the large, corporate radio stations—specifically, gangsta rap. Folami finds this artificially constructed emphasis on gangsta rap—with its anti-woman, violent, materialistic content—harmful, both to African American and white communities.

· ·

I would like to thank the Commissioners for coming to Nashville, Tennessee, to discuss these important issues of media ownership. . . .

The existing **tiered** numerical limits, set forth in the Telecommunications Act of 1996, were not "in the public interest," led to corporate **conglomeration** in radio, and did not encourage economic competition, or diversity in radio station ownership or in content. For the Hip Hop community, corporate takeover of the radio has had a deadening effect on the much needed **discourse** that was occurring among America's younger generation prior to consolidation, particularly among its young, urban, Black men, through Rap.

Historically, young urban Black men, through Hip Hop and Rap's radio air play, attained visibility from an otherwise **marginalized** existence in America. Hip Hop arose, in the late 1970s, out of the ruins of a post-industrial and ravaged South Bronx, as a cultural expression of urban Black and Latino youth, who were primarily male and who politicians and the dominant public and political discourse had written off, and, for all intent and purposes, abandoned. Rendered invisible by both White and Black politicians alike, and isolated and ignored, in what was categorized by most as a dying city, these youth decided to celebrate and live through Hip Hop and Rap.

Soon Rap would be proclaimed by some as the Black CNN, with many different Rappers giving voice to what would have otherwise remained unseen by the larger dominant American public, such as police brutality, poverty, and the conditions in America's urban centers. Moreover, some scholars contend that rap would successfully form new allegiances with counter-culture white youth who found genuine pleasure in Rap as a forbidden narrative and a symbol of rebellion, much like punk rock. Rap would defy both Black and White middle class norms with its confrontational style. Rappers, who were primarily urban Black male youth, would speak in their own voice and on their own terms, as members of a historically marginalized segment of America's population living in America's blighted urban areas.

Tiered
Ranked

Conglomeration
Joining together into one business

Discourse
Conversation; verbal exchange

Marginalized
Pushed to the edges of social standing

Today, Gangsta Rap currently dominates the nation's radio airwaves with messages of **misogyny**, violence, and excessive consumer consumption. It is largely corporate driven, heavily marketed, and commercialized by corporate media in a way that more socially conscious Rap cannot be. Gangster Rappers promote anything from sneakers, jeans, iPods, cellphones, colognes, and sports drinks. By solidifying corporate control of the nation's radio air waves, the Telecommunications Act has stifled the social commentary and diverse views in Rap that were once heard over the radio, and has encouraged the **proliferation** of Gangsta Rap and the creation of the Gangsta image that has become the **de facto** voice of contemporary Hip Hop culture. The image and the message are clear: consume, consume, consume! Overlooked for radio air play, are female rappers, and non-Gangsta Rap songs that might appeal to niche audiences or to audiences with smaller buying power. . . .

Proliferation
Spread

De facto
Actual

Although non-Gangsta Rappers find other outlets (like the Internet or satellite radio) to distribute their lyrics, such Rap does not attain the same level of visibility because those other media fail to provide inexpensive access like over-the-air radio. In addition, several studies have established that there is still a Digital Divide between Blacks and whites as to access to home computers and the Internet. There is also a racial gap in access to broadband technologies, while access to satellite radio and cable comes at a price. . . .

What was once a cultural and political expression of survival of a historically marginalized group has been hampered in a large way by limited access to the nation's radio air waves. Black male youth have historically had to navigate America's public space to become visible and assert a voice of their own, and have done so, through Hip Hop and Rap, in the face of considerable odds. The Telecommunications Act of 1996, has contributed to stifling the diversity of viewpoints in the Hip Hop community, to proliferating a very racialized and sexualized image of the Gangsta Rapper, and has served to further marginalize Black male youth who have been, and continue to be, given recent U.S. census data and studies by scholars at Columbia, Georgetown, and Princeton Universities, invisible to the American political and economic discourse.

Research and Activity Ideas

1. Over the course of the 1970s and the 1980s, the way African Americans were portrayed on sitcoms changed. Watch an episode of the 1970s television show *Good Times*. Then, watch an episode of *The Cosby Show* from the 1980s. (Both are available on DVD.) How is the depiction of African Americans different in the two shows? Explain your answer in an essay using specific examples from both sitcoms to support your response.

2. Some films have a very clear social or political message. However, it is harder to figure out the "message" in director Spike Lee's films. Some critics complain that films such as *Do the Right Thing* do not offer a specific solution to problems like racism and inner-city violence. Imagine that you are going to make a movie about issues of race and inner-city problems. What kinds of characters would you create? What specific social problems would you address? Would you supply clear solutions to these problems? If so, what kind of solutions might you suggest? What kind of tone would you use? Would your movie be humorous, dramatic, or both? Write a movie "treatment" (a synopsis that includes a list of characters with descriptions and a plot summary) describing your film.

3. Unlike other forms of African American–oriented media, black newspapers have struggled to remain in business. White-owned newspapers with greater financial resources have made it difficult for black newspapers to compete. Nevertheless, black papers have still published a great deal of high-quality journalism throughout the years. Read two articles from a white-owned newspaper, such as the *New York Times* or the *Washington Post*. Then, read two articles in a black-owned newspaper, such as the *Baltimore Afro-American* or the *Chicago Defender*. All of these papers publish much of their content online. Compare and contrast the articles in the white-owned paper and the African American-owned paper. How do the viewpoints and voices of the two papers differ? How are they similar? Explain your answer in an essay using specific examples from both newspapers to support your response.

4. In 1996, Farai Chideya launched Pop+Politics (www.popandpolitics .com), one of the first political/pop culture blogs. The blog often focuses on issues of African American interest. Pop+Politics continues to thrive today with articles about music, film, and politics. Read one of Chideya's articles on Pop+Politics. Then get involved in a discussion of the article in the comments section at the bottom of

the page. Tell Chideya what you liked and disliked about the article, as well as what you learned. If she responds to you, try to keep the discussion going with follow-up questions for the writer.

5. African American journalist Michele Norris hosted the news program *All Things Considered* on National Public Radio (NPR) beginning in 2002. Listen to two episodes of the program, which can be found online at NPR's Web site (www.npr.org). Write a review of *All Things Considered* based on the two shows you have listened to. What kinds of topics are covered on the show? Who is the show's intended audience? What did you learn from listening? Brainstorm some topics that you think would work well on the show. Then research one of the topics and prepare your own report in the style of *All Things Considered.*

 For More Information

• •

BOOKS

Berry, S. Toriano, and Venise Berry. *Historical Dictionary of African American Cinema.* Lanham, Md.: Scarecrow Press, 2007.

Cosby, Bill. *Fatherhood.* New York: Penguin Group, 1987.

Fearn-Banks, Kathleen. *Historical Dictionary of African-American Television.* Lanham, Md.: Scarecrow Press, 2006.

Howard, Josiah. *Blaxploitation Cinema: The Essential Reference Guide.* Surrey, U.K.: FAB Press, 2008.

Jaynes, Gerald D., ed. *Encyclopedia of African American Society.* Thousand Oaks, Calif: Sage Reference, 2005.

Joyner, Tom, with Mary Flowers Boyce. *I'm Just a DJ But ... It Makes Sense to Me.* New York: Grand Central Publishing, 2005.

Littleton, Darryl J. *Black Comedians on Black Comedy: How African-Americans Taught Us to Laugh.* New York: Applause Theatre and Cinema Books, 2008.

Massood, Paula J. *Black City Cinema: African American Urban Experiences in Film.* Philadelphia, Pa.: Temple University Press, 2003.

Watkins, Mel. *On the Real Side: A History of African American Comedy.* New York: Simon & Schuster, 1994.

PERIODICALS

Collier, Aldore. "The Oscars in Black and White." *Ebony* (April 2000): p. 90.

Daniels, Cora. "The Hardest Working Man in Radio." *Fortune* (December 12, 2005): p. 39.

Graves, Earl G., Jr. "Use Social Media to Enhance Face-to-Face Networking." *Black Enterprise* (September 2009): p. 6.

Hocker, Cliff. "Blacks Go Broadband: High-Speed Internet Adoption Grows Among African Americans." *Black Enterprise* (February 2008): p. 32.

Lyons, Douglas C. "Blacks and the New TV Season." *Ebony* (October 1990): p. 104.

Sturgis, Ingrid. "Adventures in the Blogosphere: As Internet Journals Come into Their Own, African American Voices Are Rising Above the Noise." *Black Issues Book Review* (January–February 2005): p. 12.

White, Paula M. "Changing Frequencies: Minority Ownership of U.S. Radio and TV Stations Remains Stagnant." *Black Enterprise* (October 1996): p. 20.

WEB SITES

The Root. http://www.theroot.com/ (accessed on November 1, 2009).

"The Telecommunications Act of 1996." *Federal Communications Commission.* http://www.fcc.gov/telecom.html (accessed November 1, 2009).

chapter five

Demographics

Chronology 268

Overview 271

Headline Makers 274
Roland G. Fryer 274
bell hooks 276
Mildred Loving 280

Topics in the News 284
The 2000 Census Provides a
    Snapshot of African
    American Demographics . .284
Drugs and Gangs Plague
    African American
    Communities 285

African American Family Life
    Undergoes Changes 291
A Black Middle Class
    Emerges 297
Great Migrations Change the
    Demographics of U.S.
    Cities 300

Primary Sources 304

Research and Activity Ideas . . .308

For More Information 309

1965 The New Great Migration begins, with blacks who had previously been making their homes in the North returning to the South.

1965 February 21 The most widely known face of black nationalism, Malcolm X, is killed in New York by a member of the Nation of Islam, a religious and political faction that he had recently left.

1965 August 11 The Watts riots begin in Los Angeles and end six days later, with thirty-four people dead as a result of looting and violence.

1967 June 12 In *Loving v. Virginia*, the Supreme Court unanimously rules that a Virginia state law banning marriages between people of different races is unconstitutional.

1968 April 4 Martin Luther King Jr., the most influential leader of the civil rights movement, is assassinated.

1970 The Second Great Migration, in which many African Americans moved from the South to points in the North and West, comes to an end.

1971 April 20 In *Swann v. Charlotte-Mecklenburg Board of Education*, the Supreme Court rules that school districts in the South can be required to bus children to schools in different neighborhoods in order to achieve racial integration.

1974 July 25 In the landmark case of *Milliken v. Bradley*, the Supreme Court rules that the Detroit city schools are barred from busing inner-city students to schools in the primarily white suburbs.

1981 bell hooks publishes her first book, *Ain't I A Woman,* a criticism of white feminism.

1984 Crack cocaine, a more potent form of powdered cocaine, is introduced in the illegal drug trade. The cheap, highly addictive drug hits poor African American communities the hardest.

1984 Bill Cosby's *The Cosby Show* goes on the air on NBC. The sitcom offers a groundbreaking television portrayal of a middle-class African American family. The show is number one in the ratings for five consecutive seasons.

1988 The Reverend Jesse Jackson begins advocating in favor of "African American" as a term of self-identification.

1990 Studies show that, on average, African American middle-school students score 20 percent lower than white middle-school students on standardized tests in reading, math, and science.

1990 January 18 The second mayor of Washington, D.C., Marion Barry, is arrested on drug charges. Despite his arrest, Barry is reelected to office in 1995.

1992 April 29   The Los Angeles riots begin after the white police officers accused of beating African American motorist Rodney King are acquitted. The riots are the worst in Los Angeles history and result in the deaths of fifty-three people.

1993   The National Youth Gang Center estimates that there are more than eight thousand gangs operating in the United States.

1995   The United States Sentencing Commission determines that crimes involving powdered cocaine should receive 1/100th of the fines and penalties for crimes involving crack cocaine.

2000   The 2000 census shows that almost 13 percent of the U.S. population is African American, with more than 50 percent of African Americans living in the South.

2002   The city of Atlanta, Georgia, sees a 114 percent increase in the number of mortgages held by single black women since 1997.

2002   The Centers for Disease Control and Prevention (CDC) reports that the birth rate among African American teenage girls has dropped by 40 percent since 1991.

2004 November 2   African Americans vote overwhelmingly for John Kerry, a Democrat, in the presidential election (88 percent of the vote vs. 11 percent voting for Republican nominee George W. Bush).

2005   African Americans account for almost 50 percent of new HIV/AIDS diagnoses in the United States.

2005 August 29   Hurricane Katrina makes landfall in southeastern Louisiana, eventually causing massive flooding and catastrophic damage to the city of New Orleans and other parts of the Gulf coast. The hurricane causes the most damage to poor, predominantly African American neighborhoods in New Orleans. More than 90 percent of New Orleanians needing evacuation assistance after the hurricane are African American.

2007   The African American population grows to over 13 percent of the total U.S. population, up from about 10 percent in 1980. The states with the most African Americans are Texas, New York, and Florida.

2007   *Black Enterprise* magazine names Washington, D.C., the most desirable place in the United States for African Americans to live.

2007   The median annual income of African American households is approximately $34,000, whereas the median income of white households is nearly $55,000.

2007   African Americans continue to have the highest rate of poverty in the

United States (24.5 percent). Hispanics are second at 21.5 percent, while the rate of poverty for whites is 8.2 percent.

2008 At the age of thirty, Roland G. Fryer becomes the youngest African American ever to receive tenure at Harvard University.

2009 A recession causes black unemployment to rise to 15 percent, whereas the country's overall rate is less than 9 percent.

2009 January 20 Barack Obama becomes the first African American president of the United States.

Demographics are data and statistics regarding the basic qualities of the general population or a segment of the population. African American demographics have frequently been difficult to assess. One reason for this is that many African Americans were not given proper names or addresses until well after the Civil War. Another reason is that after World War II, the African American population shifted dramatically from the South to the North and West. So many people moved so often that it was difficult for researchers to keep track of them. The U.S. Census 2000 is decidedly more accurate in tracking the education, marriage, and income levels of African Americans than past censuses were. Census 2000 produced a large amount of very useful data about African American demographics.

Since the civil rights era, the concept of racial integration and equal opportunity have gone hand in hand. The separation of the educational, public, and cultural lives led by whites and African Americans in the years before the civil rights movement produced dramatic differences in the quality of the lives they led. Blacks, as a whole, were far poorer and lived shorter lives than whites. It seemed clear, both to social scientists and social activists, that giving African Americans access to the same resources as whites through integration would help solve these problems. The courts and the government played a large role in effecting the changes that made integration possible. The landmark U.S. Supreme Court case *Brown v. Board of Education of Topeka, Kansas* (1954) declared segregation in public schools illegal. Later decisions pressured segregated school systems (most of them in the South) to integrate quickly. The Civil Rights Act of 1964 made discrimination on the basis of race in schools, public places, or employment decisions illegal. In *Loving v. Virginia* (1967), the U.S. Supreme Court ruled that interracial marriages are indeed constitutional. The Fair Housing Act of 1968 outlawed racial discrimination in the sale, rental, or financing of housing. These and other rulings and laws tried to break down cultural and legal barriers that kept African Americans from living, learning, and working alongside whites. Still, the pace of change was too slow to suit the courts and civil rights activists.

The courts and the Congress were not alone in moving toward integration. African Americans themselves quite literally moved—away from the segregation and often violent racism of the South toward the promise of new economic opportunity in the cities of the North and West. Fifty years after the Civil War, from approximately 1915 to 1930, more than one million African Americans fled the South. This movement became known as the

Great Migration. It was followed by an even larger movement after World War II, called the Second Great Migration. Starting in 1940, nearly 5 million African Americans continued the migration pattern northward and westward. The Second Great Migration only slowed down around 1970.

These changes in the racial makeup of the country's schools, workplaces, and neighborhoods alarmed many people. The process was far from smooth. The late 1960s saw race riots in most major cities. These riots were sparked by tension between the growing African American populations and the white power structure. Most of those rioting in these cases were African Americans. When the U.S. Supreme Court authorized the use of busing to integrate schools in *Swann v. Charlotte-Mecklenburg Board of Education* (1971), however, white Americans protested, often violently. In Boston, protests against forced busing resulted in numerous attacks and even deaths.

The various efforts at pushing Americans to integrate produce mixed results. While African Americans are much more represented in higher education and major professions than they once were, American neighborhoods remain fairly segregated along racial lines. One of the immediate results of the legal changes of the 1960s and 1970s was a demographic trend called white flight. White families who could afford to often moved away from desegregated urban neighborhoods and schools to largely white suburbs. In effect, this was segregation based on economics. Whites could afford the more expensive homes in the suburbs and the private transportation necessary to commute to and from the nearby cities for work. African Americans, in general, could not. With the loss of tax revenue from white residents, many urban centers fell into decline, and African Americans found themselves once again with substandard schools and public facilities.

Shortly before 1970, another new trend began in African American demographic movement. This trend was known as the New Great Migration. African Americans began to leave the declining big cities in the North and the West and return to the southern cities that their families had left decades before. In part this was due to the deindustrialization of the North. Towns that once thrived were now being considered part of the Rust Belt. Many African Americans, armed with a college education, returned to their former homes in the South to start businesses and families. While cities like Detroit faltered, cities like Atlanta were picking up steam. In the last few years of the twentieth century, Georgia, Maryland, and Texas became the states with the largest numbers of college-educated African Americans. California lost a great deal of its African American populace.

In 2009, the first African American president, Barack Obama (1961–), took office. Many commentators hailed his success as a sign that the United States had entered a post-racial period in which skin color no longer mattered to anyone. While Obama's election is certainly a sign that America has undergone dramatic changes since 1965, demographic data show that regardless of the many steps toward equality, African Americans are still underpaid, undereducated, and disadvantaged when compared to their white neighbors.

For instance, in 1970, the median yearly income of an African American household was twenty-two thousand dollars a year. This was fifteen thousand dollars less than the median income of a white household. Almost thirty years later, in 1999, the median African American household income had risen to almost twenty-eight thousand dollars, but white households were still making more—almost forty-five thousand dollars per year. On a more positive note, more African Americans are graduating from college and high school than ever before. In 1970, only 34 percent of African Americans were high school graduates. That number reached 80 percent by 2004, thanks in part to desegregation in schools.

Headline Makers

★ ROLAND G. FRYER
(1977–)

Roland G. Fryer has the distinction of being the youngest African American ever to get tenure at Harvard. Fryer received tenure (a lifetime appointment) in 2008 at the age of 30. Fryer's quick grasp of economics and education—especially statistics and the difficulties surrounding the black community—enabled him to finish his own education in record time and to jump ahead of his peers. Fryer claims that his motivation is simple: he wants to figure out where African Americans "went wrong." His methods are unique, and his ideas are innovative. Though young, Fryer has worked hard to accomplish much in the field of economics.

Roland Gerhard Fryer was born in Daytona Beach, Florida, on June 4, 1977. He was raised primarily by his father's mother, whom everyone called "Fat." His Aunt Ernestine and Uncle Lacey lived down the road. He spent much of his childhood at their house as well, eating dinners, playing with his cousins, and watching the family make and sell crack cocaine. Their business was profitable until one day when Fryer arrived to see police surrounding the house. Later Fryer would note that at least eight of his close family members either died young or were sent to jail. Fryer's mother had

Economist Roland Fryer in 2008. © *Ramin Talaie/Corbis*

left the family years before. When he was four, Fryer's father Roland took him to Lewisville, Texas, just north of Dallas. He spent his school years there. He returned to Daytona Beach and his grandmother in the summers.

Scared Straight

Fryer's father drank heavily. He drank so much that he eventually got fired from his job at Xerox. He once beat his girlfriend in front of his son so badly that she was hospitalized. Occasionally he would beat his son, too. Fryer did anything he could to stay out of the house and avoid his father. When Fryer was thirteen, he got a job at McDonald's. He was too young to work, so he forged a birth certificate. While he was working at McDonald's he would steal from the cash register drawer every so often. He spent his high school years doing well in football and basketball but also selling marijuana and carrying a gun. When Fryer was fifteen, his father was arrested for raping a local woman. Shortly thereafter Fryer himself was pulled over and harassed by police who thought he was a crack dealer. His near-arrest scared him so much that he declined later that evening when some friends asked him to participate in a burglary. While he stayed home, his friends were caught and sent to jail. After this, Fryer began to work harder than ever and got accepted into the University of Texas, Arlington, on an athletic scholarship.

Fryer met his future wife Lisa, an elementary school teacher, while he was in college. He earned his bachelor's degree in economics in under three years. He went on to Pennsylvania State University for his master's degree. At Pennsylvania State, he met Glenn Loury and James Heckman, two important economists who gave him a strong motivation to finish his thesis. His thesis, "Mathematical Models of Discrimination and Inequality," was strong enough to attract the attention of other researchers and academics. At the age of twenty-five he was invited to join the Society of Fellows, a prestigious teaching position at Harvard University.

Fryer does not support affirmative action or other policies or programs that give preference based on gender or race. Instead, he supports the idea of hard work and the value of providing economic motivators in education to all students regardless of race. His own challenges and successes led him to research the effects of educational incentives.

Studies African American Communities

The goal of Fryer's research is often to answer various questions about trends that affect black communities. For example, he analyzed why African Americans suffer from high blood pressure more than whites. He theorizes that perhaps this is due in part to slaves' ability to retain salt and water on the long voyage to America. He has also investigated why African American schools tend to be worse than white schools and just how much that affects academic performance.

In addition to his Harvard research, Fryer pursues several personal projects. One is working for Opportunity NYC, a nonprofit group that gives small amounts of money to needy families of inner-city students. Another of Fryer's projects is heading the American Inequality Lab at the W. E. B. Du Bois Institute for African American Research. He is also a member of the National Bureau of Economic Research. Fryer also works with economists such as Steven D. Levitt (the author of the best-selling book *Freakonomics* [2005]) and notable scholars such as Henry Louis Gates Jr. (1950–), who called Fryer a rising young star in the academic world.

In 2005, Fryer appeared on PBS's *The Tavis Smiley Show* to explain his findings and his ongoing work on race. Fryer explained that he does not believe African Americans should blame their troubles on institutions, racism, or white discrimination. Instead, he believes scientific research should carefully analyze each of the various issues confronting the African American community.

Fryer achieved a historic milestone in 2008. That year, he received tenure at Harvard University. Fryer's preference for cold hard facts makes it easier for him to deal with sensitive topics such as race and inequality. It also makes his work accepted and appreciated by progressive thinkers of all races.

★ BELL HOOKS
(1952–)

The social theorist, educator, and writer who came to be known as bell hooks was born as Gloria Jean Watkins on September 25, 1952, in Hopkinsville, Kentucky. Hopkinsville at that time was a small and segregated town, close to the booming Nashville, Tennessee, but not much else. The nature of the town and her neighborhood affected hooks. From it she learned the values of community and hard work. Her father was a custodian. Her mother cleaned the houses of local white families. Hooks grew up in a large family of mostly sisters and one brother. Her parents' long, hard hours were essential to the well-being of the family.

In her essay "Chitlin Circuit," hooks describes Hopkinsville as a place where people were content to live modest lifestyles. Hooks recalls her grandmother making soap, digging fishing worms, setting traps for rabbits, making butter, making wine, and sewing quilts. Hooks's mother was likewise hard-working. She was the main contributor to a warm and successful home. Hooks also found strength in the examples of her female black teachers. She attended Booker T. Washington Elementary School and Crispus Attucks High School. Both were segregated public schools where her teachers emphasized morale and confidence as well as education. When her school district became integrated in the late 1960s, hooks was saddened rather than happy. All the special attention that had been given to her and her race now had to be shared with others who had previously not been much a part of her life. Though her education was a good one, she also learned lessons she would later challenge, such as the importance of being loyal to a government that approved of segregation and racism.

Social theorist and writer bell hooks, c. 1995.
© Barron Claiborne/Corbis

Hooks's later writings would examine not only the race roles but also the gender roles she came across in her childhood. Her main companion was her younger brother. Hooks gradually came to recognize the difference between the roles each of them was expected to fulfill. This recognition sowed the seeds of her feminism. Indeed, at this time hooks began to be a bit of a difficult child. She often challenged and "talked back" to her elders. She was curious but at times shy, preferring to spend her time reading and writing on her own rather than socializing.

Grows Love of Poetry and Jazz in Childhood

Hooks began writing poetry at age ten. She was influenced by the rhymes she heard in songs at church. She was good at reciting poems, too. In her essay "When I Was a Young Soldier," she explains that poetry was the form of literary expression that earned absolute respect in her working-class household. Hooks would sometimes recite poems to her family. Some of her favorite poets, including Walt Whitman (1819–92) and Emily Dickinson (1830–86), were white. Among her favorite black poets were Gwendolyn Brooks (1917–2000) and Langston Hughes (1902–67). Black poets and writers were winning widespread acclaim in the 1960s. In fact, Brooks won a Pulitzer Prize for poetry in 1968. Even so, the work of white poets still tended to be the focus of most literature classes.

Hooks also liked jazz artists such as John Coltrane (1926–67) and Louis Armstrong (1901–71). She listened to the latest soul music over the radio with her sisters as they cleaned the house. Around this time she heard the name "bell hooks" for the first time. After she "talked back" to an adult in a corner store, someone remarked that she must be related to Bell Hooks, her mother's grandmother who was known locally for her defiance. When she later published a book of poetry, she did not want to be confused with another Gloria Watkins in her community, so she chose her great-grandmother's name instead. Choosing "bell hooks" symbolized her decision to be sharp-tongued (and sharp-penned) rather than obedient. Hooks chose to write her pen name in lowercase letters to emphasize the substance of her work rather than the name she had chosen.

Towards the end of her high school career, in the late 1960s and early 1970s, hooks accepted a scholarship to Stanford University in northern California. This scholarship would take her very far away from her childhood, both in physical locale and also in terms of ideas. It was a challenge for hooks to leave her small town for the prestigious university right next to the big city of San Francisco, then the center of the counterculture movement and a magnet for artists of all kinds.

Joins and Criticizes the Feminist Movement

Hooks involved herself in women's movements on campus. Although it was a relief to someone who had grown up observing females and examining gender roles, she noticed that the presence and discussion of black women in particular was nonexistent. In her first book, *Ain't I a Woman: Looking Back* (1981), hooks recalls taking a women's studies class taught by writer Tillie Olsen (1913–2007). (The title "Ain't I a Woman" is a reference to a famous 1851 speech of the same name by abolitionist Sojourner Truth.) In the class, hooks began to feel like she was not a part of, or did not belong to, the group of white women in the class who were celebrating the power of "sisterhood." Hooks would later criticize the feminist movement at that time as being too narrow. She argued that it focused only on escaping male oppression, but not oppression of all sorts. Hooks also claimed that her professors at Stanford ignored black students in their classes. Hooks explained that this furthered her distrust and desire to change the middle-class, white male-dominated social and political structure of the United States.

Despite of, or perhaps spurred on by, the difficulties she encountered at Stanford, hooks began writing her first major work, *Ain't I A Woman,* at the age of nineteen. She also took a job as a telephone operator. There, she at last found the community of black women she wanted. These women encouraged her in a way her professors and fellow students did not. Hooks felt that her co-workers at the telephone company wanted to say the same kinds of things about their lives that she did, things that would bring about change and promote understanding. Hooks struggled with finding a strong enough voice for her book in the next six years. She later said that she felt most comfortable as a writer when she felt she was speaking directly to black women. *Ain't I A Woman* not only took a long time to write, it also took a long time to see print. Publishers at that time were reluctant to take on a book dealing with issues of race and gender. Once the book was published, critical reaction to it was strong and primarily negative. However, eleven years after it was published, *Publishers Weekly* claimed it was one of the "20 most influential women's books of the last 20 years."

Focus on Education

After graduating from Stanford in 1973, hooks went on to graduate school at the University of Wisconsin. She earned a master's degree in 1976. Next she went to the University of California at Santa Cruz, where she received her Ph.D. in 1983. Her doctoral dissertation was on modern African American writer Toni Morrison (1931–), whose fiction broke ground in focusing on African American female protagonists. Hooks again struggled with racism and sexism in programs where no black women were on the faculty. Hooks took a job at Yale teaching African American studies and English literature in 1985. In a sense, hooks chose teaching at the college level to make up for what she felt was the lack in her own education. In 1988 she went to Oberlin College in Ohio to teach literature and women's studies. In 1993 she taught for a year at the City College of New York.

Hooks prizes education. At the same time, the nature of her writing and her life's work makes it hard for her to avoid being political. In 2002, she was invited to give the graduation ceremony address at Southwestern University in Texas. She criticized the Bush administration instead of giving her expected commencement speech and was booed by many members of the conservative crowd. In 2004 she returned home to Kentucky to teach there at Berea College as a distinguished professor in residence. At Berea, she offered courses and seminars in women's and African American studies in a much more desegregated society than the one she left so many years before.

While hooks is known for her commitment to teaching innovative courses and difficult subjects, her cultural studies books made her famous. After the controversial and groundbreaking *Ain't I A Woman,* she continued to publish books and essays about race and gender. She criticizes Betty Friedan (1921–2006), a well-known feminist and the author of *The Feminine Mystique* (1963), in her book *Feminist Theory: From Margin to Center* (1984). Hooks argues that Friedan's narrow, white-oriented view of housewives and mothers tends to exclude the presence of strong black women. In *All About Love* (2001), hooks examines notions of love in America, straying from her usual topics but emphasizing the same concerns about power and stereotypes. In 2004, she published *We Real Cool: Black Men and Masculinity,* an attempt to examine and explain black male identity. (The title of this work is a quote from a 1959 poem of the same name by Brooks.)

Hooks has also examined cultural concepts of beauty in such works as the children's book *Happy to Be Nappy* (1999) and a book of film criticism called *Black Looks: Race and Representation* (1992). Hooks criticized many popular mainstream black representations such as the characters in the films *The Color Purple* (1985) and *Waiting to Exhale* (1995) for fitting in too neatly with the role of victim too often assigned to black women.

★ MILDRED LOVING
(1939–2008)

Though Mildred Loving often saw herself as a simple woman from Virginia, her marriage to a white man, Richard Loving, in 1958 turned her into an icon of the civil rights movement. In the landmark court case *Loving v. Virginia* (1967) she and her husband challenged and eventually changed Virginia's antimiscegenation law (a law that makes it illegal to marry or live with someone of a different race). By doing so, they became monuments to freedom and equality.

Enjoys a Peaceful Childhood in Virginia

Mildred Delores Jeter was born in Central Point, Virginia, on June 22, 1939. Central Point was considered a relatively peaceful and accepting Southern community. Though rural, Central Point was home to many citizens of mixed races. Mildred herself was part Native American and part African American. She often identified herself as Native American.

Mildred and Richard Loving answer questions at a press conference following their victory in the Supreme Court case *Loving v. Virginia* in 1967. *Francis Miller/Time & Life Pictures/Getty Images*

Virginia had passed a law called the Racial Integrity Act in 1924. The act made it illegal for any white person in Virginia to marry anyone other than a white person. The act was influenced by the then-popular theory of eugenics. Eugenics was the groundless theory that human society could be perfected if people with "superior" genetic traits had children only with each other. In practice, eugenics had at its core many racist assumptions about different racial and ethnic groups. Some advocates of eugenics believed it was morally acceptable to kill people who they believed were fundamentally flawed. Adolf Hitler (1889–1945) was a noted believer in eugenics. During World War II (1939–45), Hitler's eugenics campaign against Jewish and Roma people was a systematic extermination of human beings that claimed more than six million lives. It became known as the Holocaust. After World War II, belief in eugenics was considered embarrassing at best, and cruel at worst. Nonetheless, the Racial Integrity Act stayed on the books in Virginia. Similar laws remained in place in fifteen other states as well. These laws all prevented couples of different races from living together or marrying. They defined a "pure white" person as someone who had only white ancestors since 1684. If a "pure white" person violated Virginia's antimiscegenation law and married someone of a different race, the maximum penalty was five years in prison for each partner.

Growing up, Mildred Jeter was unaware of this law. Her community seemed relatively open-minded, and her family had long been a part of that community. She met her future husband, Richard Loving, when she was eleven and he seventeen. Their families were friends without any racial difficulties. Eventually Mildred and Richard became more than friends. Again, no one thought anything of it within their town. When Mildred became pregnant at age 18, she and Richard decided to marry, since having a child out of wedlock was not nearly as acceptable at the time as being in a mixed-race relationship.

The Lovings Are Arrested

Mildred apparently did not know much about the law preventing her marriage. However, her soon-to-be-husband Richard knew enough to suggest they go to Washington, D.C., to get married. They were legally married there on June 2, 1958. Afterwards, they returned home ready to start their new life together. But on the morning of July 11, 1958, at around 2:00 A.M., they awoke to police standing over their bed. Even though they had a valid marriage license, they were arrested. They were both charged with living together as husband and wife in violation of Virginia's antimiscegenation law.

Richard Loving was released after one night in the Bowling Green jail. Mildred was held for days. Afterwards, they went to live with their families until they could figure out what to do. In 1959, their criminal case came before a Virginia court. The court, under Judge Leon M. Bazile, sentenced them to a year in prison, but gave them the alternative of moving away from Virginia for at least twenty-five years. Bazile's rationale behind his upholding of the law was "The fact that [God] separated the races [by continents] shows that he did not intend for the races to mix." After Judge Bazile's ruling, the Lovings moved to Washington, D.C. Washington, D.C., was about an hour and a half away from their hometown. They came back for brief visits with their families. They could only visit so long as they did not travel together.

The Lovings moved to a lower-income neighborhood in Washington, D.C. While they were living in that city, the Lovings had two more children. Richard worked as a bricklayer and Mildred stayed home with the children. Mildred Loving was frustrated by the distance between her and her family and the economic troubles that went along with having three children. She began to think more and more about challenging Virginia's Racial Integrity Act. Loving took matters into her own hands and wrote to U.S. attorney general Robert Kennedy (1925–68) in 1963. She asked him to consider her case. Kennedy contacted an attorney in Virginia, Bernard S. Cohen of the American Civil Liberties Union. Cohen took on the Lovings' case. He recognized it as potentially central to the civil rights movement that was beginning to take hold of the country at that time. Cohen would later say that he knew the Lovings' case was going to be important. He also thought it was a stroke of good fortune that the case would be called *Loving v. Virginia*.

Cohen and another attorney, Phillip J. Hirschkop, got the Supreme Court of the United States to hear the case. In the meantime, the Lovings tried to remove themselves from the legal proceedings as much as possible. They preferred to go on with their lives and hope for the best. In an interview in the *Washington Evening Star* in 1965, when their case was starting to gain national attention, Mildred Loving explained that she and Richard believed that the law should allow people to marry anyone they want.

The Supreme Court heard the Lovings' case in 1967. Cohen and Hirschkop argued that laws that discriminate on the basis of race are unconstitutional. On June 12, 1967, the Supreme Court voted 9-0 that the Virginia law and other states' similar antimiscegenation statutes were indeed unconstitutional (Alabama was the last state to repeal its laws regarding racial marriages in 2000). This came to be known as the "Loving Decision," calling to mind not only the name of the couple but also the cause they fought for.

The Lovings Return to Virginia

After their trial and the resulting spotlight that followed the Lovings, they quietly moved back to their home in Virginia and settled down there. Mildred stayed home with the children. Richard was a construction worker and contractor. He built a house for them to live in, and they enjoyed living near their families. Mildred desperately needed that support after tragedy struck. A drunk driver hit their car and killed Richard in 1975 at the age of 41. Mildred lost an eye in the same accident. She never remarried and continued to live in the home her husband had built until her death. She died of pneumonia in 2008, one month short of what would have been her and Richard's fiftieth anniversary.

In 1996, Richard Friedenberg directed a movie about the Lovings' saga entitled *Mr. and Mrs. Loving*. Mildred herself said not much was accurate about the film's portrayal of her life save for the fact that the Lovings had three children. The Lovings' case has continued to remain important in American politics. It has also changed the demographics of the country. Now that mixed-race couples can marry freely, there are more children of mixed races. Miscegenation is much more widely accepted and appreciated than in previous American eras. June 12 is an unofficial holiday, "Loving Day," created to commemorate the Lovings and similar couples. Subsequently, the Lovings' story had an effect on the debate over gay marriage rights. In a rare press statement on the fortieth anniversary of her court case in 2007, Loving stated that she believed that all Americans, regardless of their race, sex, or sexual orientation, should have the same freedom to marry. Loving also said that she believes the government is not entitled to deny some people's basic civil rights because of other people's religious beliefs. Loving's championing of love and loyalty above unfair laws and prejudices made her a symbol of equality and perseverance.

Topics in the News

❖ THE 2000 CENSUS PROVIDES A SNAPSHOT OF AFRICAN AMERICAN DEMOGRAPHICS

The first U.S. census was taken in 1790. A census is a complete count of the population of a country performed by the government. At the time of the first census, the country's population was almost four million people. Almost seven hundred thousand of those people were slaves. An official U.S. Census Bureau was formed in 1903 to gather statistics and demographic information about the rapidly growing country. Today, the census is primarily used to determine the population of states in order to determine how many seats each state gets in the House of Representatives and the Electoral College. However, the information the census provides is much more extensive than a simple head count. The census is used to divide money among the states, to track immigration levels, and to track changes in education levels and income figures. The population census is taken every ten years. The national census in 2000 showed a marked rise in black achievement and notable demographic changes from previous decades.

In 2000, the census showed that the United States had a population of 281.4 million people. Almost 13 percent of the U.S. population were African American. More than 50 percent of polled blacks lived in the South. The smallest percentage (less than 10 percent) lived in the West. New York and Chicago were the cities with the largest black population in 2000, together totaling 9 percent of the black population overall. Most African

The 2000 Census showed that African Americans are attaining higher levels of income than they ever have before. *AP Images*

Americans live within cities, while white Americans tend to live in suburbs of major cities.

African Americans are graduating from high school and seeking college education in greater numbers than ever before, and the gap in educational achievement between African Americans and whites is decreasing. About 80 percent of African Americans under the age of twenty-five reported being high school graduates. Black women are more likely than black men to have a bachelor's degree. According to the 2000 census, approximately 9 percent of African Americans were unemployed, while only 4 percent of whites were unemployed. Twenty-eight percent of black families made $50,000 or more per year, compared to 52 percent of white families. What this demographic information shows is that the typical African American is making strides in education, employment, and income but that the majority of white Americans continues to have an easier time moving ahead financially.

Demographers anticipated the 2010 census would probably show lower incomes and home ownership across the board due to the recession that began in December of 2007. Predicting what will happen beyond 2010 is tricky. Many things can happen to affect population growth and the outcome of a census. However, assuming that the population will continue to grow more or less as it has in recent years, the U.S. Census Bureau projected that the population of the country in 2050 will be 419 million people. Approximately 14.6 percent of the population will be African American. This is not a significant population increase compared to Hispanics and Asian Americans, whose populations are predicted to at least double. However, it is a higher growth rate than that of non-Hispanic whites, who are estimated to actually decline from 69 percent of the population in 2000 to 50 percent in 2050. Immigration will likely be a large part of this shift, as will education (more educated populations tend to have fewer children) and miscegenation (people of two different races marrying and producing offspring who are more difficult to classify).

❖ DRUGS AND GANGS PLAGUE AFRICAN AMERICAN COMMUNITIES

Thanks to the civil rights movement and changes in the law, African Americans have enjoyed tremendous advances over the last forty years. At the same time, the African American community has confronted a unique and difficult set of problems involving illegal drug use. African Americans suffer disproportionately from drug addiction and the social problems associated with drug use and the drug trade. African Americans are less likely than whites to seek treatment for drug addiction. They are much more likely to be arrested and imprisoned for drug possession and trafficking. And the gang violence associated with the drug trade in American cities is much more likely to affect blacks than whites. The reasons for these difference are complex and controversial.

Crack Cocaine Epidemic Begins in the 1980s

The form of the illegal drug cocaine known as "crack" surfaced in the United States in 1981. Crack is cocaine mixed with either baking soda or lye and sold in a hardened "rock" form that is smokable. It costs much less money than powder cocaine. It is also highly addictive. The first so-called "crack house"—a house or apartment where users gather to smoke the drug—was reported by police in Miami, Florida, in 1982. At first, drug enforcement officials did not see crack as a major problem. Most users appeared to be middle-class whites using the drug recreationally. However, the drug's cheap price soon made it popular with poorer customers, many of whom were African American. By 1987, the number of people using cocaine and suffering health problems related to cocaine use increased dramatically. National health statistics show that cocaine-related health emergencies increased by 12 percent in 1985—and by 110 percent in 1986. Within just a couple of years, the crack trade dominated the poor African American neighborhoods of several American cities. Prices kept dropping and purity levels increased in the late 1980s, making crack even more dangerous and addictive.

Many law enforcement experts believe crack was primarily responsible for increased gang violence in the 1980s and 1990s. A 1988 study by the

The development of crack cocaine as a relatively cheap and highly addictive drug created a large increase in gang activity and drug use in low-income African American communities.
© Darrin Jenkins/Alamy

Bureau of Justice Statistics showed that 32 percent of all homicides in New York City were crack-related. Washington, D.C., which has one of the largest black populations in the country, was dubbed "the murder capital" in the late 1980s due to its increase in crack-related violence. The news media reported on this crack-related crime frequently, and public alarm grew. The administration of President Ronald Reagan (1911–2004) responded by declaring a "war on drugs." A key feature of this war on drugs was required minimum sentencing for drug offenses.

The application of drug laws stirred considerable controversy in the 1980s and 1990s. Evidence suggests that the crack sentencing laws have been applied more harshly to African Americans than to whites. For instance, according to some sources, by 1989 70 percent of crack users in New York were upper-income earners and primarily white; however, by 1999, 94 percent of those actually sentenced to jail time for crack use were black or Hispanic. By 2007, although only 25 percent of crack users were black, more than 81 percent of those convicted of crack-related crimes were black.

While crack seems to be related to a spike in imprisonment rates for African American men, the lives of African American women and children were also negatively affected by rising rates of crack use in the late 1980s. Use of crack cocaine by pregnant women causes a variety of birth defects. A high number of special-needs babies being born to crack-addicted mothers in the 1980s gave rise to the crisis of the "crack baby" in foster care systems nationwide. These babies are much harder to care for than healthy babies. While the stereotype of the "crack baby" of the 1980s was that of an infant born to a crack-addicted, single, African American mother, the reality was more complex. During the height of the crack epidemic, doctors and hospitals did not compile formal statistics on the number of babies born with signs of pre-birth cocaine exposure. Infants were not routinely tested. Infants born in hospitals serving mostly black patients were much more likely to be tested than infants in hospitals serving mostly white patients, which may have led to an overreporting of the number of black babies testing positive for drugs. The perception that African American babies were more likely to be exposed to crack than white babies was not based on hard evidence, but the perception shaped public policy and cultural attitudes toward African American mothers.

By the early twenty-first century, most criminologists (scholars who study the causes and nature of crime) agreed that the crack epidemic had ended and that crack cocaine use was declining. In early 2009, President Barack Obama (1961–) said that he plans to refocus anti-drug efforts on treatment and counseling rather than tough sentencing.

Marion Barry Rises, Falls, and Rises Again

Marion Barry (1936–), the former mayor of Washington, D.C., was a major player in the civil rights movement, but his story—and his legacy—is a complicated one. Barry was born to Mississippi sharecroppers. He picked cotton for most of his childhood. The notion of hard work led him to college at a time when protest movements were picking up speed and becoming national news. In 1964 he abandoned his doctoral program in chemistry to work for the Student Nonviolent Coordinating Committee (SNCC), a group that blended Malcolm X's ideas of black power with Martin Luther King Jr.'s more peaceful protests. Barry eventually moved to Washington, D.C., where he spearheaded the Free D.C. movement, which was designed to get the city's largely black population the right to vote and have representation in Congress. Until the 1960s, citizens of Washington, D.C., could not vote in national or local elections. Although the District of Columbia Home Rule Act was passed in 1973, citizens continued to have limited power over their own government. Many D.C. license plates read "Taxation without Representation," a reference to their limited voice in Congress.

Because of his efforts to help the city, Barry became Washington, D.C.'s second elected mayor in 1979. As mayor, he implemented a number of programs designed to help the city financially. Though many think the city improved during this time, there were rumors of corruption and abuse of the city's budget. Allegations came to a head in 1990 when Barry was arrested for smoking crack cocaine in a hotel room. Barry went to prison for six months, a relatively short sentence in the heyday of the crack epidemic.

Washington D.C. mayor Marion Barry after his indictment on drug charges in 1990.
© Bettmann/Corbis

Despite his arrest and conviction, Barry was again elected mayor in a controversial election in 1994. He served until 1999. There were many conflicts during his last term. When it ended, much of the city seemed relieved. His legacy is thus a complicated one. Few contest his allegiance to and hard work for the civil rights movement, but many have criticized his financial and legal problems since then.

Gangs and Violence Plague the Large Cities

The 1980s saw an explosion in gang violence. According to law enforcement agencies, gang members are almost all male, about 40 percent are under eighteen, and 84 percent are black or Latino (49 percent Latino, 35 percent black). The rising rates of gang violence in general therefore affected African American teens disproportionately. According to a 1996 report by the Bureau of Justice Statistics, violent crimes committed by youths as a whole increased by 172 percent between 1985 and 1994. For African American youths, the increase was 261 percent. Though black male teenagers only made up 1 percent of the population during this period, they accounted for 17 percent of murder victims and 30 percent of murderers.

An organization called the National Youth Gang Center (NYGC) began collecting statistics on gang activity from law enforcement agencies in 1996. Their research shows that most large American cities had gang problems prior to 1990. Large cities remain the areas most likely to have gang problems. The NYGC reported in 1996 that there were more than thirty thousand active gangs in the United States. That number declined steadily to about twenty thousand in 2003. After 2003, however, it climbed every year, reaching about twenty-seven thousand in 2007.

The spread of gang activity is due in part to the rising demand for drugs. The illegal drug trade funds the activities of some American gangs. The fact that gang violence spiked around the same time crack cocaine became a widely publicized problem led the public to connect the two trends. This led to the stereotypical picture of a gang member being an inner-city black teen who sells crack. However, some sociologists question how big a role drugs play in gang activity. Many gangs are too unorganized to manage the distribution of drugs in a profitable way. Law enforcement teams find that many serious drug dealers leave their gangs in order to have more order and independence. Thus, the appeal of profits from the drug trade is not always the reason African American teens enter gangs. They are more likely influenced by their peers and the promise of some kind of social network they may be lacking in school or at home.

In the early twenty-first century, strides have been made in reducing gangs by providing more police and better social and employment choices for gang members. Even so, as of early 2009 it was estimated that there were one million gang members in the United States and that gang-related crimes accounted for 80 percent of all crimes.

Black Men Are Imprisoned at Higher Rates

As of May 2009, there were more than two hundred thousand federal prisoners in the United States. The majority of the prisoners were serving sentences between five and ten years long, and more than 50 percent of the

A gang unit officer searches a group of African Americans suspected of being gang members in the violent area of south-central Los Angeles in 2007. *Robert Nickelsberg/ Getty Images*

total crimes committed were drug-related. Over 90 percent of federal prisoners were male, and almost 40 percent were black. By contrast, African Americans make up just 13.5 percent of the nation's population. These numbers suggest that the criminal justice system treats African Americans unfairly, especially since the rate at which crimes are committed has fallen to its lowest level since the 1960s. Black males are imprisoned at more than six times the rate of white males, and black females at four times the rate of white females.

Differences in sentencing for drug crimes partly explain these figures. Because crack was seen as a greater threat to society as a whole than marijuana and powder cocaine, crack-related crimes brought stiffer sentences. While both blacks and whites use crack cocaine, blacks are more likely to be arrested for crack use. Once arrested, African Americans are less likely than whites to have enough money to afford a private attorney who could shield them from a prison sentence.

Another factor related to higher imprisonment rates for African Americans is poverty. Poverty is statistically connected with imprisonment. In 2007, 53 percent of the jailed population had earned less than ten thousand dollars before their incarceration. As of 2006, 24.2 percent of African Americans nationwide were living in poverty, compared with just 8.2 percent of white Americans. Statistically, this makes African Americans more likely to go to prison.

The high number of black men in prison takes a toll on African American communities and the country as a whole. Five percent of all state tax dollars collected in the United States go to corrections, including prisons and rehabilitation programs. The increase in the number of black males in prison also affects their families because the imprisoned men are not able to earn an income and provide for their dependents.

Some experts suggest that the United States should combat these alarming rates of incarceration by reviewing sentencing policies and imprisoning fewer drug-related offenders. Most drug-related crimes occur on a small, personal level. Very rarely are large-scale international drug deals involved. In early 2009, President Barack Obama announced that he plans to work to reduce the mandatory sentencing levels for crack cocaine.

❖ AFRICAN AMERICAN FAMILY LIFE UNDERGOES CHANGES

There have been many significant changes to marriage and family life in the African American community since the 1970s. Black female students are increasingly outperforming their black male counterparts in school. An increasing number of African Americans are choosing to marry persons who are not also African Americans. As many as 70 percent of African American mothers are single and raising children on their own. African American teenage girls are becoming pregnant at a much higher rate than teenagers of other races. Gay and lesbian couples and families are becoming increasingly visible in the African American community.

Educational Achievement

Black middle school students scored approximately 39 percent lower than whites in 1970 on standardized tests such as reading, math, and science. In 1990, they scored only 20 percent lower. By 2007, the difference had dropped to about 6 percent, according to a study by the National Assessment of Educational Progress (NAEP). Thanks to school integration and early education programs like Head Start, more middle-class black students are increasing their test scores and graduation rates. Inner-city schools still struggle, as do rural schools. Despite the benefits of desegregation, blacks seem to do better in predominantly black schools rather than more integrated schools. One reason black schoolchildren are doing better overall is the economic advances of their parents. As a group gets wealthier, its children tend to perform better on standardized tests. This is in part due to the fact that school systems are based on property taxes. The best schools are generally in the wealthiest neighborhoods. The rise of charter schools and private schools affect these demographics as well.

The Wealthiest African American of the 20th Century

Oprah Winfrey—talk show host, actress, and philanthropist—has the distinction of being not only the wealthiest African American of the twentieth century but also one of the wealthiest women in the world. The fact that Winfrey is a "double minority" and came from a poor, rural background in Mississippi makes her rise to fame and fortune all the more remarkable.

Winfrey was born to an unwed teenage mother whose income came from cleaning houses. She ran away from home at age thirteen. Eventually Winfrey went back to high school and began working in radio. She won a full scholarship to Tennessee State University, a historically black college. As a college student she studied media and communication. From there her career skyrocketed. She now spends time influencing not only the nation but also the world. While some worry that Winfrey's influence is too great, she shows no sign of slowing down. Her story continues to fascinate people the world over.

Despite these changes, one educational statistic has remained constant: black males do not do as well as black females on educational tests, school performance, and college advancement. Significantly more black women than black men graduate from colleges and professional schools. Several theories have been advanced to explain why this could be happening. Many appear to be based on racial stereotypes in addition to actual learning and education. For instance, there are theories that the black male is seen as a potential threat in the classroom, while the black female is more of a victim. Another stereotype is that black males tend to spend their time in athletic pursuits rather than academic ones. The prevalence of these misconceptions in the primary and secondary classroom—particularly in inner-city schools—may lead some teachers to alter their methods of instruction to fit their views. Another issue is that most inner-city black children (over 70 percent) are being raised by their mothers and grandmothers. School systems, too, are primarily matriarchal (run by women), with female teachers outnumbering male teachers. This could lead to compliance on the part of black female students, who are comfortable with the role of women in power, and a sense of rebellion in young black males who miss their fathers and resent the lack of male involvement in their lives. Also, after high school, many black men choose to get jobs to support their families rather than continue their education.

While more African Americans and Americans overall are attending college than in previous years, minorities are still underrepresented in college faculties across the country. A 2000 report by the American Council on Education showed that only 6 percent of college and university faculty are African American. Many of these faculty members teach at community colleges and historically black schools.

The Rate of Interracial Marriage Is Rising

Along with desegregation in the public sphere, the civil rights era saw a good deal of desegregation in the private arena as well. More minorities and whites were working alongside one another, going to schools together, and getting married to each other. The case that sparked the reform in the area of marriage law was the landmark *Loving v. Virginia.* Decided in 1967, *Loving* overturned and declared unconstitutional a law in the state of Virginia that banned interracial marriage.

Prior to *Loving v. Virginia,* which altered the laws of marriage across the states, miscegenation (the mixing of races, either through marriage or cohabitation) was illegal in many states. Antimiscegenation laws prohibited whites from mixing with other races, most often African Americans but also Native Americans and Asians. After the civil rights era, members of all races had greater economic motives and means to move across the United States. More mixed-race relationships naturally occurred. When Mildred Jeter (1939–2008), who was black, married Richard Loving, who was white, in Washington, D.C., in 1958, they did not realize their marriage would be punishable by law once they returned to their home state of Virginia. Just weeks after they returned to Virginia, they awoke in the middle of the night to find themselves being arrested by policemen standing over their bed. Their arrest prompted them to move away from Virginia. With the help of the American Civil Liberties Union (ACLU), they successfully won their case in court years later. After their success, they returned to Virginia to be close to their families. Although Richard died in a car crash shortly afterwards, Mildred became a symbol of civil rights and freedom. She never remarried and lived in the home he had built for them until she died in 2008.

After the Lovings' lengthy legal battle, many other states repealed their own similar laws because the Supreme Court had declared them unconstitutional as violations of the Fourteenth Amendment. Some states, where racism was particularly deep-rooted, waited to officially repeal their laws. They waited both as an act of defiance of the Supreme Court and also as a way to condemn interracial marriage. Alabama was the last state to officially revoke its antimiscegenation law in 2000.

The rate of interracial marriages has increased since it was made legal in 1967, but is still relatively rare. © Neil McAllister/Alamy

The number of interracial marriages has increased dramatically since *Loving* was decided in 1967, but it still remains relatively rare. According to the 2000 U.S. Census, Native Americans are the race most likely to marry another race: 56.7 percent of Native Americans are members of an interracial marriage. African Americans are less likely to marry outside their race. Only 7 percent of blacks marry someone of another race. The number of African Americans in interracial marriages is higher among young people, among people who live in cities, and with the attainment of higher education.

According to the 2000 Census, there were 287,576 interracial marriages in the United States. A black man and a white woman was a much more common pairing than a black woman with a white man. Hispanic-white marriage is the most common type of intermarriage in America.

Black Single Parents Face Challenges

Over the last several decades, family structures in the United States changed. Divorce became more socially accepted, and common, in the 1970s and 1980s. Currently in the United States, approximately one half of marriages end in divorce. Trends show that marriages (and partnerships in general) last longer in wealthier communities. Data also show that black women are the least likely to have successful marriages. Black couples in general marry less frequently than white couples, get divorced more frequently, and are less likely to remarry.

Financially, divorce takes its toll on most families, regardless of race. The financial impact can be particularly difficult for black families. Black men earn less money on average than white men, while black women only make, on average, as much as white women (which is less than white men make). Thus, divorce often hits black families—whose income levels are already less stable than those of whites—harder than white families.

In addition, black males have higher rates of being absentee fathers. Of the twenty-four million children without fathers in this country, the majority are African American. This leaves black mothers (and often their mothers as well) with most of the financial burden. Traditionally, the African American community has been more close-knit than most white communities. Many single black parents turn to neighbors and other family members for help. On the upside of this trend in single parent homes, many new homeowners are unmarried African American females. In Atlanta, a city with 100,000 more unmarried black women than black men, mortgages to such women rose 114 percent from 1997 to 2002.

Children of divorced families are affected in many ways. Generally, children of divorced or single parents do worse in school and have more behavioral problems than children from two-parent homes. African American boys can be negatively impacted by the lack of a positive adult male role model in the home. Some people argue that the high rate of absenteeism among black fathers is partially to blame for high drop-out rates and high levels of gang involvement in low-income black communities. However, a 2005 study in the *Journal of Family Issues* argued that the rate at which African American men are absentee fathers is often overstated. The study found that young black men (age twenty-two and under) who become fathers are no less likely to be involved with their children than fathers of other races.

Teenage Pregnancy Becomes More Common

Teenage pregnancy is a problem among all races, but the rate of African American teenage births is almost double that of white teenage births. In 1995, black teens were responsible for 23 percent of all teen births. Some progress has been made since then. The Centers for Disease Control and Prevention (CDC) reported that the teen birth rate had fallen by 2002. For black teens, the rate was down by over 40 percent. For teens aged fifteen to seventeen, the rates had been cut in half since 1991.

One of the biggest difficulties associated with teen pregnancy is financial strain. Teenagers have less money saved than do their parents. They also have fewer ways to earn money while in school and tend to earn lower wages. A pregnant teenage girl who wants to keep her child faces the hard decision of either staying in school and hoping her family will help with the child or dropping out and not receiving a high school diploma.

The Most Conspicuously Absent Father in the United States

President Barack Obama is an example of someone who grew up without a father. President Obama now speaks publicly about the importance of good male role models, especially in the African American community, where many believe fathers are needed most. His memoir, *Dreams from My Father* (1995), was one of the best-selling books of 2008, the year he was elected president.

Barack Obama at age ten with his father. *AP Images*

Obama's family was comfortably middle-class. He spent much of his childhood in exotic locales like Indonesia and Hawaii. Even so, the absence of his father was keenly and bitterly felt. His parents met while they were in college. They divorced when Barack was only two. His father moved back to his native country of Kenya after finishing his master's degree at Harvard University. Obama only saw his father once after that, when he was ten years old. He spent much of his life pondering the man's absence. Obama was raised by his mother, her second husband, and his grandparents, all of whom were fairly well-to-do and educated.

Either way is a hard road. Many teens find themselves working long hours for little pay. For African American communities, this route is often even more difficult because African Americans still earn lower wages on average than their white counterparts in the same jobs. For a pregnant teenager whose father does not live with the family, the new child relies almost solely on its grandmother for financial support.

In 1991, 46 percent of unwed teenage pregnancies ended in abortion, 44 percent were carried to term and kept, and only 2 percent were given up for adoption. The adoption process is a difficult one. Many American families choose to adopt from foreign countries, where there is little chance the mother might want the baby back. This puts another strain on pregnant African American teens, who often do not see adoption as a possibility.

African American Gay and Lesbian Families Struggle to Gain Acceptance

In 2003, the Supreme Court ruled in *Lawrence v. Texas* that laws specifically prohibiting homosexuality are unconstitutional and a violation of the Fourteenth Amendment. However, in the early 2000s gay couples still did not receive the same rights as non-gay unions. Many gay and lesbian activists argue that the Supreme Court's 1967 decision in *Loving v. Virginia,* which held that state laws prohibiting interracial marriage are unconstitutional, means that it is also unconstitutional for states to deny gay couples the right to marry. Mildred Loving herself stated her support for gay marriage rights before she died in 2008.

Gay couples and families often have a hard time dealing with discrimination. Gay black couples have perhaps an even harder time. Gay black men often deny the fact that they are gay, not wanting to seem weak or effeminate in the face of stereotypes that suggest black man are—or should be—strong and aggressive. Many black gay men and lesbians seek out community. The National Coalition of Black Gays was founded in 1979. A number of other groups have been formed to combat AIDS and to help black gay men and lesbian women fit in and find support. The Pentecostal Faith Temple of Washington, D.C., supports gay rights, as do many other black churches.

Pop cultural icons often help black gays gain acceptance. Gay performers such as RuPaul (1960–), writers such as James Baldwin (1924–87) and Countee Cullen (1903–46), politicians such as Barbara Jordan (1936–96), and television characters such as Lafayette Reynolds (played by Nelsan Ellis) on HBO's series *True Blood* have garnered a cult following among all races and sexual orientations. These icons go a long way to help black gays and lesbians gain acknowledgment and equality.

❖ A BLACK MIDDLE CLASS EMERGES

Since the civil rights movement of the 1960s, African Americans have made great strides in the main areas that contribute to a successful middle class: education, occupation, and income. During the 1950s and 1960s, several U.S. Supreme Court decisions and congressional acts broke down old cultural and legal barriers that kept blacks out of good schools and good jobs. Among these legal decisions and new laws were the 1954 U.S. Supreme Court decision *Brown v. Board of Education,* which declared segregation in schools unconstitutional, and the Civil Rights Act of 1964, which made racial discrimination in employment and education illegal. Changes such as these allowed African Americans access to better schools. They also gained access to better-paying jobs that required advanced skills. This helped bring many

African Americans into the middle class, which had previously been dominated by whites.

Advances Since the 1960s

In 1960, only 20 percent of African Americans had graduated from high school. This was less than half the national average for whites. By 2003, that number had risen to 80 percent, which was less than 10 percent lower than the national average for white students. The rates at which African Americans earned college degrees also increased dramatically. According to the 2000 U.S. census, 14.3 percent of African Americans over the age of twenty-five had a college degree. This was significantly less than the 26.1 percent of whites over twenty-five who had a college degree; however, it was a dramatic increase over the rate in 1960, when only 3.5 percent of African Americans older than twenty-five had a college degree (and only 8.1 percent of whites). The increased rate at which African Americans are graduating from high school has had a huge impact on the rise of the black middle class.

A large, stable middle class means less crime, better neighborhoods, and a higher level of education for all. An economic boom in the 1960s swelled the ranks of the middle class of all races; legal desegregation allowed African Americans to take advantage of the strong economy. In 1960, only 10 percent of African Americans belonged to the middle class. During the 1960s and early 1970s, African Americans showed dramatic upward mobility, a term demographers use to describe one generation achieving wealth at a greater level than the generation before them. In 1962, only one in five black

The emergence of the black middle class in the second half of the twentieth century resulted in more African American families owning their own homes. © Palmer Kane Studio/Alamy

The Cosby Show

One of the first popular portrayals of upper-middle-class African Americans came some twenty years after the civil rights movement. *The Cosby Show* first aired in 1984 and was an instant success among viewers of all races. Centered on comedian Bill Cosby's character Heathcliff Huxtable and his family, the show presented a model of African American family life that was dramatically different from those seen in such hit shows of the 1970s as *Sanford and Son* (1972–77) and *Good Times* (1972–79). *Sanford and Son* focused on the struggles of a poor black junk dealer and his son. *Good Times* dealt with the lives of an African American family living in a Chicago housing project. Cosby's Heathcliff Huxtable, by contrast, was a successful doctor. His wife Claire was an attorney. The family of five lived comfortably in a brownstone in Brooklyn, New York.

This portrayal of a black family being successful and relatively unconcerned with race was a first on television. The show was sometimes criticized for being too "white" and not addressing serious race issues. Nevertheless, it was number one in the ratings for five consecutive seasons and ran for eight years.

males was born into a class higher than his father's. By 1973, that figure was one in three. This emerging black middle class was fairly stable, meaning that once middle-class status was achieved, it was maintained. About half of African Americans born into the middle class in 1973 remained middle-class in adulthood.

Vulnerability to Economic Downturns

Unfortunately, African Americans tend to be hit harder by economic downturns than whites, in part because they may not have a network of middle-class family members to turn to for help. During the economic downturn of the late 1970s, many African Americans lost financial ground, although they regained their footing in the 1980s and 1990s. However, as the world entered a severe recession in 2008 and 2009, African Americans again found themselves disproportionately affected. Home ownership, one of the key indicators of middle-class status, spiked for the African American population—and the U.S. population as a whole—at the turn of the twenty-first century, as the housing industry enjoyed a boom. By 2004, about half of African American families owned their own homes (and about three-fourths of whites), up from 44 percent in the early 1990s. The economic downturn of 2008 began in 2007 in the housing market, when home owners began defaulting on high-risk subprime mortgages. African Americans were much more likely to hold one of these risky mortgages: 52.5 percent of black homeowners had these risky subprime mortgages, as opposed to 17.4 percent of whites. Huge numbers of borrowers had the bank foreclose on their loans, but blacks were hit hardest, with one in ten black homeowners losing their homes as opposed to one in twenty-five white homeowners.

Despite advances in educational options and job availability, blacks' incomes are still lower than those of whites. African Americans own more of their own businesses than they did a generation ago, and those businesses no longer solely serve the black community. However, African Americans do not move up the corporate power structure as easily as white Americans do. In addition, due to the problems of the previous generation's employment levels, many African Americans do not have significant inheritances or pensions. As a result, they must work harder and longer than many middle-class whites. While white families have money invested in stocks, African Americans have fewer investments overall. For example, a 2007 study by the federal government found that white families invest 29 percent of their assets in stocks, bonds, and other similar investments. Black families on average invest only 15 percent in the same areas. African American families put a majority of their assets in housing, the study found. Even so, African American families are less likely to own their own homes. When they do, the homes tend to be in lower-income neighborhoods. Due to a lack of savings, many middle-class blacks feel they are just a paycheck away from poverty.

❖ GREAT MIGRATIONS CHANGE THE DEMOGRAPHICS OF U.S. CITIES

Since 1965, the African American population has not only grown in size, its composition and location also have changed dramatically. Many African Americans who moved out of the South in the years following World War II returned to the South in search of work or to reunite with their families as part of what is known as the New Great Migration. Several urban areas in the South have become centers of African American wealth and opportunity. However, African Americans also continue to suffer the consequences of poverty and natural disasters.

African Americans Leave the South

During the years between 1910 and 1970, 5.6 million African Americans left their homes in the South to find better lives elsewhere in the country. This movement came in two large waves. Between 1910 and 1930, more than a million African Americans moved away from the South in what was known as the First Great Migration. Another bigger wave, known as the Second Great Migration, came after World War II ended in 1945. Demographically speaking, the movement caused a relatively stable population of blacks in the South to head elsewhere, to cities and states that were previously more or less off-limits due to distance or race relations. The manufacturing industry boomed in big midwestern and northeastern cities in the early twentieth century, and African Americans found work in factories that allowed them a much better standard of living than they had on farms in the South. As schools were desegregated in the 1950s and 1960s, new educational opportunities also attracted African Americans to major urban centers outside the South.

Many black southerners who relocated during the Second Great Migration had to leave their families and friends behind. They did so to better themselves and achieve more than they could in what had always been a segregated and racially biased South. In addition, southern farms no longer needed as many workers, regardless of race, due to the rise of machinery and technology. This Second Great Migration found many blacks moving from places such as Alabama, Texas, and Louisiana to places such as California, Michigan, Illinois, and New York.

The civil rights movement peaked during the 1960s, and the South saw many incidents of racially motivated violence and unrest. As the benefits of the civil rights movement began to be seen and the unrest died down, many African Americans who had migrated away from the South reevaluated their decision to move away. The jobs in northern and midwestern factories involved long, hard hours. The manufacturing industry in America faced new foreign competition, and factory jobs were harder to find. Meanwhile, the South developed strong, urban economic centers of its own, offering African Americans appealing job opportunities. For these reasons, the Second Great Migration came to an end around 1970.

Other demographic changes happened after the civil rights movement. More blacks were bused to white schools, and more blacks could afford to move to the suburbs. More interracial marriages were legal and accepted, thanks largely to the Supreme Court's decision in *Loving v. Virginia.* As a result, more children of mixed races were born. Incomes of African Americans rose, as did education levels. What was once exclusively

The availability of good-paying jobs in the auto industry brought many African Americans north in the mid-twentieth century. © *Bettmann/Corbis*

The Richest and Best

P rince George's County in Maryland is the wealthiest black community in the country. Bordering Washington, D.C., the county is home to many politicians, lawmakers, and engineers, which accounts for the relatively high median household income (above eighty thousand dollars per year). Over 60 percent of the county's residents are African American. Many have college educations. Despite such positive statistics, Prince George's County also has accounted for 20 percent of the murders in Maryland since 1985.

According to a 2007 list by *Black Enterprise* magazine, Washington, D.C., is the most desirable place for African Americans to live due to the education level of the general populace and the opportunities for high-level employment. Cities like Atlanta, Georgia, and Raleigh, North Carolina, which are the capitals of their states, also appeal to African Americans. They have many universities (some historically black) and thriving economies full of black-owned businesses, thanks to the New Great Migration. Atlanta is home to the world headquarters of AT&T, Coca-Cola, and Delta Airlines. Its airport is a major international hub for the eastern United States. Raleigh has grown thanks to the Research Triangle, a section of the state of North Carolina that supports profitable medical and scientific research.

black culture became popular culture to all races. This mix was not always successful, though. Crime rose in many urban areas. Working-class European Americans in many northern cities were resentful of new African American arrivals who they believed were taking their jobs. Tensions erupted into full-scale riots in many major cities in the late 1960s. By the early 1970s, many African Americans were ready to go back to their southern roots, where the economy had changed for the better and where they could more easily benefit their old communities.

The Return South

The population of the Sun Belt, which stretches across the southern United States from Florida to California, has grown significantly since the 1970s. African Americans have contributed to that growth. The Sun Belt has always attracted northerners thanks to its warm climate. Between 1950 and 1990, the Sun Belt states' population grew substantially. For example, Arizona's population grew by 388 percent and Florida's by 366 percent. By contrast, the population of the rest of the United States grew by only 64 percent during the same time. After 1970, industries began to appear in the South where there had once been farms. These industries hired workers who tended not to unionize, which was a perk for southern business owners. Cities like Atlanta, Miami, and Houston became international hubs. The military established many bases in the South. This also attracted African Americans, who found the military lifestyle earned them both respect and a decent living. Air conditioning made it easier for older people of all races to be comfortable in the South. As a result, a vast number of retirees moved to be by the warmth of the coast in their later years; 20 percent of new Florida residents each year are at least sixty–five.

Another important aspect of this demographic influx into the South from approximately 1970 to the present—commonly referred to as the New Great Migration—is that many of the African Americans who have moved to the South are better educated than before. For example, from 1995 to 2000, Maryland, Georgia, and Texas were the states that gained the most black college graduates. This resulted in more black-owned businesses than before, a distinct shift from just fifty years earlier.

In addition to internal domestic migration, immigration from abroad (foreign countries) has contributed to the growth of the African American population in the South. Many Afro-Caribbean Americans continue to move from their island homes to the South, especially to Florida. These immigrants, from places like the Bahamas, Haiti, and Jamaica, bring their own customs to the southern black population. The South continues to grow, both financially and in terms of population, thanks in large part to thriving African American communities.

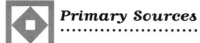

Primary Sources

 SUPREME COURT'S *LOVING V. VIRGINIA* DECISION (1967)

The selection that follows is an excerpt from the Supreme Court's unanimous opinion in the landmark case of *Loving v. Virginia* (1967). Mildred and Richard Loving were an interracial couple arrested for breaking a Virginia law against interracial marriage in 1957. The Lovings challenged the law before the U.S. Supreme Court in 1967. Chief Justice Earl Warren presented the unanimous decision of the Court. In its decision, the Supreme Court ruled that Virginia's antimiscegenation laws (laws prohibiting a person from legally marrying or cohabitating with a person from another race) were unconstitutional and violated the Fourteenth Amendment. The *Loving* case, therefore, made it illegal for any state to have laws prohibiting marriage between people of different races. This excerpt from the ruling explains the initial case and charges, whereby the Lovings were arrested in their own home while they slept, and goes on to refute their conviction.

Abode

Home or place of residence

Virginia judge Leon M. Bazile upheld a Virginia law prohibiting interracial marriage when he ruled against Richard and Mildred Loving for violating the statute in 1959. *Grey Villet/Time & Life Pictures/Getty Images*

In June 1958, two residents of Virginia, Mildred Jeter, a Negro woman, and Richard Loving, a white man, were married in the District of Columbia pursuant to its laws. Shortly after their marriage, the Lovings returned to Virginia and established their marital **abode** in Caroline County. At the October Term, 1958, of the Circuit Court of Caroline County, a grand jury issued an indictment charging the Lovings with violating Virginia's ban on interracial marriages. On January 6, 1959, the Lovings pleaded guilty to the charge and were sentenced to one year in jail; however, the trial judge suspended the sentence for a period of 25 years on the condition that the Lovings leave the State and not return to Virginia together for 25 years. He stated in an opinion that:

> "Almighty God created the races white, black, yellow, malay and red, and he placed them on separate continents. And but for the interference with his arrangement there would be no cause for such marriages. The fact that he separated the races shows that he did not intend for the races to mix."

After their convictions, the Lovings took up residence in the District of Columbia. On November 6, 1963, they filed a motion in the state trial court to vacate the judgment and set aside the sentence on the ground that the statutes which they had violated were **repugnant** to the Fourteenth Amendment. The motion not having been decided by October 28, 1964, the Lovings instituted a class action in the United States District Court for the Eastern District of Virginia requesting that a three-judge court be convened to declare the Virginia antimiscegenation statutes unconstitutional and to enjoin state officials from enforcing their convictions. On January 22, 1965, the state trial judge denied the motion to vacate the sentences, and the Lovings perfected an appeal to the Supreme Court of Appeals of Virginia. On February 11, 1965, the three-judge District Court continued the case to allow the Lovings to present their constitutional claims to the highest state court.

The Supreme Court of Appeals upheld the constitutionality of the antimiscegenation statutes and, after modifying the sentence, affirmed the convictions. The Lovings appealed this decision, and we noted probable jurisdiction on December 12, 1966. The two statutes under which appellants were convicted and sentenced are part of a comprehensive statutory scheme aimed at prohibiting and punishing interracial marriages. The Lovings were convicted of violating 20-58 of the Virginia Code:

> "Leaving State to evade law. If any white person and colored person shall go out of this State, for the purpose of being married, and with the intention of returning, and be married out of it, and afterwards return to and reside in it, cohabiting as man and wife, they shall be punished as provided in 20-59, and the marriage shall be governed by the same law as if it had been solemnized in this State. The fact of their cohabitation here as man and wife shall be evidence of their marriage."

Section 20-59, which defines the penalty for miscegenation, provides:

> "Punishment for marriage. If any white person intermarry with a colored person, or any colored person intermarry with a white person, he shall be guilty of a felony and shall be punished by confinement in the penitentiary for not less than one nor more than five years." . . .

There is **patently** no legitimate overriding purpose independent of **invidious** racial discrimination which justifies this classification. The fact that Virginia prohibits only interracial marriages involving white persons demonstrates that the racial classifications must stand on their own justification, as measures designed to maintain White Supremacy. We have consistently denied the constitutionality of measures which restrict the rights of citizens on account of race. There can be no doubt that restricting the freedom to marry solely because of racial classifications violates the central meaning of the Equal Protection Clause.

These statutes also deprive the Lovings of liberty without due process of law in violation of the Due Process Clause of the Fourteenth Amendment. The freedom to

Demographics
....
PRIMARY SOURCES

Repugnant
Offensive and inconsistent with

Patently
Clearly and plainly

Invidious
Hostile and with an evil purpose

marry has long been recognized as one of the vital personal rights essential to the orderly pursuit of happiness by free men.

Marriage is one of the "basic civil rights of man," fundamental to our very existence and survival.... To deny this fundamental freedom on so unsupportable a basis as the racial classifications embodied in these statutes, classifications so directly subversive of the principle of equality at the heart of the Fourteenth Amendment, is surely to deprive all the State's citizens of liberty without due process of law. The Fourteenth Amendment requires that the freedom of choice to marry not be restricted by invidious racial discriminations. Under our Constitution, the freedom to marry, or not marry, a person of another race resides with the individual and cannot be infringed by the State.

These convictions must be reversed.

It is so ordered.

◆ TEN PLACES OF 100,000 OR MORE POPULATION WITH THE HIGHEST PERCENTAGE OF BLACKS OR AFRICAN AMERICANS: 2000

The following chart is from the U.S. Census Brief *The Black Population: 2000,* which highlights data from the 2000 census that relates specifically to the African American population. This brief reveals that in 2000, the African American population was highly concentrated. That means that the percentage of African Americans in a given city or county in the United States is either very high or very low, when compared to the percentage of African Americans nationally. For example, the census showed that 64 percent of counties in the United States had a black population of under 6 percent, but in 96 counties—95 of which are in the South—blacks account for 50 percent or more of the population. This chart shows that eight of the ten U.S. cities with the highest African American population are in the South. Interestingly, however, the two cities with the highest percentage of African Americans are in the Midwest. Detroit and Chicago (just thirty minutes from Gary, Indiana) attracted large numbers of blacks during the Great Migration (1910–70).

• •

Ten Places of 100,000 or More Population With the
Highest Percentage of Blacks or African Americans: 2000

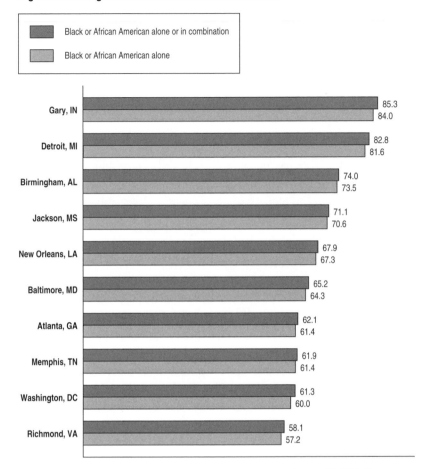

Black or African American alone or in combination

Black or African American alone

Place	Alone or in combination	Alone
Gary, IN	85.3	84.0
Detroit, MI	82.8	81.6
Birmingham, AL	74.0	73.5
Jackson, MS	71.1	70.6
New Orleans, LA	67.9	67.3
Baltimore, MD	65.2	64.3
Atlanta, GA	62.1	61.4
Memphis, TN	61.9	61.4
Washington, DC	61.3	60.0
Richmond, VA	58.1	57.2

Source: U.S. Census Bureau, Census 2000 Redistricting Data (Public Law 94-171) Summary File, Table PL 1.

Research and Activity Ideas

1. Every ten years, the U.S. Census Bureau assesses the demographics in the country. Data about wealth, population, children, and education are calculated and analyzed. Think of a measurable factor that affects the African American population that you think should be calculated but currently is not. Write a report explaining how you would go about gathering the information that you believe is being left out.

2. Prepare a speech about the value of a college education for African Americans. In your speech, explain at least three ways that higher education helps not just the person being educated but society as a whole. Propose at least one change to our country's educational system that you believe would help African Americans pursue college degrees in higher numbers.

3. Write a report about changes to America's black population. What do you think will have happened to some of the main demographics of the population—income, education, employment, home ownership, and the number of children born—by the year 2020? by 2050? What factors influence your analysis?

4. Take your own census of your classmates. Remind them that their answers will remain anonymous. Ask them about housing, education, how many siblings they have, their parents' employment, race, gender, and anything else that you think matters statistically. Now ask them where they think they will be in fifteen years. Will their demographics have changed much? If you can, conduct a similar census of another class (of students your age) nearby or elsewhere in the United States. How do their results vary?

5. Some African Americans, like Roland G. Fryer and Oprah Winfrey, have succeeded despite their poor and difficult beginnings. Fryer was raised primarily by relatives who made and sold crack cocaine. Winfrey was raised by a single mother and often wore dresses made of potato sacks to school. Conduct research to find some other examples of people in our lifetime who have risen above their humble beginnings (not necessarily African Americans). Write an essay explaining how you think this happened. Was it something inside of them or help from the outside that made a difference? Explain.

6. Conduct research on the ten large U.S. cities with the highest percentage of African Americans. Write a report in which you discuss what these cities have in common and how they differ in terms of such factors as climate, education, employment and industry, and anything else you

think might be significant. Based on your analysis, make a prediction about the African American population in these areas: will it grow, shrink, or remain about the same in ten years? in twenty years? Use research to back up your prediction.

 For More Information

BOOKS

hooks, bell. *Ain't I a Woman: Black Women and Feminism.* Boston: South End Press, 1981.

hooks, bell. *Black Looks: Race and Representation.* Boston: South End Press, 1992.

Kennedy, Randall. *Nigger: The Strange Career of a Troublesome Word.* New York: Vintage, 2002.

Newbeck, Phyl. *Virginia Hasn't Always Been for Lovers: Interracial Marriage Bans and the Case of Richard and Mildred Loving.* Carbondale, Ill.: Southern Illinois University Press, 2005.

Obama, Barack. *Dreams from My Father: A Story of Race and Inheritance.* New York: Three Rivers Press, 2004.

Tolliver, Susan. *Black Families in Corporate America.* Thousand Oaks, Calif.: Sage, 1998.

PERIODICALS

"A Virtuous Circle: Black and White (Academic Achievement of Black Middle Class) (American Survey)." *Economist* 324:7768 (July 18, 1992): p. A27(1).

Dubner, Stephen J. "Toward a Unified Theory of Black America." *New York Times Magazine* (March 20, 2005): p. 1.

Jenkins, Jeanne E., and John Guidubaldi. "The Nature-Nurture Controversy Revisited: Divorce and Gender as Factors in Children's Racial Group Differences." *Child Study Journal* 27:2 (1997): pp. 145–60.

Johnson, Kevin. "Report: Gang membership on the rise across U.S." *USA Today* (January 30, 2009), reprinted in *Arizona Republic.* http://www.azcentral.com/arizonarepublic/news/articles/2009/01/30/20090130gns-gangs0130.html (accessed September 30, 2009).

Jones, Lisa. "Rebel Without a Pause." *Village Voice Literary Supplement* (October 1992): p. 10.

WEB SITES

DeShay, Akiim. "The African American Middle Class." *BlackDemographics.com.* http://www.blackdemographics.com/middle_class.html (accessed September 30, 2009).

"Fryer, Roland." *Harvard University Department of Economics.* http://www .economics.harvard.edu/faculty/fryer/cv/RolandFryer (accessed September 30, 2009).

"United States Census 2010." *U.S. Census Bureau.* http://www.census.gov/ (accessed September 30, 2009).

U.S. Supreme Court. *Loving v. Virginia,* 388 U.S. 1 (1967). *FindLaw for Legal Professionals.* http://caselaw.lp.findlaw.com/scripts/getcase.pl?court=US&vol= 388&invol=1 (accessed September 30, 2009).

OTHER

"Interview with Tavis Smiley." *The Tavis Smiley Show.* PBS (March 30, 2005).

chapter six

Education

Chronology *312*

Overview *315*

Headline Makers *318*
Joe Clark. *318*
Johnnetta B. Cole *321*
Michael Eric Dyson *326*
Harry Edwards *330*
Henry Louis Gates Jr.. . . .*333*
Rod Paige *338*

Topics in the News *343*
Black Studies Programs Are
    Established in Higher
    Education *343*
Courts Order School Busing
    to Achieve Integration . . .*346*

School Administrators
    Propose Ebonics to Aid
    Black Students. *352*
Charter Schools Provide an
    Alternative to Minority
    Students *354*
States Take Over Failing
    Inner-City Schools *358*
Historically Black Colleges
    and Universities Face
    Challenges *363*

Primary Sources *369*

Research and Activity Ideas . . .*375*

For More Information *376*

Chronology

1965 March 5 The Freedom School, one of the nation's first integrated schools, is burned to the ground in Indianola, Mississippi.

1965 April 9 Congress enacts the Elementary and Secondary Education Act of 1965 (ESEA), a landmark legislative act intended to close the achievement gap between students from low-income families—a large percentage of whom are minorities—and those from privileged families.

1966 February 1 Dr. Samuel P. Massie becomes the first African American professor at the U.S. Naval Academy.

1966 December 29 In *U.S. v. Jefferson County Board of Education,* a U.S. Court of Appeals declares that the federal government can withhold federal funding from schools that refuse to desegregate.

1968 May 11 During Alfred University's annual Parents' Day celebration, a group of students and faculty members stage a demonstration, calling for scholarships for African American students and for African American history to be added to the school's curriculum.

1968 November 6 Students at San Francisco State University begin a five-month strike that prompts the school to establish the first black studies department in a four-year college.

1968 December 23 In *Powe v. Miles,* a federal court decrees that the portions of private colleges that receive public funding are subject to the Civil Rights Act. African American students benefit from this ruling because it requires private institutions to follow affirmative action policies, or those programs that attempt to replace discriminatory practices with equal opportunities for people of all races.

1969 The Ford Foundation grants $1 million to Howard University, Yale University, and Morgan State University to prepare faculty members to teach courses in African American studies.

1969 April 22 At City College in New York, 250 African American and Puerto Rican students begin a protest that closes the campus and continues until May 15, 1969. Among the group's demands is the establishment of a School of Black and Puerto Rican Studies at the college.

1969 June 2 In *U.S. v. Montgomery County Board of Education,* the Supreme Court rules that schools must hire a certain number of minority teachers based on a defined ratio. As a result, one out of every six faculty and staff members at a school must be of a different race than the majority of faculty at that school.

1971 April 20 In *Swann v. Charlotte-Mecklenburg Board of Education,* the

Supreme Court rules that district courts can require schools to bus students outside of their neighborhoods in order to achieve racial balance.

1973 December 14 The New York Board of Regents orders colleges not to allow minorities living in on-campus housing to segregate themselves.

1974 September 14 In Boston, angry whites throw rocks and shout racial slurs at African American students being bused to white schools as part of an integration plan. The incident is one of many that will affect Boston public schools for the rest of the decade.

1976 February 1 Negro History Week, founded by Professor Carter Woodson's Association for the Study of Negro Life and History in 1926, is expanded into Black History Month.

1977 May 11 The National Association for the Advancement of Colored People (NAACP) files suit against the U.S. Department of Health, Education, and Welfare. The NAACP charges that the federal agency has been negligent in enforcing the integration of vocational education.

1978 June 28 In *Regents of the University of California v. Bakke,* the Supreme Court prohibits the use of a racial quota system (a requirement that a fixed number of minority applicants be admitted every year) in college admissions.

1979 August 15 In Ann Arbor, Michigan, the school board approves a program that will teach "Black English" to all teachers at Martin Luther King Elementary School.

1983 February 7 In Philadelphia, a U.S. district judge rules that once school districts have initially achieved racial integration, they are not required to maintain racial balance among their faculties by constantly reassigning teachers.

1984 As part of the ongoing *Geier v. Alexander* case, the U.S. District Court grants a Stipulation of Settlement Agreement to the plaintiffs and defendants. The purpose of the settlement is to improve higher-education opportunities for African Americans and increase the numbers of African American students in predominantly white universities.

1986 June 16 A test given to two hundred thousand teachers in Texas (the Texas Examination for Current Administrators and Teachers, or TECAT) is formally challenged by teachers' unions on the grounds of racial bias. Eighteen percent of African American teachers and six percent of Hispanic teachers fail the test, while only one percent of white teachers fail it.

1992 City Academy High School, the nation's first charter school, opens in St. Paul, Minnesota, with a student body that is approximately ninety-percent minority.

1994 Elaine R. Jones is named the first female director-counsel of the NAACP's Legal Defense and Educational Fund (LDF), which has been responsible for major civil rights litigation related to education. Under Jones's leadership, the LDF defended affirmative action at the University of Michigan in the U.S. Supreme Court case *Gratz vs. Bollinger* (2003).

1994 January 25 Reauthorizing the Elementary and Secondary Education Act of 1965, Bill Clinton signs the Improving America's Schools Act (ISA).

1997 October 25 In Philadelphia, African American women participate in the Million Woman March, a movement focusing on education and health care.

1999 Thirty years of court-supervised desegregation ends in the Charlotte-Mecklenburg school district, which had been at the center of the school busing controversy in the early 1970s.

2002 January 8 President George W. Bush's No Child Left Behind Act (NCLB) is signed into law. It reauthorizes federal programs that aim to improve the performance of elementary and secondary schools by increasing state, district, and campus accountability standards.

2003 June 23 The Supreme Court rules that public institutions of higher education can use race as one of many factors in the admissions process.

2007 According to the U.S. Census, nineteen percent of the African American population has completed four or more years of college, as opposed to thirty-two percent of the white population.

2007 June 28 The Supreme Court rules that race cannot be a factor in assigning students to high schools in Louisville, Kentucky, and Seattle, Washington.

Overview

With its landmark decision in *Brown v. Board of Education of Topeka, Kansas* (1954), the U.S. Supreme Court breathed life into the Fourteenth Amendment's equal protection clause. The Court recognized both civil and political rights for African Americans. Such rights are often referred to as "first generation rights." In the decades following *Brown,* African American students began to insist upon more than civil and political liberties. They wanted schools—segregated or not—to affirm their economic, cultural, and social rights as well. Known as "second generation rights," these are liberties endorsed by the United Nations' *Universal Declaration of Human Rights* (1948).

In the South, many school districts responded to *Brown's* ruling that elementary and secondary schools desegregate "with all deliberate speed" by instituting what they called "freedom of choice" plans. Freedom of choice plans allowed parents to select any school within the district for their children to attend. The plans were supposed to provide for integration and racial balance. These plans did transfer some African American students into formerly all-white schools. No white student in any southern state, however, chose to attend schools that were primarily African American. Because most students remained where they were, schools remained segregated, or made up of students of only one race. The persistence of school segregation caused a series of lawsuits to be filed against school districts during the 1960s and 1970s. These lawsuits were heard by various federal courts, including the U.S. Supreme Court. In several of these cases, the courts ruled that a school's compliance with desegregation orders would determine its eligibility for federal funding.

In 1971, the Supreme Court ruled in *Swann v. Charlotte-Mecklenburg Board of Education* that the school district of Charlotte, North Carolina, was required to bus its students across district lines in order to achieve integration. The ruling set the precedent for African American education for the entire decade. Busing, however, became a controversial topic. African American parents were upset by the fact that for every seven African American students who were bused, only one white student was bused. They also argued that the staff and students at white schools had not been prepared for the arrival of African American students. As a result, they said, African American students were often received with discrimination and even violence.

African American students in colleges and universities also experienced racism on and off campus. Demands for second-generation rights, however, resulted in the creation of African American studies programs at both black and white colleges and universities all over the United States. By 1970, these programs had been instituted at universities such as San Francisco State, Harvard, Yale, and Ohio State. Growing numbers of African American students were on college campuses. African American curricular programs increased as well. In response, many organizations and African American student unions were formed to support these students and recruit new students. One important recruitment strategy for colleges was to prepare high school students for higher education by emphasizing the fields of science, technology, and engineering. The National Society for Black Engineers was founded by two undergraduate students at Purdue University as the Society of Black Engineers. It later grew into a national group. It is a particularly successful example of these kinds of organizations.

In part because of the changes taking place in colleges and universities during the late 1960s and 1970s, African Americans began to see changes in their public elementary and secondary schools as well. For the first time, many schools acknowledged the need for multicultural education in the classroom. Schools began providing students with the appropriate curriculum plans and textbooks. Black History Month was established as a yearly observance in 1976. African Americans were afforded the unprecedented opportunity to learn about the accomplishments of their people in a school setting.

Nevertheless, equal education for African Americans continued to be a problem in the 1980s and 1990s. The gap between academic achievement on standardized tests for whites and African Americans had begun to close. Many people argued, however, that African American students remained at a disadvantage. As evidence, they pointed to the disproportionate (higher than average) numbers of African Americans in low-level courses, remedial classes, and special education programs. Annual evaluations showed that disparity among racial and ethnic student populations persisted in America's schools. The disparity was most prominent in math and science. In addition, funding for students at predominantly minority urban schools fell well below that of predominantly white suburban schools. This is mainly because, in most states, revenue from property taxes is used to fund many schools. Wealthier neighborhoods (which tend to be white) pay more money in property taxes than poorer neighborhoods (which tend to have higher minority populations).

In the late 1990s and early 2000s, lawmakers attempted to address these disparities. For example, the No Child Left Behind Act of 2001 provides funds for students to transfer to higher-performing schools or receive free tutoring to increase academic-achievement levels. In response, public schools began to devote more money to support diversity training and multicultural and bilingual educational programs. Along with these changes came greater parental involvement within the African American community. Parents increasingly became aware of their rights. Parents have a right to know how their children's schools are performing in comparison to state goals and standards. They also have a right to know if their children's teachers are fully qualified and if student populations within the schools are making adequate yearly progress.

Educational research has increasingly shown that a person's culture and experiences are fundamental to the acquisition of knowledge. As a result, learning opportunities for African Americans are more numerous than ever before. Today, elementary and secondary educators can turn to resources aimed specifically at the African American community. For example, some software programs teach reading by drawing on the students' familiarity with rap lyrics or traditional clapping and chanting games that many African American girls learn to play at a young age. Schools are looking beyond the conventional, traditional perspectives and expectations of education. Such schools are successful not only in the elementary and secondary education of African American students, but also in the preparation of those individuals to attend college and have more access to jobs on par with whites.

Headline Makers
• •

★ **JOE CLARK**
(1939–)

Joe Clark became famous as principal of Eastside High School in Paterson, New Jersey. Clark patrolled the hallways with a bullhorn and a baseball bat, and he often used controversial methods of disciplining students. A former drill instructor in the U.S. Army, Clark believes that education is a mission that requires students to be held to high expectations, to be confronted when they fail to meet those expectations, and to be punished if they interrupt or impede the educational process. His forceful management style and extreme disciplinary tactics put him in the national spotlight when he was deemed a model educator by President Ronald Reagan (1911–2004). Clark was also the subject of the 1989 film *Lean on Me*.

Born May 7, 1939, in Newark, New Jersey, Joe Louis Clark learned about responsibility, hard work, and the value of education early in his life. He worked while attending high school to help support his mother and his siblings. In 1958, he joined the U.S. Army Reserve, where he served as a drill sergeant. After earning a bachelor's degree from William Paterson College, Clark attended Seton Hall University. He obtained both master's and doctoral degrees. In the late 1960s, Clark began his career as an educator in Paterson, New Jersey. He taught grade school and then took a position as the director of camps and playgrounds in Paterson. From the 1970s to the early 1980s, Clark served as an elementary school principal before assuming the position that would make him the center of a nationwide controversy: principal of Eastside High School in Paterson, New Jersey.

High school principal Joe Clark in 1988. *Yvonne Hemsey/Getty Images*

Transforming Eastside High

Eastside High School was an inner-city school that had been devastated by violence, vandalism (willfully destroying or defacing of public property), drug use, and gang activity. Ninety percent of the school's approximately 3,200 students were African American or

Hispanic. Most came from poor families. Fights in classrooms and hallways were common. Teachers as well as students frequently found themselves in confrontations involving weapons. Drug dealers conducted business inside and outside the school building. Students smoked marijuana in the bathrooms and crowded hallways. The school had the appearance of a war zone. Graffiti covered the school's walls and hallways, and broken windows, doors, and furniture were familiar sights.

As a result of the school's atmosphere, most students and teachers were constantly afraid that violence might erupt. The quality of instruction at the school was not good. Little actual learning took place. In addition to high truancy (students skipping school) and dropout rates, the students at Eastside had standardized test scores that were among the lowest in the state of New Jersey.

On the first day of school at Eastside High in September 1982, a student was stabbed. On the first day of school in 1983, the students arrived at a school that had undergone a great transformation. Clark had vowed to make Eastside High a place where students would feel safe and be able to learn without serious distractions. He had spent the summer overseeing a renovation of the building to fix broken windows, busted door locks, and dilapidated fences. He also reorganized the school's administrative structure, which means that several staff members who did not meet Clark's standards were dismissed. He established a clearly defined chain of command and system of problem-solving channels. His goal was to more effectively maintain order among both students and staff.

Clark's philosophy of education is that all students deserve a good education but should be removed from the school environment if they are not willing to work toward that end. As a consequence, he completely reworked student policies. Under Clark's management, students and faculty were required to wear photo identification badges and uniforms because Clark believed that such a dress code created a level playing field. As students entered Eastside High that first day of school in 1983, Clark greeted them with the bullhorn that would become part of his daily routine.

Clark believed that strict discipline created an environment where the students could excel academically. Therefore, he demanded that students and staff adhere to school regulations with no exceptions. Students who chose not to comply with Clark's rules were suspended. Teachers who disagreed with his policies were asked to leave. During the new principal's first week of school, he expelled around 300 students. The school's newly implemented suspension policy had zero tolerance for verbal assault, fighting, drug possession, vandalism, graffiti, tardiness, and wearing hats.

Clark was a highly visible presence in the halls of Eastside High. He visited classrooms, talked with students, made daily announcements over the public address system, and praised the teachers he felt were performing well. In an effort to stop drug deals, Clark increased campus security and kept exit doors chained to keep out dealers. Clark wanted to make it clear to the students at Eastside High that he was not going to tolerate troublemakers roaming the halls. As a result, he consistently suspended and expelled violators of school policies throughout his tenure at Eastside High. After only two years under Clark's leadership, the governor of New Jersey declared the school a model school.

Clark Becomes a National Figure

In December of 1987, Clark's strict disciplinary methods garnered national attention. He expelled more than sixty students whom he judged to be hindering the education of other students. This group included many students over the age of eighteen who were well short of credits for graduation. The Paterson school board began insubordination (disobedience to authority) proceedings against him. He was charged with denying these students due process, their right to fair treatment under the law. At the same time, he was charged with violating city fire codes for chaining most of the school's doors shut. Despite the opposition Clark faced from the school board, he had a great deal of support from parents and students in the community. They rallied behind him at board meetings. Clark found even more support from the Reagan administration. A White House official offered him a government post in the Office of Policy Development, but Clark refused, saying that he remained committed to his students at Eastside High.

The school board's insubordination proceedings were eventually dropped. Clark also allowed some of the expelled students to come back. The controversial principal continued to be the focus of widespread media coverage, however. He appeared on the cover of *Time* magazine in February 1988. He also appeared on numerous news programs and television talk shows to discuss educational reform, particularly in urban schools. The U.S. secretary of education praised Clark's tough stance in the midst of social crisis and upheld him as an example of what strong leadership can accomplish in inner-city schools. Even so, Clark was not without his share of critics. They said that troubled, disruptive students needed an alternative means of education, not harsh discipline and expulsion. Newspaper editorials called for his resignation. A very critical *New York Times* opinion piece accused Clark of being abusive to students and teachers.

Life After Eastside High

After suffering a bout with pneumonia and undergoing open-heart surgery in May of 1989, Clark resigned from Eastside High School in June.

A month later, Clark's book, *Laying Down the Law,* was published. This work describes Clark's time at Eastside High, his philosophy of education, and the reasons for his actions as a principal. Clark believes most school administrators, teachers, and parents are either unable or unwilling to see the main issues affecting schools. As a result, they settle for poor academic performance and disruptive behavior by students. Clark argues that students in such environments miss the opportunity to learn the skills that they need to be successful members of society. The harsh reality, he explains, is that not all students can be saved from a life of violence, ignorance, and corruption. Those students should be removed from the ones who do have productive futures, he concludes. The book was met with both praise and criticism. Clark spent the next several years lecturing all over the country.

In August 1995, Clark became the director of the Essex County Juvenile Detention Center in Newark, New Jersey. The center was an over-crowded facility that had been under the supervision of a federal judge for various violations. There, Clark once again found himself at the center of controversy. His forceful approach to discipline conflicted with state regulations for juvenile detention facilities. Clark's response to charges against his extreme disciplinary actions was characteristic of his days at Eastside High School. Clark defended his methods by stating that the children in his care were not beaten or abused, but they were held account-able for their actions. After numerous clashes with state officials over the confinement and punishment of violent inmates, Clark resigned from the detention center on January 4, 2002.

Despite his aggressive attitude and rebellious actions throughout his career, Clark has consistently drawn praise from supporters. In the early 2000s, he became a keynote speaker at various venues. He shares his success stories and strategies for education reform, school management, and drug prevention in inner-city schools.

★ JOHNNETTA B. COLE
(1936–)

Johnnetta B. Cole was the first African American female president of Spelman College, the nation's oldest institution of higher learning for African American women. Cole has been a dynamic presence in the world of academia (colleges and universities) for many years. In addition to her work as an educator and an administrator, she is a respected anthropologist. (Anthropology is the scientific study of the origins and nature of human beings.) Her book *All American Women: Lines That Divide, Ties That Bind* was a landmark in women's studies because of the

insightful way it brought together issues of race, class, and gender. Throughout her career, Cole has been an advocate for historically black colleges and universities (HBCUs). She is convinced that these schools provide African American students more opportunities not only to excel but also to discover their heritage.

Johnnetta Cole was born in Jacksonville, Florida, on October 19, 1936, to an ambitious, highly educated family. In 1901, Cole's maternal great-grandfather (her mother's grandfather), Abraham Lincoln Lewis, co-founded the Afro-American Life Insurance Company of Jacksonville. Cole's father, John Betsch Sr., was also an insurance agent, and he joined his wife's family business. Mary Frances, Cole's mother, taught English and worked as a registrar at Edward Waters College before she also joined the family insurance business. Both of Cole's parents were college graduates. They instilled the value of education in all three of their children: Johnnetta, her older sister Marvayne, and younger brother John Jr.

Former college president Johnnetta B. Cole speaks at the Essence Music Festival in 2008. *AP Images*

Cole was a precocious child, meaning she was mature and advanced at an unusually young age. Cole finished high school at the age of fifteen. She entered Fisk University in the summer of 1952 under its early admissions program. There, she befriended Arna Bontemps (1902–73), an award-winning writer, university librarian, and historian of African American culture. Bontemps's position at Fisk allowed the young Cole to see firsthand a hero of the African American community at work.

After a year at Fisk University, Cole joined her sister at Oberlin College. Her intention was to study medicine. However, while taking an anthropology class about racial and cultural minorities, Cole became interested in the African diaspora. She began studying how, despite being scattered all over the world, people of African descent were able to retain their cultural traditions and identities. Cole was inspired and intrigued by what she was learning. She decided to change her major to anthropology.

Training in Anthropology

Cole graduated from Oberlin in 1957 with a bachelor's degree in anthropology. Next, Cole enrolled in the anthropology graduate program at Northwestern University. There, she studied under Melville Jean

Herskovits (1895–1963), an anthropologist noted for having established the study of the "New World Negro" as a new field of research. She also studied under Paul James Bohannan (1920–2007), whose work includes *Africa and Africans,* a study of African economic and legal anthropology. Cole earned a master's degree in anthropology in 1959. While she was at Oberlin, she fell in love with Robert Cole, a white graduate student in economics who had grown up on a dairy farm in Iowa. When the couple went to Jacksonville to visit the Betsch family, white extremists threatened to bomb the family's insurance company. Nevertheless, the two were married in 1960. They moved to Liberia in West Africa for two years to conduct research.

In Liberia, Cole carried out field studies in local villages, and her husband did economic surveys of the area. In 1962, the Coles' first child, David, was born in Monrovia, which is the capital of Liberia. Soon afterward, the family returned to the United States. The Coles began teaching at Washington State University. Johnnetta was named Outstanding Faculty Member of 1965, despite having only a part-time position. In 1966, she had her second son, Aaron, followed by a third son, Che, four years later. She received her Ph.D. in anthropology in 1967 and then became assistant professor of anthropology at Washington State University. She helped found the school's black studies program, serving as its director.

In 1970 Cole accepted a tenured faculty position at the University of Massachusetts at Amherst. She taught there for thirteen years. She was instrumental in developing the university's Afro-American studies program. She also acted as a liaison—a person who establishes and maintains communication and cooperation—between the university and other schools in the Connecticut River Valley area. Cole taught courses in Afro-American studies and anthropology. She also served as provost of undergraduate education.

Cole and her husband divorced in 1982 after twenty-two years of marriage. The next year, she was named a 1983 Russell Sage Visiting Professor of Anthropology at Hunter College of the City University of New York. During her time at Hunter College, Cole directed the Latin American and Caribbean studies program. She also taught anthropology courses. Cole recognized that feminist studies had traditionally focused on white, middle-class women. As a result, she conducted fieldwork that included studies of households headed by women, racial and gender inequality in Cuba, the lives of Caribbean women, how women age, Cape Verdean culture in the United States, and labor in Liberia. This abundance of research culminated in the publication of *All American Women: Lines That Divide, Ties That Bind* (1986). It was a groundbreaking book.

Critics praised it for the way it combined African American studies, cultural anthropology, and women's issues.

"Sistah Prez"

On April 5, 1987, Cole made history when she was named the first African American woman president of Spelman College. Spelman College was founded in 1880 by abolitionists from New England. It is a private school located in Atlanta, Georgia. It had been headed by white women until an African American man, Albert Manley, became president in the 1950s. After Cole became president, it was not long before she was known around campus as "Sistah Prez." She was widely acknowledged as a compassionate, approachable, and exceptional leader. Cole taught classes each semester. She also focused on making Spelman a center of African American scholarship. She wanted it to be a place where teachers, community leaders, artists, and scholars alike could find information about the history and accomplishments of African American women. She also established new academic programs for students. Cole partnered with six major corporations in Atlanta to create a mentorship program. The program gave promising Spelman students the opportunity to work with CEOs of the companies.

One of Cole's primary responsibilities at Spelman was raising money for the college. She estimated that the task consumed half of her time as president. Comedian and television personality Bill Cosby (1937–) donated $20 million to Spelman at her inauguration. Cole was grateful, but she did not hesitate in the following months to remind people that schools can

Johnetta Cole made history in 1987 when she became the first female African American president of Spelman College, a historically black college in Atlanta, Georgia.
© Tami Chappell/Reuters/ Corbis

never have enough money to educate the leaders of tomorrow. Cole proved to be effective at getting donations for Spelman. For example, by the end of only one fundraising campaign, Cole had raised $114 million.

Even as she was busy with her duties at Spelman, Cole was giving interviews, serving on the boards of many corporations, editing anthropology books, and collecting numerous awards and honorary degrees from various organizations and colleges. She was also steadily writing. In addition to scholarly articles, Cole published *Conversations: Straight Talk with America's Sister President* (1993). The book highlights the importance of education, tolerance, and greater social awareness in achieving equality for both sexes and all races.

In 1997, the president of Emory University in Atlanta invited Cole to help foster relations between the school and the African American community. Cole decided to resign from her post at Spelman. Before she went to Emory, she took a year off to write *Dream the Boldest Dreams: And Other Lessons of Life* (1997). The book is filled with sayings and short passages. It explores how learning certain lessons can make life easier. It also gives suggestions about ways people can be more fulfilled. For instance, the book encourages people to get involved in community service and to be willing to work hard for the things in life that truly mean something.

Later Career and Retirement

While at Emory, Cole served as a Presidential Distinguished Professor of anthropology, women's studies, and African American studies. She stayed at Emory until she learned of the state of affairs at Bennett College for Women in Greensboro, North Carolina. Like Spelman, Bennett is an HBCU. In fact, they are the only two colleges in the United States that were founded specifically for the higher education of African American women. Bennett College has a prestigious history dating back to 1926. However, it had been poorly managed for several years. As a result, enrollment numbers were decreasing, accreditation levels were falling, and debt was mounting. Cole had always been an advocate for the higher education of African American women. Thus, she accepted the position of president of the college and took on the challenge of turning the school around.

During her time at Bennett, Cole established the "Revitalizing Bennett Campaign" to address the school's three-million-dollar deficit. Former president Bill Clinton (1947–) and Oprah Winfrey (1954–) headlined fundraising events. The university raised close to $50 million under Cole's management. That was enough to free the college from financial probation. It was also enough to renovate three historic buildings on campus and improve many other buildings. Cole also found time to collaborate with fellow educator Beverly Guy-Sheftall (1946–). Their anthropological research resulted in the work *Gender Talk: The Struggle for Women's Equality in African American Communities* (2003).

In 2005, Cole submitted her resignation from Bennett College because she felt some faculty members were hindering her leadership efforts. The school's board rejected her resignation. Encouraged by supporters, she withdrew her resignation and served as president of Bennett College until she retired in June 2007. She continued to serve on the board of the school's Johnnetta B. Cole Global Diversity and Inclusion Institute, which was founded in March 2004.

Throughout her career, Cole has served on the board of directors for numerous organizations. Those organizations include the American Council on Education, Sisterhood in Support of Sisters in South Africa, the Association of American Colleges, the Global Fund for Women, and the Points of Light Initiative Foundation. She was also the first woman ever elected to the board of Coca-Cola Enterprises. Since the mid-1980s, Cole has been involved with a number of Smithsonian programs. She has been a member of the scholarly advisory board of the National Museum of African American History and Culture ever since the museum opened. On February 9, 2009, Cole was named the director of the Smithsonian National Museum of African Art in Washington, D.C. In addition to organizing fundraising efforts, one of her most important roles at the museum is educating the public about the African diaspora.

★ MICHAEL ERIC DYSON
(1958–)

Michael Eric Dyson is often called "the hip-hop intellectual." He has introduced popular culture—from gangsta rap to Malcolm X to hip-hop music to comedian Bill Cosby—into the world of academia (colleges and universities). His reputation does not rest solely on his cultural studies, however. Scholars also consider him a cutting-edge historian whose work has provided a critical, intellectual perspective of historical figures who have influenced African American society.

A Hard-Working Son and Scholar

Dyson was born on October 23, 1958, in Detroit, Michigan. His mother, Addie Mae Leonard, had picked cotton in Alabama before moving to Detroit. In Detroit, she worked in the city's school system. When Dyson was two, his mother married Everett Dyson. Everett Dyson was a father of four sons, and he soon adopted his wife's young boy. Dyson's father worked full-time at an automobile factory. He also worked part-time at a gardening nursery. Dyson helped out at the nursery starting at the age of twelve.

When Dyson's father was laid off from the automobile factory after thirty-three years, he started his own lawn care service. He also began searching the city for discarded metal to sell to junkyards. Both jobs involved help from his sons.

Dyson attended public schools in Detroit. His teachers recognized his intellect and also his talents as both a speaker and a writer. By encouraging him to be proud of his African American heritage, Dyson's fifth-grade teacher influenced him to learn more about the history of his people. Dyson's seventh-grade English teacher noticed his gift for public speaking. Dyson honed his skills by giving speeches to the congregation of his church. After listening to Martin Luther King Jr.'s "I've Been to the Mountaintop" speech (given on April 3, 1968, just a day before he was assassinated), Dyson was inspired to enter a speech contest, which he won.

Scholar Michael Eric Dyson in 2008. *Mathew Imaging/ WireImage*

Dyson was too young in the 1960s to have been active in the civil rights movement, but he was affected by two particular events during those years. In July 1967, when Dyson was eight, a riot broke out in Detroit after police arrested more than eighty people at an after-hours club. By the time the riot was over, more than forty people were dead, at least four hundred injured, and thousands arrested. For Dyson, the event was a disturbing introduction to curfews imposed upon the African American community and what could happen when people broke it. When Martin Luther King Jr. (1929–68) was assassinated the next year, Dyson felt that his childhood innocence had died as well; the nine-year-old boy became afraid of standing in front of windows and doors at night.

In 1971, Dyson met Baptist preacher Frederick G. Sampson II, who quickly became the boy's mentor. With help from Sampson, Dyson received a scholarship to Cranbrook, a boarding school in Bloomfield Hills, Michigan, a city thirty miles outside Detroit. Dyson had always gone to school with African Americans. At Cranbrook, he found himself surrounded by white classmates. Many of his fellow students were hostile. They addressed him with racial slurs, vandalized his dorm room, and destroyed his possessions. Dyson began to defend himself from their attacks. Within two years he was expelled from the school.

Early Career Struggles

After returning home to Detroit, Dyson earned his high school diploma in 1976. In 1977, he married his girlfriend, who was pregnant at the time. Dyson began working a series of different jobs to support his family. He worked as a welder, a clerk at a Chrysler automobile plant, a manager-trainee in a fast-food restaurant, and a janitor in the Detroit city schools. His wife, an aspiring actress, worked as a waitress. Nevertheless, Dyson had to apply for welfare. He and his wife divorced in 1979.

Dyson was determined to provide his son a better future than the welfare system. Encouraged by Sampson, he became an ordained Baptist minister by the time he was twenty-one years old. Being a minister rekindled Dyson's love for public speaking. He moved to Tennessee, where he attended divinity school at Knoxville College. He later transferred to Carson-Newman College in Jefferson City, Tennessee, where he earned a bachelor's degree in 1982. He also received the school's Outstanding Graduate in Philosophy Award. While working toward his undergraduate degree, Dyson worked full-time at a factory. In addition, he served as a pastor at three churches. He was fired from two churches. The first one fired him because he wanted to allow three women to become deacons. The second fired him because he questioned why his predominately white congregation did not invite other African Americans to speak at the church.

After he graduated from college, Dyson worked as a freelance journalist. He focused much of his work on African American popular culture and music. He accepted a graduate fellowship at Princeton University. While he worked on his master's and doctoral degrees, he served as assistant director of a poverty project at Hartford Seminary in Connecticut. He also taught ethics and cultural criticism at Chicago Theological Seminary. He received his master's degree in 1991. One year later, he received the National Magazine Award from the National Association of Black Journalists for his freelance writing. His writing had appeared in such periodicals as *Vibe*, *Atlantic Monthly*, and *New Republic*. He earned his Ph.D. from Princeton in 1993. He continued his teaching career as an assistant professor at Brown University in Providence, Rhode Island.

Many academics do not show a scholarly interest in popular culture. Dyson, however, recognized the importance of modern-day personalities such as filmmaker Spike Lee (1957–), basketball star Michael Jordan (1963–), and singer Michael Jackson (1958–2009) in mainstream American culture. These personalities are also important to African American culture, gender, race, religion, and class. In 1993, Dyson published his first book, *Reflecting Black: African-American Cultural Criticism,* a collection of essays about these men and other African American icons. The book also included pieces discussing discrimination, including one about racism in the seminary.

In 1994, Dyson published another book, *Making Malcolm: The Myth and Meaning of Malcolm X*. He was inspired to write the book when a group of African American students at Brown University objected to the enrollment of white students in a course he taught about Malcolm X (1925–65). The book was targeted at the general public. It blended biography with social and cultural criticism, and it was a critical and popular success. In addition to being named a Notable Book of 1994 by the *New York Times*, *Making Malcolm* was selected as one of the twentieth century's most outstanding books by *Black Issues Book Review*.

The Professor of Gangsta Rap

Dyson moved to the University of North Carolina, Chapel Hill, in the mid-1990s. He was a professor of communication studies. He was also the director of the school's Institute of African-American Research. He began writing articles about contemporary gangsta rap artists such as Ice Cube (1969–) and Tupac Shakur (1971–96). He came to be regarded as an expert on the social and cultural importance of rap music. He was asked to testify about the subject before a congressional subcommittee. At the university, Dyson's most popular class was one he taught about the effects of gangsta rap on the values of American society, especially within the African American community. His study of rap music led to his next book, *Between God and Gangsta Rap* (1995). His next work, *Race Rules: Navigating the Color Line* (1997), explored racial divisions in America and divisions within the African American community in pieces featuring a number of public figures, including O. J. Simpson (1947–) and Colin Powell (1937–). In 1997, Dyson accepted a position as a distinguished visiting professor at Columbia University. His course on gangsta rap continued to be in high demand.

Two years later, Dyson became the first Ida B. Wells-Barnett University Professor at DePaul University in New York. That position allowed him time to research the life and works of Martin Luther King Jr. Dyson's studies of King culminated in his 2000 work *I May Not Get There with You: The True Martin Luther King, Jr.* One year later, he published a book on the life of Tupac Shakur, a rap artist who was murdered in 1996, entitled *Holler If You Hear Me: Searching for Tupac Shakur*. Dyson then took a job as an Avalon Foundation professor in the humanities and African American studies at the University of Pennsylvania. There, he once again focused his teachings on gangsta rap. He also explored hip-hop music and the lyrics of Shakur.

Dyson has been a very productive writer during the 2000s, publishing *Open Mike: Reflections on Philosophy, Race, Sex, Culture and Religion* (2002), *Why I Love Black Women* (2003), *Mercy, Mercy Me: The Art, Loves, and Demons of Marvin Gaye* (2004), *Is Bill Cosby Right? Or Has the Black Middle Class Lost Its Mind?* (2005), *Pride* (2006), *Come Hell or High Water: Hurricane Katrina and the Color of Disaster* (2006), *Know What I Mean? Reflections on Hip Hop* (2007), and *April 4, 1968: Martin Luther King's Death and How it Changed America* (2008). Each of these works has been critically acclaimed. All have further reinforced his reputation as "the hip-hop intellectual." He received both the NAACP Image Award for Outstanding Literary Work, Non-Fiction and the BET/General Motors Black History Makers Award in 2005.

Dyson hosted a daily talk show called *The Michael Eric Dyson Show* from January 2006 to February 2007. His goal with the show was to fill the void in radio talk shows for African Americans. In 2007, Dyson moved to Washington, D.C., to serve as University Professor of Sociology at Georgetown University. At Georgetown, his course load included theology, English, and African American studies classes. In April 2009, he launched a new version of *The Michael Eric Dyson Show*. His first guest on the daily talk show was Oprah Winfrey (1954–). Additionally, he is a frequent guest on CNN, National Public Radio, and HBO's *Real Time with Bill Maher.*

★ HARRY EDWARDS
(1942–)

Harry Edwards is internationally known for leading the "Revolt of the Black Athlete," a movement that led to a boycott of the Olympic Games in Mexico City in 1968. Edwards is also recognized as one of the world's preeminent specialists in the field of sports psychology. Over the years he has remained an outspoken and sometimes defiant supporter of African American athletes. He is also an expert on the role of race in both professional and amateur sports. Edwards is a professor of sociology (the study of society, social institutions, and social relationships). In addition, he has worked with professional sports teams—including the San Francisco 49ers—and once served as a consultant for Major League Baseball's Office of the Commissioner.

Athletics Provide Academic Opportunities

The second of eight children, Edwards was born on November 22, 1942, in East St. Louis, Illinois. His family lived in such poverty that they often had to boil water they collected from a drainage ditch so that they had water to drink. His father, an ex-convict, encouraged his son to be an athlete. Edwards's father realized that playing sports could provide a future for an African American from their part of the country at the time. Edwards excelled in football, basketball, and track and field in high school. He received an athletic scholarship to attend Fresno City College in California.

Edwards attended Fresno for two years before transferring to San José State College on a scholarship for track and field. There, in addition to becoming a nationally ranked track and field athlete, he played for the college's basketball team. Despite his success in sports, Edwards, along with other African American student-athletes, encountered campus-wide discrimination. African Americans, for example, were not allowed housing in school facilities. Campus officials were afraid that white students would move out if African Americans moved in. Edwards could not pledge a fraternity, nor could he enjoy access to the university's recreation center or campus restaurant. The academic restrictions he faced were most frustrating to Edwards. Typically, African American athletes were advised to take only "easy" courses. The administration feared that allowing student-athletes a challenging course load would cause their grades to dip, making them ineligible for sports. Edwards, however, was a serious student who wanted more. He petitioned the college so that he could major in sociology. When he graduated in 1964, he was the first African American student-athlete to graduate from the school since the early 1950s.

Because of his strength, stature, and athletic ability, Edwards received offers to play professional football from the Minnesota Vikings and the San Francisco 49ers. Rather than pursue a career as an athlete, Edwards instead chose to attend graduate school. He accepted a Woodrow Wilson fellowship to Cornell University in 1966 and worked on his master's and doctoral degrees in sociology. Living in upstate New York allowed him access to lectures given by Malcolm X and other civil rights activists in New York City. Edwards increasingly made a connection between their messages and the discrimination suffered by African American athletes.

The Revolt of the Black Athlete

After receiving a Ph.D. in sociology in 1967, Edwards returned to San José State as a part-time professor and coach. Edwards wanted to improve living conditions and academic opportunities for African American students at the school. Therefore, he presented a list of civil rights violations to the school administration. For the most part, the administration ignored the violations. Angered by this reaction, Edwards co-founded the United Black Students for Action (UBSA). He rallied his supporters and led a movement that made history. For the first time ever, a National Collegiate Athletic Association (NCAA) Division I football game was canceled because of an on-campus protest. The effectiveness of this event prompted Edwards to turn his attention to promoting what was by then known as the "Revolt of the Black Athlete" on a national level.

The USBA evolved into the Olympic Project for Human Rights (OPHR). The OPHR had the specific purpose of demonstrating to the world that the United States exploited African American athletes. Edwards argued that the United States used African American athletes to project an image of racial harmony and equality that was false. According to Edwards, oppression of African Americans was as widespread as ever. Those African Americans who allowed themselves to be used by the government to show this false image of race relations betrayed their people, he concluded. Edwards faced personal attacks—such as the killing of his pets and Ku Klux Klan threats—but he did not stop his campaign. He led the OPHR in a victorious demand that South Africa and Rhodesia be banned from participating in the 1968 Olympics because of their apartheid (a legal system of racial separation) practices. The highlight of the OPHR's involvement in the Olympics in Mexico City came on October 19, 1968. When American medalists Tommie Smith (1944–) and John Carlos (1945–) stood on the winners' podium while the national anthem played, both men bowed their heads and raised black-gloved fists in a Black Power salute. Their intention was to show solidarity in an international statement of protest against racism and human oppression. Smith and Carlos were stripped of their medals, and they were required to leave the Olympic Village.

Career as an Academic and Consultant

In 1970 Edwards accepted a post at the University of California, Berkeley. He continued to fight for social and racial equity for all African Americans, especially athletes. After six years at Berkeley, Edwards was denied tenure by a university committee because he had not been notably published in academic journals. His publications to that point consisted of one book, *Revolt of the Black Athlete* (1970), and essays and articles in such periodicals as *Sports Illustrated.* Because of both his reputation as a crusader and his popularity with his students, Edwards received an outpouring of support from fellow sociologists, athletes, members of the clergy, and, of course, students. When Jerry Brown (1938–), the governor of California, wrote letters protesting the university's decision, the committee's ruling was reversed.

Throughout the years, Edwards has focused on the physical and psychological health of amateur and professional athletes. In an age of performance-enhancing drugs, he has cautioned athletes against taking steroids. In addition, he urges coaches and managers not to ignore drug use. He is also an advocate for the hiring and promotion of African American coaches and managers. In 1987, Los Angeles Dodgers general manager Al Campanis (1916–98) said on national television that African Americans were not suitable for management positions in Major League Baseball. In response, the commissioner of Major League Baseball hired Edwards to help teams employ African Americans in the business sector of professional baseball.

In the late 1980s and early 1990s, Edwards also served as a consultant to the Golden State Warriors, San Francisco's professional basketball team, and the San Francisco 49ers. Edwards helped facilitate (bring about and make easier) communications between African American players and mostly white coaching staffs. He traveled with the teams and did psychological evaluations of draft prospects. Perhaps most importantly, Edwards counseled the athletes themselves about practical issues. Those issues included investments, education, dealing with management, and career options after professional sports.

Edwards is generally regarded as the first academic to establish the legitimacy of the idea that sports are a reflection of society. He retired from the University of California, Berkeley, in June 2000. On February 14, 2008, he was inducted into the African American Ethnic Sports Hall of Fame. His opinions remain highly respected. He is often called upon to assess situations involving contemporary athletes. For instance, he was involved in the psychoanalysis of the controversial football star Terrell Owens (1973–) following his apparent breakdown. After football player Michael Vick (1980–) pled guilty to dogfighting charges in 2007, National Football League Commissioner Roger Goodell (1959–) enlisted Edwards's help in creating the league's new personal conduct policy. Ultimately, Edwards sees himself as a role model—not as a former athlete, but as a man who passed on a career in professional sports to become an academic.

★ HENRY LOUIS GATES JR.
(1950–)

Henry "Skip" Louis Gates Jr. is renowned (widely known and respected) for his cultural studies of African American literature and history and their impact on American oral and literary traditions. Gates was the first African American to earn a Ph.D. from Cambridge University. He was also instrumental in expanding Harvard University's African American studies program. He has dedicated his career to gaining more

popular and academic recognition of African American literary works. He has written and edited numerous articles and books in his field. He is perhaps most highly regarded for his contribution to the comprehensive reference book *Africana: The Encyclopedia of the African and African American Experience* (1999) and for hosting and producing several documentary series on PBS.

Academic Excellence

Gates was born on September 19, 1950, in Keyser, West Virginia, a valley town surrounded by the Allegheny Mountains. His father worked as a loader at the local paper mill during the day and as a janitor at the town's telephone company at night. His father was also a gifted storyteller. Gates's mother, a housecleaner, was interested in the messages of civil rights leader Malcolm X. She did not agree with his views that the races should live separately, and instead taught her children how to live in an integrated society. Gates's mother became the first African American member of the Parent Teacher Association in their school community. Gates attended Davis Free School, the area's only elementary school. He was an excellent student. In the fifth grade, he learned about Africa and the civil rights movement in the United States from lessons on current events. Gates began to develop an appreciation for the contributions and sacrifices African Americans had made—and were making—to the culture and history of the United States.

At the age of twelve, Gates experienced a significant change in his life when his mother was hospitalized with clinical depression. Gates was afraid she was going to die, so he bargained with God: If God would let his mother come home from the hospital, then Gates would devote his life to Christ. His mother did return home, and Gates lived up to his word. He became active in his church. Encouraged by his uncle, a Methodist minister, he attended a summer church camp that fostered his intellectual growth. He explored ideas and issues about religion and race.

In 1964, Gates fractured his hip playing touch football. While the doctor, a white man, was examining him, he asked Gates what he planned to be when he grew up. Gates replied that he wanted to be a physician himself. When the doctor quizzed Gates about his knowledge of science, he answered the man's questions correctly. At the end of the examination, the doctor incorrectly diagnosed Gates's hairline fracture as a psychosomatic illness, which is an injury caused by mental or emotional disturbance. As a result of the diagnostic error, Gates's leg did not heal properly, and he now walks with a cane.

After graduating as valedictorian of his high school class in 1968, Gates entered Potomac State College of West Virginia University. He planned to go to medical school. His discovery of fascinating new horizons in his history and literature courses, however, changed his career plans. Gates's literature professor recognized his student's academic talent and advised him to apply to Ivy League schools. Gates was soon accepted at Yale University. In 1973, he graduated with honors from the prestigious university with a B.A. in history.

Gates won a fellowship to study at Cambridge University in England. There, he met Nobel laureate Wole Soyinka (1934–), a Nigerian playwright who convinced him to study literature along with history. Soyinka introduced Gates to the mythology and writings of the Yoruba people in Nigeria. Soyinka inspired Gates to focus on the background of African American literature and its relationship to the literary traditions of Africa and the Caribbean.

Success in Teaching and Writing

During graduate school, Gates worked as a London staff correspondent for *Time* magazine. He received his master's degree from Cambridge in 1974. Next, he returned to the United States and to Yale University. He was a lecturer at Yale while he worked on his Ph.D. in English language and literature. Gates earned his doctorate in 1979, and he became an assistant professor at Yale. Shortly thereafter, he published an essay called "Preface to Blackness: Text and Pretext," which appeared in the book *Afro-American Literature: The Reconstruction of Instruction* by Robert Stepto and Dexter Fisher. In 1980, Gates began work on his Black Periodical Literature Project. The project focused on nineteenth-century African American literary works from periodicals. Gates became well known in the world of African American scholarship when he rediscovered and republished Harriet E. Wilson's *Our Nig* (1859), the first novel published by an African American woman. When it was originally published, the novel had been ignored. It was credited to a white man at a later time. By researching and verifying the original work, Gates both extended the history of African American literature by more than thirty years and influenced scholarship in literature by African American women.

In 1981, Gates received a 150,000-dollar grant from the MacArthur Foundation. He dedicated much of the grant to his Black Periodical Literature Project. In 1984, he was promoted to associate professor of English and the director of the Department of Afro-American Studies at Yale. That same year, Gates published and edited *Black Literature and Literary Theory*. The book challenged the traditional Western literary canon by proposing an African American literary canon. A "literary canon" is the group of books from a particular time period or place that are considered to be the best or most important. Gates followed that book with *The Signifying Monkey: Towards a Theory of Afro-American Literature* (1989), a work that defined a critical approach to African American literature. *The Signifying Monkey* won the American Book Award and the Anisfield-Wolf Book Award for Race Relations. In 1990, Gates used the book's ideas about African American vernacular (slang, informal language) to defend the rap group 2 Live Crew against obscenity charges in Florida, maintaining that the group's lyrics reflected the African American mythic tradition and its rich, symbolic language.

In 1988, Gates accepted a job as a full professor of English and Africana studies at Cornell University. Also that year, he was named the W. E. B. Du Bois Professor of Literature. He thus earned the distinction of being the first African American male to hold an endowed chair at Cornell. One year later, he joined the faculty of Harvard as chair of the Department of African American Studies. He remained at Harvard until 2006. When Gates first came to Harvard, the department consisted of one white professor and only a few students. Within a few years, Gates had recruited some of the country's most prominent African American intellectuals, including Cornel West (1953–). Gates and West co-authored *The Future of the Race* (1996).

Multimedia Projects

Gates made a pledge with some of his colleagues in the 1970s to fulfill W. E. B. Du Bois's dream of publishing the African American equivalent of the *Encyclopaedia Britannica*. Gates fulfilled that pledge by working under an advisory board headed by Soyinka to co-edit the *Encarta Africana* (1999). *Encarta Africana* was published on CD-ROM. In print, the volume was published under the name *Africana: The Encyclopedia of the African and African American Experience*. The work included more than three thousand articles. It is an African American reference book of unprecedented scope. In 1999, Gates created Africana.com to provide corrections and revisions to *Encarta Africana*. The site was purchased by AOL Time Warner the next year. Gates developed an interactive online course about the Harlem Renaissance. He also coordinated the production of *The Wonders of the*

African World (1999), a six-part miniseries for PBS. In the miniseries, a team of scholars spent a year traveling through twelve countries in Africa collecting evidence of African cultures from the past.

During the 2000s, Gates continued to work tirelessly on multiple projects. In 2002, after extensively researching the authenticity of the handwritten manuscript, he published the only known novel written by a female African American slave. *The Bondwoman's Narrative* is an autobiographical novel written by Hannah Crafts during the 1850s. For PBS, Gates produced and hosted *America beyond the Color Line* (2004), *African American Lives* (2006), and *Oprah's Roots* (2007). Gates also published books expanding on those documentaries. These projects used genealogical research (information about a person's ancestors and relatives) and genetic mapping to help the celebrities he interviewed— actress Whoopi Goldberg (1955–), music producer Quincy Jones (1933–), Dr. Ben Carson (1951–), and actor Chris Tucker (1972–), for example— learn more about their heritage. The projects also gave Gates the opportunity to explore his own ancestry. He discovered that one of his ancestors was John Redman. Redman was a free African American man who fought in the American Revolution. As a result, Gates was inducted into the Sons of the American Revolution in 2006. Gates's genealogical investigations also led to his editing the *African American National Biography* (2008), which contains many of the stories he had collected during his research of family history. He even co-founded AfricanDNA, an organization that allows people to receive the same genetic testing, matching, and genealogical exploration that was done for the subjects of his *African American Lives* series.

Gates has been the recipient of more than fifty honorary degrees from such institutions as Dartmouth College, Emory University, and New York University. He has received numerous other awards, ranging from the George Polk Award for Social Commentary in 1993 to the 2008 Ralph Lowell Award from the Corporation for Public Broadcasting. In 1997, Gates was named one of *Time* magazine's "25 Most Influential Americans." He was elected to the Academy of Arts and Letters in 1999.

Gates next published *Lincoln on Race and Slavery* (2009). It is a volume filled with definitive texts and historical notes gathered from President Abraham Lincoln's personal letters, speeches, and official documents. The work follows his PBS documentary *Looking for Lincoln* (2009). Gates is an influential critic of both African American and white culture. He writes articles for *Time* and the *New Yorker*. He is also the editor-in-chief of TheRoot.com, a daily online magazine for African Americans.

★ **ROD PAIGE**
(1933–)

Rod Paige first distinguished himself as a college football coach, but his commitment to education has extended far beyond the playing field. Drawing from his vast personal experiences in education, Paige was the first African American to serve as U.S. secretary of education. In the George W. Bush administration, Paige was instrumental in drafting President Bush's No Child Left Behind Act of 2001. He also helped ensure that the policy was implemented throughout the nation.

Early Education in the Segregated South

Paige was born June 17, 1933, in the segregated town of Monticello, Mississippi. He was the oldest of five children. Paige grew up in a household that understood the value of books and education. His father was a school principal. His mother was a librarian. As a young boy, Paige engaged in lively discussions about his favorite books and literary characters with his parents and siblings. Paige went to Monticello's Lawrence County Training School, a segregated school for first through twelfth graders. When he realized the differences between his school and the school for white students—the white school had a nice gym, while his school had no gym at all, for example—he got angry. He began to feel the need to prove that he was as smart as white students. He felt this need not only when he was in grade school, but also years later when he was in college and graduate school.

Paige attended Jackson State College in Jackson, Mississippi, after graduating from high school in 1951. He played on the school's football team. In 1955, he graduated with honors, earning a bachelor's degree in physical education. He took a job teaching and coaching at a high school in Clinton, Mississippi, after graduation. Soon, he was drafted by the U.S. Navy and moved to San Diego, California. In July 1956, Paige married his college girlfriend Gloria Crawford. A few days later, Paige received orders to ship out to Okinawa, Japan. In Japan, he served as a medical corpsman.

When Paige returned to the United States, he took a job as the head football coach at Utica Junior College in Mississippi. He remained there until 1962, when he left to coach at Jackson State University. Seeking a life beyond football, he decided to pursue a master's degree. At that time, no graduate schools in Mississippi accepted African Americans. Instead, Paige enrolled at Indiana University. He earned both master's and doctoral degrees in physical education. He wrote his dissertation (a very long paper that a student must write to earn a doctoral degree) on the response time of offensive linemen.

Paige worked briefly as an assistant football coach at the University of Cincinnati after completing graduate school. In 1971, he accepted a position as head coach and athletic director at Texas Southern University in Houston. He accepted on condition that he also be granted faculty status. Impressed by Paige's intelligence and leadership abilities, university president Granville Sawyer happily agreed. While coaching at Texas State University, Paige grew more and more discouraged by the ever-increasing commercialism in intercollegiate athletics. As a result, he turned his focus from sports to academics. Several teams in the National Football League were interested in hiring him as a coach. Paige instead focused his attention on education. He left coaching completely in 1984 to become dean of Texas State University's College of Education.

U.S. Secretary of Education Rod Paige in 2004. *Mark Wilson/Getty Images*

A Committed Educator

Texas State University's education program flourished under Paige's control. At one point, around thirty-three percent of teachers and administrators working in the Houston Independent School District had graduated from the College of Education at Texas State University. During his ten years as dean, Paige established the university's Center for Excellence in Urban Education, a research facility that addresses instructional and managerial concerns in urban schools.

In 1989, Paige believed that the citizens of Houston wanted a change in the city's vision for public school education. He ran for a seat on the Houston Independent School District (ISD) school board. He hoped his experience in the field of education would make up for his inexperience in local politics. Paige won the election. Paige was one of four new members of a nine-member board. All of them were prepared to lead Houston ISD in a new direction. At the time, Houston ISD was the nation's seventh largest school district. With Paige serving as committee chairperson, the Houston ISD school board drafted the Declaration of Beliefs and Visions. The declaration was a statement of the district's purpose and goals. It called for reform through decentralization, which is the process of taking authority away from one person or group and distributing it among many people or groups. Additionally, schools would be responsible for developing a challenging core curriculum.

The curriculum was to prepare all students—whether bound for college or headed straight into the workforce—for life after graduation. Furthermore, the declaration proposed that district policies hold teachers accountable for the quality of classroom instruction.

Joan Raymond, the superintendent of Houston ISD, opposed the Declaration of Beliefs and Visions. After battling with the school board for a year, she was fired. Her replacement, Frank Petruzielo, supported the document's reforms. Paige was still not satisfied. He felt that the new superintendent viewed the declaration as a fast fix to many of the district's problems, not a long-term instrument of change. In 1992, Paige was elected president of the Houston ISD school board. Two years later, Petruzielo left the district. Paige resigned from his position at Texas Southern University and was hired as the Houston ISD's new superintendent.

Paige was superintendent from 1994 to 2001. He concentrated on implementing the reforms set forth in the Declaration of Beliefs and Visions. For instance, he created the Peer Examination, Evaluation, and Redesign (PEER) program. The PEER program was designed to facilitate partnerships with business and community professionals who would recommend ways to improve the Houston ISD. Paige made sure that Houston ISD teachers' salaries were competitive with other large school districts in Texas. He also instituted teacher incentive pay to recognize those instructors who demonstrated outstanding job performance and innovative approaches to education. This system of financial reward required a new system for evaluating teachers and administrators.

The state of Texas audited (performed a formal financial investigation of) Houston ISD in 1996. Paige saw an opportunity to use the results of the audit to his further his goals for the district. To help relieve school overcrowding, Paige began contracting with private schools to accept Houston ISD students who were struggling academically. He also established a system of charter schools. Campus administrators with decision-making power over such issues as textbooks, classroom materials, and personnel headed the charter schools. Paige also privatized school maintenance, employee benefits, and food services, which means he changed those businesses from being run by the government to being run by private individuals and companies.

Many teachers were critical of Paige. Some teachers did not believe that relying on students' scores on standardized tests was a good way to measure learning. They also felt Paige had given principals too much authority in making personnel decisions on their campuses. Others disagreed with the decentralization of special education. They argued that such programs were best served from district offices rather than individual schools. When a 390-million-dollar bond election failed, it was evident that many members of the Houston ISD were dissatisfied with the Declaration of Beliefs and Visions. Nevertheless, Paige stayed true to his vision of reform. People soon began to appreciate his leadership and the improvements he was making. In 1998, a record 678-million-dollar bond issue was passed. A bond issue is a way for the government to borrow the money it needs to run schools.

In 1999, the Council of the Great City Schools awarded Paige the Richard R. Green Award for Outstanding Urban Educator. That award was followed by the National Association of Black Educators Superintendent of the Year award. In recognition of his contributions to the city of Houston's development, *Inside Houston Magazine* designated Paige as one of the twenty-five most powerful people in Houston. In 2001, the American Association of School Administrators named him National Superintendent of the Year.

Secretary of Education

In December 2000, president-elect George W. Bush (1946–) offered Paige the post of U.S. secretary of education. As governor of Texas, George W. Bush was impressed by both Paige's management style and his reforms. Bush often spoke of Houston ISD as a model for other urban schools. He was confident Paige could help improve schools all across America.

On January 24, 2001, Paige became the first superintendent and the first African American ever to serve as U.S. secretary of education. As head of the Department of Education, Paige gained the support of both Republicans and Democrats. He immediately devoted his energies to the No Child Left Behind Act of 2001 (NCLB). NCLB addressed many of the same issues Paige had dealt with in Houston ISD schools. Its goal was to give every child—regardless of race, religion, or nationality—the opportunities and resources to achieve academic success. NCLB empowered parents, especially those whose children attended low-performing schools, with a voucher plan. The voucher plan would allow them to have their children attend private schools at no cost to them if their local public school district did not improve within a set time period. NCLB also called for standardized testing, greater accountability, and local control for teachers and school administrators.

Educational organizations throughout the country opposed the standardized testing mandated by NCLB. They contended that an emphasis on standardized tests detracted from real classroom learning because they forced teachers to devote the bulk of their time to test preparation. Many state legislatures protested the high standards of achievement set forth in NCLB. The act's new standards meant that some schools that had formerly been considered excellent now had failing status. Several states even

U.S. Secretary of Education Rod Paige talks with students in 2003.
AP Images

considered rejecting federal funding so they would not be required to comply with NCLB's guidelines. In response to such opposition, Paige went on a six-month tour to win support for NCLB. He visited school facilities and spoke at town hall meetings. He encouraged parents, teachers, principals, and administrators to work together and be active participants in the educational process. By June 2003, every state had put an approved accountability plan into place. The accountability plans reflected Paige's philosophy of education: every child deserves equal access to an education, and educational excellence should be the standard for every school.

On November 15, 2004, Paige announced his resignation from the Department of Education. In March 2005, he accepted a position as a public policy scholar at the Woodrow Wilson Center in Washington, D.C. He began work on a project addressing the achievement gap between African Americans and other races. He also became a trustee of the Thomas B. Fordham Foundation, a nonprofit think tank committed to the belief that all children deserve a high-quality education. In March 2007, Paige published *The War against Hope: How Teachers' Unions Hurt Children, Hinder Teachers, and Endanger Public Education*. The book challenges the methods of the National Education Association, among other groups. Paige also co-founded Chartwell Education Group, a consulting company based in New York. Using his experience as both an educator and an administrator, Paige helps Chartwell provide education-related services—including guidance on policy and how to comply with current laws—to state and local governments, corporations, and other foundations.

❖ BLACK STUDIES PROGRAMS ARE ESTABLISHED IN HIGHER EDUCATION

The civil rights movement during the 1960s inspired African Americans to express pride in their African heritage more publicly than ever before. When the slogan "Black Power" entered the public arena in 1966, African American youth especially found a new sense of empowerment, or sense of high self-esteem. African American activism on college campuses became widespread. Those students demanded a voice in their higher education. Many African Americans thought that schools were teaching from a perspective that did not recognize and represent the lives and concerns of African Americans. For instance, they wanted more teaching on the history of their African American and African ancestors. They also wanted courses that focused on the contributions of African Americans to society and on the social problems in their communities. The result was the field of African American studies, also known as black studies, Afro-American studies, Pan-African studies, and Africana studies.

Students Demand Ethnic Studies

The nation's first African American studies programs were created in response to a student protest. At the predominantly white San Francisco State College (now University), for example, the Black Student Union (BSU) and Third World Liberation organized a strike. The strike lasted from November 6, 1968, to March 20, 1969. The students committed violent acts such as setting fires in the library and planting a bomb in administrative offices during school hours. The groups issued a list of demands, including calls for specific teachers to be given certain jobs, but their central goal was the formation of a department of black studies. While not all of the striking students' demands were met, San Francisco State College did establish the nation's first college of ethnic studies. This included the first black studies department in the country. Now a part of San Francisco State University's curriculum, the student strike is taught in history and social justice courses. Its most lasting effect is that it laid the groundwork for African American studies programs in other colleges and universities.

Supporters of African American studies said it was important to have teachers and administrators who understood and were sensitive to the educational needs of African Americans. They also wanted courses that were relevant to the African American experience. Most early courses taught works by such African American scholars as W. E. B. Du Bois (1868–1963), John Hope Franklin (1915–2009), and Benjamin Brawley (1882–1939). Students also read works by James Baldwin (1924–87), Frederick Douglass (1818–95), and Malcolm X (1925–65). African American studies programs

Students demonstrate against police during a faculty strike at the San Francisco State College. Faculty and students began the strike in 1968 to force the school administration to establish a black studies department, among other demands. *Vernon Merritt III/ Time & Life Pictures/ Getty Images*

bring together many different academic subjects, so the courses that could be offered seemed to be endless in possibility. In the late 1960s and early 1970s, typical courses included Africana: A Study in the Problems of Emerging Nations, Jazz Styles and Techniques, Black Capitalism, Pan-Africanism: The Politics of Integration, and Community Studies: Problems in Community Living.

Achievements in African American Studies

Professor Molefi Kete Asante (1942–), head of African American studies at Temple University, is credited with founding the nation's first doctoral program in African American studies in 1988. The first student to earn a Ph.D. in African American studies was Adeniyi Coker, a Nigerian. The first African American to obtain a doctoral degree in African American studies was Mark Hyman, and the first white person was Cynthia Lehman. Temple University set the precedent for doctoral programs in African American studies that were soon developed at other institutions.

One of the nation's most renowned African American studies programs can be found at Harvard University in Cambridge, Massachusetts. In 1989, historian and literary critic Dr. Henry Louis Gates Jr. (1950–) accepted a post at Harvard. He was to be the chairman of the Department of African American Studies. At the time Gates arrived at Harvard, the department consisted of only one white professor and a few students. Within only a short time, Gates had recruited some of the country's most prominent African American thinkers. These included Cornel West (1953–), with whom he wrote *The Future of the Race* (1996). He also recruited philosopher Anthony Appiah (1954–), noted sociologist William Julius Wilson (1935–), and African art expert Dr. Suzanne Blier (1948–). From 1991 to 2003, Gates raised more than forty million dollars in donations for the department, which expanded into the Department of African and African American Studies. In 2001, the department instituted a Ph.D. program. Today, Harvard's Department of African and African American Studies serves thousands of students.

The nation's bad economy during the mid-1970s until the early 1980s led to criticism of African American studies programs. Many colleges and

First African American President of a Large State University

Clifton R. Wharton (1926–) was the first African American to receive a Ph.D. in economics from the University of Chicago. He was also the first African American to head a Fortune 500 company and the first African American U.S. deputy secretary of state. In the world of education, however, he is known for serving as the first African American president of Michigan State University. He accepted the job in 1970, a turbulent time in American history. Demonstrations, riots, and sit-ins were common on college campuses during the 1960s. At the time Wharton began his tenure, four students were killed and nine others wounded during a Vietnam War protest at Kent State University. Once a visiting professor at the University of Singapore, Wharton shared his views of Asian culture with Michigan State's student body. He even suspended classes for educational seminars about Indochina, the French colony that in part became Vietnam, and distributed information about how to conduct safe, effective protests.

In 1978, Wharton began his tenure as the longest-serving chancellor of the State University of New York system. It was the nation's largest university system, with sixty-four campuses. There, he initiated a study of the university's two most pressing problems. One was the need to elevate the national reputation of the school's graduate and professional schools, and the other was the need to avoid unnecessary administrative delays so that the school's business could get done in a timely way. Wharton campaigned for legislation that would allow campus administrators to have more flexibility in funding decisions. Wharton considers this legislation to be one of his major contributions to the university.

universities were struggling with budget cuts. Administrators began to question whether these programs made financial sense, especially given their relatively new status in higher education. Even some prominent African American scholars criticized African American studies programs because they perceived the courses to be of low academic value. Some people argued that the courses were taught by unqualified instructors. Nevertheless, black studies programs have continued to grow over the years. Significant developments in the discipline include the rise of professional organizations such as the National Council for Black Studies. Also, African American studies programs have expanded to include African American women's studies and classical African studies.

❖ COURTS ORDER SCHOOL BUSING TO ACHIEVE INTEGRATION

Education in the United States was segregated up until 1954. This means that black and white students could not attend the same schools. This system of segregation became illegal in 1954 when the U.S. Supreme Court ruled on the landmark case *Brown v. Board of Education* that schools could no longer be segregated. A follow-up case a year later, commonly known as *Brown II*, ordered that public schools be integrated. Integration, or desegregation, means blending students of different races in the same schools, instead of having separate schools for blacks and whites. Even though the Supreme Court ordered it, many city and state governments continued to resist desegregation. Some white schools responded by trying to close public schools rather than allow African Americans to attend. Others enacted "freedom of choice" plans that allowed students to select what schools they wanted to attend. Not surprisingly, these measures did little more than continue the cycle of segregation. By the mid-1960s, only slightly more than two percent of African American students in the United States attended integrated schools.

Supreme Court Rulings Spur Faster Integration

In 1968, however, the Supreme Court ruled in *Green v. School Board of New Kent County* that the New Kent County School Board's "freedom of choice" plan was unacceptable. The Court ordered that school boards all over the country must immediately start integrating their schools. The problem of school integration, however, was that whites and blacks tended to be segregated by neighborhood; when students attended schools near where they lived, the schools were naturally segregated. School districts would have to find some artificial way to achieve school integration. Some districts decided to bus students to schools farther away from where they lived as a way to accomplish this goal, although it was not until three years later that busing became mandatory in some districts.

In the 1971 case *Swann v. Charlotte-Mecklenburg Board of Education*, the Supreme Court decided that integration had not been fast or effective enough. It found that the Mecklenburg County school district in North Carolina had knowingly taken steps to prevent integration within its schools. The district did this by drawing geographical zones that created segregated schools, as almost all of the African American students

Students in the Charlotte-Mecklenburg School District participate in busing to achieve integration. The busing program became the model for school integration throughout the 1970s. *AP Images*

in the county lived in Charlotte. As a result, the Court ordered the Charlotte-Mecklenburg School District to bus its students, both white and African American, up to fifteen miles across city lines to achieve desegregation. This ruling became the model for education for the entire decade.

Most of the desegregation court cases during the 1960s addressed segregation created by specific policies in southern schools. Busing also became an issue in the North and West. In the early 1970s, voters in Denver had elected opponents of busing to the city's school board. A federal judge in Colorado, responding to a suit filed by a group of eight Denver families seeking improved school integration, ruled that the school board had deliberately segregated schools by shifting neighborhood school boundaries and building schools in locations that served a racial majority. Some white parents protested the judge's call for forced busing. They demonstrated, holding signs that read, "No one asked us what we want." Others' reactions were more violent. One-third of the city's buses were destroyed by arsonists (people who set destructive fires on purpose). Also, someone exploded a pipe bomb on the front porch of Wilfred Keyes, the leader of the group of eight families that had filed suit against the Denver public school system to force integration of the school system. When the case got to the Supreme Court, the Court ordered Denver to remedy its racial imbalance by busing. This decision led to more than twenty years of forced busing in Denver. Approximately one-quarter of the city's students were bused to schools outside their neighborhoods. When many white

White Flight

"White flight" is a trend in which upper- and middle-class whites move out of racially mixed urban neighborhoods and into mostly white suburbs (neighborhoods outside of the city). The beginnings of white flight came in the aftermath of World War II (1939–45). At this time, growing numbers of African Americans migrated to U.S. cities for better employment and educational opportunities. When *Brown v. Board of Education* required schools to desegregate, many white families chose to leave the city rather than have their children attend school with African American students. The whites established suburban neighborhoods that were, for the most part, segregated in practice.

One devastating effect of white flight is urban decay, the process by which an urban area falls into a state of disrepair due to a lack of tax revenue, or funding. In areas of urban decay, abandoned property invites vandalism, and schools have less financial support than they once did. Both crime rates and unemployment figures increase. All of these factors contribute to the gap in education between inner-city students and more affluent, or wealthy, suburban students. Although white flight continues to occur throughout the nation, some areas are seeing a recent trend referred to as "gentrification," a process in which wealthy whites move back into an urban area, driving up the cost of living so that the current residents are displaced.

families responded to the Supreme Court's decision by moving, Denver public schools lost approximately 7,000 students in the summer of 1975. In the fall of that same year, around 100 students per week left for suburban schools.

Boston Busing Causes Riots, Fights

In Boston in 1972, *Morgan v. Hennigan* was filed in a U.S. District Court in Massachusetts. The plaintiffs, or people bringing the lawsuit, charged that Boston public schools were unconstitutionally segregated. Judge W. Arthur Garrity found that the Boston Independent School District School Committee had intentionally resisted desegregation by maintaining separate school systems. Boston appealed the decision to a higher court, asking the court to undo the lower court's ruling. The appeals court refused. Thus, a plan to integrate Boston schools was put in place in 1974.

Boston police stand in front of South Boston High School to protect incoming African American students to the formerly segregated school in 1974. *Lee Lockwood/Time & Life Pictures/Getty Images*

This began with busing students from the African American area of Roxbury to the mainly white neighborhood of South Boston.

Buses carrying African American students pulled up at South Boston High School for the start of the school year. An angry white mob greeted them by throwing rocks and rotten tomatoes at the buses and shouting racial slurs. Nine African American students were injured when the windows on their buses were broken. Not long afterwards, leaders in the African American community got a call that protesters were going to attack the buses again. The leaders managed to stop the buses from getting to South Boston High. It was lucky they did. A mob of 2,000 protestors had been waiting for the buses to arrive so that they could turn them over and set them on fire.

As the school year went on, some white parents staged a boycott. This means they removed their children from the public schools. Instead, they sent them to nighttime tutoring sessions. Those white students who stayed at the school sat across the room from their African American classmates. Hostility in the school continued to build. Multiple fights occurred on a daily basis. In December, an African American student stabbed a white student, inciting a riot by whites seeking revenge. To avoid further violence, all African American students were secluded, or hidden away, in an office. Their parents had to send five buses to the school. Three were decoys, and only two actually carried the students to safety.

Despite the number of problems caused by mandatory busing at South Boston, the following school year saw larger numbers of students being bused. Approximately twenty-five thousand students of all races were forced to attend schools outside of their neighborhood districts. The cost of busing these students exceeded fifty-six million dollars, causing significant tax increases in Boston to pay for the program. In Charlestown, an area in northern Boston, both African American and Latin American students were bused to Charlestown High School. White students from Charlestown were bused to Roxbury. Once again, racial strife ran rampant. During the first week of school, parents held protests against busing. Those students whose parents had not moved them to private schools boycotted the Charlestown schools.

African American students at Charlestown High faced taunts and physical attacks by white students on a daily basis. In response, they created the Minority Students' Council and met with the school's headmaster, demanding that he ban racial profanities, or foul words, and slurs. The day following the meeting, 175 white students boycotted school and presented their own list of demands. Their demands included punishing African American students for making obscene gestures and comments to white female students. A few days later, four white males were arrested for attacking an African American male in the hallways. Five African American students were suspended for three days for getting involved in the fight. The next morning, African American students refused to get off the buses when they arrived at Charlestown High. The white students staged a sit-in on the school's main stairs later in the school year. African American students had to be locked in upstairs classrooms for safety reasons. In spite of the repeated dangers and everyday persecution, African American students continued to attend Charlestown High.

Busing was overwhelmingly disliked all over the United States. One 1972 survey found that seventy-three percent of the population—African American and white alike—opposed busing. Indeed, members of white communities were not the only ones upset. A number of African American parents were upset by the fact that for every seven African American students who were bused, only one white student was. Furthermore, they said, the staff and students at white schools had not been prepared for the arrival of African American students. The students endured discrimination and even violence at their new schools. President Richard Nixon (1913–94) himself criticized court-ordered busing, arguing that it affected neighborhoods in a negative way by dividing them. The president asked Congress to ban busing, but his efforts were futile. Busing continued to be upheld by the Supreme Court as a constitutional process by which schools could and should integrate.

Council of Independent Black Institutions Supports African-Centered Schools

Founded in 1972, the Council of Independent Black Institutions (CIBI) supports independent African-centered schools. The group was born from black scholar Molefi Kete Asante's concept of "afrocentricity," a discipline that focuses on African culture and its contributions to the development of Western civilization. Afrocentricity offers an alternative to the traditional Eurocentric (centering on the values and historical perspective of the white European tradition) model of anthropology. The purpose of CIBI is to reconstruct African culture and to ensure that Africa's cultural history is part of the lives of African Americans today. To this end the CIBI provides schools with African-centered curriculum materials for all ages—infancy through post-graduate levels—and in all subject areas. It also provides methods for implementing and evaluating those programs. The CIBI works internationally to promote African-centered education. It does this through student exchange programs, where students visit and attend school in a different place; conventions, where people from different places come together to focus on a common topic; and computer networking.

The CIBI calls for states and districts to build stronger public schools and offer more opportunities for parents to choose where their children go to school. In particular, the CIBI believes that those in government should be obligated to provide African Americans equal access to a quality education within their own neighborhoods rather than force African American students to attend white schools. Greater choice within communities would eliminate the need for busing. The group promotes the improvement of African American educational opportunities through the establishment of charter schools. CIBI also argues for strengthening existing magnet schools and supplying parents with school vouchers to pay for private schools.

The Council of Independent Black Institutions supports African-centered schools like this one in Tallahassee, Florida. © *Jeffery Allan Salter/Corbis*

Supreme Court Reconsiders Court-Ordered Busing

In *Milliken v. Bradley* (1974), the Supreme Court made a landmark decision when it struck down a district-court ruling that called for busing between Detroit's African American schools and suburban white schools. The Supreme Court ruled that schools could bus students only within their own districts and not across district lines. This ultimately meant that suburban students could not be used to desegregate inner-city schools. Consequently, the upper and middle classes, predominantly white, moved from urban areas to settle in suburbs, essentially segregating schools once again.

In 1977's *Milliken II,* the Supreme Court shifted its focus from busing to the improvement of schools. The Court agreed that the purpose of integration was to give African Americans access to a better education. The Court recognized that all students could benefit from being educated in their neighborhood schools if those schools were of acceptable quality. Finally, in 1991, the Supreme Court ruled in *Board of Education of Oklahoma v. Dowell* that schools were released from busing if they had taken all practical steps to achieve integration. Even so, busing programs continued in some areas of the country into the twenty-first century.

❖ SCHOOL ADMINISTRATORS PROPOSE EBONICS TO AID BLACK STUDENTS

The term "Ebonics" was coined in 1973 by Dr. Robert L. Williams (1930–), a director of African American studies at the University of Missouri. The word is a combination of "ebony," meaning black, and "phonics," which refers to the sounds words make. Williams used "Ebonics" to refer to a way of speaking by some African Americans. Some linguists (scholars of language) consider Ebonics, which is now also known as African American Vernacular English (AAVE), to be a separate language. Other linguists consider it a dialect, or variety, of English. Although Ebonics had been recognized by linguists for some time, it was not a source of public attention until 1996. That year a school board in Oakland, California, passed a resolution to start using Ebonics in the classroom.

The decision to use Ebonics was an attempt to address a significant problem. Many African American students in the Oakland Unified School District did not do as well in school as their white peers, especially on standardized tests. Education advocate Toni Cook (1944–) campaigned for the formation of a district task force to study the statistics and make recommendations for educational programs that would boost the achievement of African Americans.

After an eight-month evaluation, the task force proposed that the schools expand what was known as its Standard English Proficiency (SEP) program. In response to the task force's suggestions, the Oakland school board passed a resolution that recognized Ebonics as the "primary language of African American children." Ebonics would become part of the language arts curriculum in Oakland schools. The resolution called for using federal bilingual education funds to hire linguists who had studied AAVE to train teachers about Ebonics. The goal of this training was for teachers to learn how to better help African American students improve their standard English-language skills.

Only hours after the proposal had been passed, Ebonics became the subject of widespread controversy in the United States. With little regard to the proposal's wording, the media reported that the Oakland Unified School District had accepted Ebonics as a separate language. Reports said the district planned to teach the "broken English" and unconventional grammar of Ebonics to its student body. Cook and members of the Oakland Unified School District issued statements to explain what the proposal had actually said. However, Ebonics continued to be the topic of radio and television programs as well as newspapers and magazines. Well-known African Americans such as civil rights leader Jesse Jackson (1941–) and actor Bill Cosby (1937–) spoke out against the resolution.

A U.S. Senate hearing was held on January 23, 1997. Linguists joined educators from Oakland to testify about the benefits of teaching Ebonics. Michael Casserly (1948–), the executive director of the Council of the Great City Schools for the U.S. State Department, provided testimony that summarized data from fifty urban school districts across the nation. He gave statistics from 1992–1993 showing that 60.7 percent of white elementary students scored above the national average in reading. By high school, that percentage had increased to 65.4 percent. In contrast, only 31.3 percent of African American elementary students scored above the national average in reading. That percentage had dropped to 26.6 percent by high school. Casserly intended to illustrate that taking into account the everyday language characteristics of African American students could help ease the educational problems they faced. Nevertheless, the federal government and the California legislature both passed bills to ensure that bilingual funding could not be used to teach Ebonics. In April 1997, the Oakland school board cut the term "Ebonics" from any of its educational plans or programs.

Although the controversy over Ebonics has died down since 1997, many linguists and educators continue to study Ebonics as an issue that goes beyond language. They argue that the debate about Ebonics is really a debate about culture and how U.S. schools are failing to meet the needs of

African American students. Several of the ideas concerning the use of Ebonics in schools presented by the Oakland school board have been supported by educational research. For instance, educators now more readily acknowledge the fact that African American students may benefit from teaching materials specifically targeted for speakers of AAVE, even though AAVE may not be what is considered standard English. Ongoing research is being conducted to determine the relationship between both AAVE and African American culture and the development of reading and writing skills.

❖ CHARTER SCHOOLS PROVIDE AN ALTERNATIVE TO MINORITY STUDENTS

Since the 1990s, one major trend in educational reform that particularly benefited African American students was the growth of charter schools. As of 2010 there were more than four thousand charter schools in the United States. A charter school is a public school that operates independently of the local school board, often with an educational philosophy different from other schools in the area. Charter schools are designed to address the particular needs of a given community of students. For example, one charter school might focus on artistically gifted students, while another might be a school for special education students. The makeup of the student body in charter schools varies from school to school, depending on what the mission of the charter is. Students who attend charter schools are not assigned to go there. Rather, they are there by choice.

The first charter school legislation was enacted in Minnesota in 1991, followed by California in 1992. Since then, charter schools have been one of the fastest-growing advancements in educational reform. They have received bipartisan support (meaning support from both major political parties) from state legislators, governors, U.S. secretaries of education, and U.S. presidents. President Bill Clinton (1946–), for instance, called for the establishment of three thousand charter schools by the year 2002. President George W. Bush (1946–) issued a call in 2002 for three hundred million dollars to support charter schools. As of 2009, there were forty-six hundred charter schools in the United States, serving around 1.4 million students.

Success of Urban Charter Schools

Many charter schools have been established to prepare low-income, inner-city minorities (also known as disadvantaged students) for higher education. Urban charter schools in California, Michigan, Texas, and New York serve a high percentage of African Americans and Hispanics. These minority groups tend to be from low-income families. In its 2005 Annual

Survey of America's Charter Schools, the Center for Education Reform found that approximately 63 percent of the students in a typical charter school qualify for the U.S. Department of Agriculture's free and reduced-price lunch program. At the predominantly black Codman Academy Charter School in Dorchester, Massachusetts, 79 percent of students qualify.

Charter schools are not required to follow a traditional public school system curriculum that tells them what and how they must teach. Therefore, most charter schools offer special programs specially designed for their students. A number of charter schools that serve mainly black students include African American history as part of their core curriculum. African American cultural events and mentoring programs with members of the African American community help students understand their rich heritage and promising future.

In general, the performance of charters schools dealing with minority students is better than that of traditional public schools. The Center for Education Reform reported that forty-six percent of African American eighth graders in charter schools passed the mathematics section of Michigan's 2004 state assessment test, as compared with only 21 percent of African American students statewide. The growing numbers of charter schools between 2000 and 2010—as of 2010, one in every eighteen public schools in New York City was a charter school—indicates that parents, community members, educators, and politicians all have confidence in their reliability and effectiveness, especially for minority students. A rigorous study published in 2009 revealed that this confidence was well-founded: the study found that charter schools in New York outperformed traditional public schools, and that they had success in shrinking the achievement gap between poorer African American students and wealthier white students. New Jersey's charter schools have also received favorable attention for succeeding where most public schools in the state have failed: in the poor, urban neighborhoods. Test scores at the Discovery Charter School, North Star School, and Robert Treat School of Newark, New Jersey, were far above those of the area public schools.

Some of the success of charter schools can be attributed to the sense of belonging these schools foster in minority students. Faculties at predominantly African American charter schools encourage students to believe that they have the potential to become great community leaders. In the majority of charter schools, faculty members lead classroom discussions about responsibility and character. They teach students the importance of helping and supporting each other. As a result, the school environment is one of acceptance, respect, and trust. Another major factor in the success of urban charter schools is that students are often in school longer. The school

The Implications of No Child Left Behind for African American Parents

The No Child Left Behind (NCLB) Act of 2001 empowered African American parents by emphasizing the importance of parental involvement in their children's school systems. It guaranteed them the right to access school data in order to evaluate the academic progress of their children. As outlined by NCLB:

- Parents have the right to know how their children's school is performing overall in comparison to state academic standards and whether it is meeting annual state goals for student achievement, called "Adequate Yearly Progress (AYP)."
- Parents have the right to information about the AYP of subpopulations within the school.
- Parents have the right to request documentation of a teacher's qualifications.
- Parents can transfer their children to higher-performing schools or obtain special tutoring to raise their children's academic achievement.

year at many charter schools starts earlier and ends later than traditional schools. The school day also starts earlier and ends later. At Newark's Team Academy, for example, students arrive at 7:30 A.M. and leave at 5:00 P.M.

Because of this supportive school culture, violence in charter schools is typically less prevalent than in regular public schools. Even when they are located in the same neighborhoods with violent public schools, charter schools are, on the whole, safer and more peaceful. One reason for the lack of violence or disruption among students at charter schools is the fact that the students are held to high standards of behavior. At Roxbury Preparatory Charter School in Boston, Massachusetts, once a district full of racial violence, students are held to a strict code of conduct. They wear uniforms, walk silently in a line down the hallway from class to class, and raise their hands to ask questions. They receive demerits for such rule violations as chewing gum, misbehaving on school buses, being tardy to class, not finishing homework on time, and engaging in disruptive or disrespectful behavior. Ultimately, students at charter schools are taught to accept

responsibility for themselves and their actions in order to maintain structure and focus, as well as peace, in the school.

Critics Challenge Charter School Movement

Opponents of charter schools have argued from the beginning that charter schools hurt students who remain in conventional schools because they take resources away from quality public schools. State funding for a school is based on the number of students enrolled there. If a large number of children choose to attend charter schools instead of their neighborhood schools, then the school districts lose a significant amount of money. Critics point out the fact that taxpayers are supporting charter schools even though they may have no voice in how the school is operated. (Public school districts are governed by a board of directors elected by the community.) People who challenge charter schools contend that the schools are not held accountable for issues ranging from student performance to financial management. A charter school can, however, be closed if it fails to perform or uphold its mission, which in turn disrupts the education of the students who must then find a new school.

African American parents sometimes choose to send their children to charter schools like this one in New Jersey to avoid the problems often found in the urban public schools they would normally attend. © Najlah Feanny/ Corbis

A major source of contention with charter schools in the twenty-first century is segregation. Critics argue that charter schools catering to African American and economically disadvantaged children are creating segregated schools no different from those schools that were ordered by the Supreme Court to integrate in the 1960s and 1970s. A study conducted by Harvard University in June 2003 revealed that 70 percent of African American students in Massachusetts charter schools attended schools comprised of 90 percent minority students. A lack of diversity, say opponents of charter schools, means an incomplete education. Still, charter schools have clearly succeeded in giving urban African American students educational opportunities they formerly lacked. The success of charter schools serving African American communities has resulted in thousands of students applying for admission. According to the Inner City Foundation in Los Angeles, charter schools in African American and Hispanic neighborhoods have waiting lists of more than 5,000 students. In response to increased interest, communities will most likely continue to pursue charter schools as innovative alternatives to traditional public schools.

❖ STATES TAKE OVER FAILING INNER-CITY SCHOOLS

Serious problems exist in urban schools. These are a direct reflection of the conditions of the inner cities in which they are located. During the 1960s, urban areas from Los Angeles, California, to Newark, New Jersey, experienced outbreaks of violence. These areas had largely African American populations. The underlying causes were injustices that had plagued African American neighborhoods for years. Such problems include inadequate schools, high unemployment, poor housing, and rising costs of living. Decades after this violence erupted, these same problems continue to plague inner cities. The education of children in these communities has continued to suffer. When gang activity, widespread drug use, and daily violence dominate urban communities, the same troubles unavoidably make their way into the neighborhood schools. Consequently, students who attend these schools struggle to learn for reasons that extend beyond academics. They often come from broken homes. Some live in substandard housing or are hungry when they come to school. Some fear for their safety both in and outside of school.

When wealthy families leave urban areas for mostly segregated suburban neighborhoods, inner-city schools lose tax dollars. As a result of losing wealthy residents while steadily gaining more poor immigrants, a large number of inner-city schools cope with a devastating poverty that cannot be easily overcome. In addition to majority populations of low-income students, urban schools serve a large percentage of minorities.

Schoolbooks holding up a broken desk are evidence of a lack of school funding at a Manhattan school in 2001. African Americans often must attend poorly-funded schools because they live in poor urban areas. © *James Leynse/ Corbis*

On average, as of 2010 inner-city schools receive 797 dollars less per child than suburban schools. This means each inner-city classroom of twenty students receives 15,940 dollars less than its suburban equivalent. Whereas students in suburban schools work on new computers and play in well-equipped gyms, children in overcrowded inner-city schools do not have enough chairs for everyone. Students must share old textbooks. Even outdated computers are of little use because old school buildings are not wired for today's technology. The schools are subject to vandalism and graffiti. Inner-city school buildings are also dilapidated, or broken down, and dangerous. They often have broken windows and backed-up toilets that spill sewage on bathroom floors. Moreover, many facilities lack heat and air-conditioning. With no money available for repairs, the problems only get worse as the buildings age.

Educational studies show that the inequality in resources between urban and suburban schools leads to lower test scores and lower graduation rates in urban schools. These studies also indicate that inner-city students make the decision to drop out of school as early as fifth grade. Early signs include skipping classes, frequent absences, and being held back to repeat a grade. Thus, it is no surprise that one of the biggest challenges inner-city schools face is motivating students to stay in school and remain focused on future employment goals. People who argue for urban school reform point to the alarming numbers of African American males who are currently in prison. They say that urban schools choose to allow these at-risk students to "fall through the cracks."

More School Accountability Leads to Takeovers

In the 1990s, state takeovers of public schools came to the forefront of education as a strategy for inner-city school reform, particularly during the years from 1995 to 1997. During this period, 38 percent of the decade's takeovers occurred. Boston, New York, Cleveland, Chicago, Baltimore, Oakland, and Washington, D.C., school districts were taken over during the 1990s. In all of these districts combined, the average African American enrollment was 69.7 percent, as reported by the National Center for Educational Statistics in 2001.

In the early 2000s federal and state educational agencies created policies to make schools more accountable, or responsible, for their students' education. One such program is the No Child Left Behind Act of 2001 (NCLB). A main focus of NCLB is the educational success of minority students. The act states that if a school is receiving certain federal funds and fails to demonstrate good yearly progress for five straight years, the school district must make fundamental reforms. Options given to districts that have not met standards include reopening schools as charter schools—most of which are comprised mainly of minorities—and replacing all or most of the schools' staff. Another alternative a district has is turning over the operation of failing schools to its state educational agency.

The reasons for takeovers are generally the same from district to district. Schools turned over to the state have poor financial management and underperforming students and faculty. Most of the schools serve low-income and disadvantaged populations, including African Americans. Sometimes states plan an immediate state takeover of a school or district in trouble. However, most of the time, a school or school district receives a series of penalties before actually being taken over.

Mayor Takes Control of Detroit's Public Schools

One of the most highly publicized state takeovers during the 1990s involved the Detroit public school district. Between 1950 and 2000, the city's population had dropped from two million to one million. Families chose to leave Detroit and move to suburbs for a variety of reasons. One was the declining quality of its public services, including the public school system. As more people left, the city lost more and more tax revenue, and public services continued to decline. By 1997, schools in the city of Detroit were in dire need of help. Detroit was almost ninety percent African American and was the poorest city in America. About 108,000 of its 180,000 enrolled students lived in poverty. The school dropout rate in Detroit was a little over 26 percent, and scores on the standardized Michigan Education Assessment Program (MEAP) had shown little or no progress for several years. At the beginning of the 1998–1999 school year,

Detroit schools had a shortage of five hundred teachers. It also lacked three hundred substitute teachers. This meant that core subjects sometimes did not have instructors. School buildings in the district were in serious need of repair. One elementary school in a particularly poor section of Detroit had to evacuate students from the building because of a carbon-monoxide (a poisonous gas) leak from an old coal-burning furnace.

In response to the crisis, Michigan's governor, John Engler (1948–), championed Senate Bill 297. The legislation handed over the running of the city's public schools to Detroit mayor Dennis Archer (1942–). Engler's bill called for the removal of the school's superintendent, along with the district's school board. The board was composed of eleven elected members. In their place would be a chief executive and a six-member commission appointed by Archer. This would last until the election of a new school board in five years.

The planned state takeover of Detroit schools inspired heated debate from its beginnings. Opponents of the takeover bill argued that Engler was an enemy of public education. Their evidence was that he passed legislation that permitted the creation of charter schools, which drew students away from the struggling public schools. Several state senators questioned whether removing a school board that had been elected by the general public was legal. Backed by the NAACP (National Association for the Advancement of Colored People) and New Detroit (a coalition of community leaders dedicated to maintaining positive race relations), some challengers alleged that the bill was racist. They said it would overrule the voting power of African Americans, who had elected the school board. Still others argued that Engler was proposing an experiment, not a solution. They said that any takeover would merely transfer the control of millions of dollars in bond money from one entity to another.

Backers of the bill were quick to point out that the Detroit school district had failed miserably in managing its schools. They said that, more importantly, it had failed in educating its students. Simply put, Detroit schools were in crisis and needed fundamental change. Business professionals in the Detroit area agreed. They showed that graduates of Detroit public schools lacked the reading and math skills to function in the job market. Many supporters of a state takeover were confident that a school board appointed by the mayor would have more professionalism and expertise in management and decision making.

Senate Bill 297 became the Public Act 10 of 1999 on March 26, 1999. With modifications made by Mayor Archer, the act granted the mayor's office authority to order mandatory after-school classes and summer school for students performing below academic standards. In addition, teacher training would be intensified, and schools would be policed by members of the community. To achieve what legislators, educators, and parents alike wanted for Detroit's schools, Archer requested that the state provide him with clearly defined standards for the Detroit public school system. Additionally, he proposed hiring 1,200 new teachers.

The state-imposed takeover of Detroit public schools lasted for six years. During that time period, the district saw little improvement. Enrollment continued to decline. It fell from around 180,000 students to approximately 140,000 by 2005. While 48.5 percent of seniors scored at the lowest level on the MEAP in 1999, the figure had increased to 59.1 percent in 2005. Compared with other students in the state, Detroit students' scores are frequently half of the state average. Improvements in financial management were also lacking. In the years from 2000 to 2005, the district had deficits, meaning it spent more money than it brought in.

In November 2005, resentful Detroit voters elected a new board of education. They were once again seeking leadership for their inferior schools. Only three years later, however, the state of Michigan was once again planning to take control over the financial operations of the Detroit public school system. After months of controversy surrounding the district's finances, the district revealed a deficit of $408 million. This prompted hundreds of layoffs and other budget cuts. The state had to give the Detroit school system money so that it could pay its employees as well as vendors who were threatening to sue because of unpaid invoices. In an attempt to

The Michigan Department of Education appointed Robert Bobb as an emergency financial manager for the Detroit Public Schools in 2009 when the school system reached a financial crisis. *AP Images*

intervene, the Michigan Department of Education appointed Robert Bobb as an emergency financial manager for the district. He oversaw all financial decisions in the district, including budgeting and contract negotiations.

Still, Detroit schools were in financial crisis as of 2009. One school asked the community for donations of toilet paper because it had no money for supplies. On May 13, 2009, Bobb shocked the nation when he appealed to U.S. Secretary of Education Arne Duncan (1964–) for federal disaster funding. He wanted the Detroit public school system to be put under a presidential emergency declaration. Bobb argued that the district's educational situation is similar to the one schools in New Orleans faced after Hurricane Katrina, a 2005 disaster that devastated the city. In response, Duncan said that he supports another state takeover of Detroit schools, with Detroit's new mayor, Dave Bing (1943–), in charge.

Other School Takeovers

The challenges faced by Detroit's schools are extreme, but not unique. Several urban school districts taken over by the state have remained troubled. Others have made improvements. Philadelphia's school district (which has a student body that is about 65% African American) was taken over by Pennsylvania in 2002, and various private companies and institutions (including local universities, nonprofit groups, and for-profit companies) were put in charge of managing the schools. By 2006, Philadelphia schools were showing marked improvement in student achievement.

❖ HISTORICALLY BLACK COLLEGES AND UNIVERSITIES FACE CHALLENGES

Historically black colleges and universities (HBCUs) were established to provide higher education for African Americans during a time of segregation, when black students were not allowed to attend college with white students. The oldest HBCU, Cheyney University in Pennsylvania, dates back to 1837. Most organized colleges and universities began to emerge after the Civil War (1861–65), when newly freed slaves looked to education as a way to improve their lives both socially and economically. Groups such as the American Missionary Association and the Freedmen's Bureau worked to establish private colleges and universities specifically for the education of African Americans. In 1890, the Second Morrill Land Grant Act specified that states receiving federal land-grant funds must either open their white agricultural and mechanical schools to African Americans or provide money for similar schools for African Americans. Some of the schools were founded as religious seminaries or normal schools (schools for the training of teachers). Others were founded as technical colleges, which provided agricultural and technical courses. These schools produced a number of leading engineers and scientists.

The Higher Education Act of 1965 defines an HBCU as "any historically black college or university that was established prior to 1964, whose principal mission was, and is, the education of black Americans, and that is accredited by a nationally recognized accrediting." HBCUs are valuable alternatives for African Americans who have faced discrimination and have often been excluded from majority white colleges and universities. They provide students with not only a quality education but also a link to their African American cultural history.

HBCUs make up about 3 percent of the nation's colleges and universities. These schools include the prestigious Howard University, founded in Washington, D.C., in 1886; Spelman College, founded in Georgia in 1881; and Bethune-Cookman University, founded in Florida in 1904. More than half of all African American public school teachers and approximately 70 percent of African American dentists have earned their degrees at HBCUs. Many well-known athletes, celebrities, writers, and politicians are graduates of HBCUs. They include Hall of Fame National Football League player Walter Payton (1954–99), actress and comedienne Wanda Sykes (1964–), Nobel Prize-winning writer Toni Morrison (1931–), and former U.S. secretary of education Rod Paige (1933–).

Graduates of the historically black Howard University wait for their commencement ceremony in 1996. © *Annie Griffiths Belt/Corbis*

Enrollment in HBCUs Declines After Civil Rights Era

Before desegregation, HBCUs were responsible for the education of 90 percent of those African Americans who received a higher education in the United States. The civil rights movement and affirmative action policies of the 1960s, however, opened up all institutions of higher learning to black students. Black students had more options to choose from, and HBCUs began to see a decline in enrollment. During the 1970s and early 1980s, African Americans increasingly enrolled in predominantly white colleges and universities that had formerly denied them admittance. The decline in African American enrollment was at least partially offset by an increase in the number of non-African American students attending HBCUs. From 1986 to 1996, enrollment in HBCUs increased by 25 percent. This figure includes a large number of non-African Americans. By the 2000s, almost one out of every five students at HBCUs was white, and an additional thirteen percent were foreign students.

The increased presence of non-African American students and faculty in HBCUs has highlighted the need to preserve the unique identities of HBCUs. Unlike mainstream colleges and universities, HBCUs provide African Americans with a source of ethnic pride. They offer programs designed to meet the specific needs of the African American community, while also serving as keepers of African American history and heritage.

Since the 1970s, presidential administrations have acknowledged the contribution of HBCUs to both the past and the future of African American scholars. They have done this with a variety of legislative acts. In the late 1970s, President Jimmy Carter (1924–) established a White House initiative program with the purpose of strengthening and expanding the capacity of HBCUs. A few years later, President Ronald Reagan (1911–2004) issued an executive order aimed at reversing some of the effects of prior discriminatory actions against HBCUs. Congress also increased federal funding to HBCUs at this time. In 1989, President George H. W. Bush (1924–) expanded Reagan's executive order. He created the President's Advisory Board on Historically Black Colleges and Universities. This group is a Department of Education commission that reported directly to him and the Secretary of Education about issues involving HBCUs. These issues included how to increase attention these schools get from private companies.

Challenges Faced by HBCUs

Throughout the years, HBCUs have had to deal with shortages in funding. This lack of funds has left them struggling to stick to their budgets while maintaining high educational standards. They have not historically received the same level of state and federal funding as mainly white colleges. For this reason, these schools have been forced to rely heavily on

Some Historically Black Colleges and Universities

The United States is home to more than one hundred HBCUs, many of which are located in the South, where freed slaves began their formal educations. Some examples are listed below.

Four-Year Public Schools
- Grambling State University (Louisiana)
- Lincoln University (Pennsylvania)
- Morgan State University (Maryland)
- Prairie View A&M University (Texas)
- Virginia State University (Virginia)

Four-Year Private Schools
- Bethune-Cookman College (Florida)
- Fisk University (Tennessee)
- Shaw University (North Carolina)
- Spelman College (Georgia)
- Tuskegee University (Alabama)

private donations and money from such groups as the United Negro College Fund. Even these resources fall short of what HBCUs need. The financial status of many African American students who attend HBCUs also contributes to the challenges the schools face. Schools like Bennett College and St. Augustine College, both private schools in North Carolina, have been on probation for financial problems and have faced losing their accreditation, which is like a license for colleges. When a college loses accreditation, it also loses access to federal grant programs, which further hurts the college. Some African American educators worry that HBCUs might either be closed down or become a part of white schools. Despite persistent financial troubles, however, supporters of HBCUs remain confident that these schools will go on and continue to provide high-quality education that is both empowering and affordable.

HBCUs have had a harder time recruiting and keeping talented teachers more so than other colleges and universities in the nation. This is mainly because of the rising number of employment opportunities available to African Americans. Prior to the 1960s, teaching was one of the few professions open to African Americans with college degrees, and black teachers could only teach at institutions for black students. This began to change as the federal government passed laws prohibiting discrimination in employment because of the civil rights movement. Career opportunities began to open up for qualified African American professors at white universities and colleges. Those jobs typically pay more than what the limited budgets of HBCUs can offer, and it is easier to gain recognition as a scholar. As a result, HBCUs do not always attract the most celebrated or experienced educators, and teacher turnover rates tend to be greater.

Many HBCUs offer open enrollment, meaning anyone with a high school degree or the equivalent can attend on demand. In contrast, most four-year colleges and universities practice selective admission, meaning students must apply by submitting evidence of their academic abilities (such as standardized test scores and transcripts) and the college admission committee chooses only highly qualified candidates for admission. Because of open enrollment, HBCUs must also manage the academic problems that arise from enrolling students who are not academically prepared for college. This lack of academic preparation is partly due to the elementary and secondary schools that many African Americans attend. Many African Americans attend underfunded schools in poorer neighborhoods that do not provide the same quality of education as schools in wealthier areas. African American students who excel in high school most often choose to attend larger, more prestigious colleges rather than HBCUs. When average students have not been taught basic skills in secondary schools, HBCUs have the added responsibility of helping students make up for what they missed in their early schooling. HBCUs do also attract strong students. This is especially true of schools like Florida A&M, which consistently recruits National Achievement scholars; Morehouse College in Georgia, which graduates many Rhodes scholars; and Howard University in Washington, D.C., which draws students with its renowned law school.

Critics of HBCUs question the importance of HBCUs in the twenty-first century. Some argue that the mission and purpose of the schools are no longer relevant in a society of equal educational opportunities and affirmative action. The harshest attacks come from opponents who argue that HBCUs are academically inferior to predominantly white colleges and universities. They point to the achievement gap between African American students who attend HBCUs and those who attend traditionally white schools, pointing out lower SAT scores and high school grade-point averages. Furthermore, critics say, HBCUs cannot offer African American students the same quality of education as predominantly white colleges. They say this is due to poor funding that prevents them from having the resources and facilities to prepare African Americans for the technological demands of the twenty-first century. The global economic crisis of 2008

The United Negro College Fund

Founded in 1944, the United Negro College Fund (UNCF) has become one of the nation's best-known charities. Its mission is:

- to enhance the quality of education by providing financial assistance to deserving students,
- to raise operating funds for member colleges and universities, and
- to increase access to technology for students and faculty at historically black colleges and universities (HBCUs).

UNCF is the most successful advocate for the higher education of African Americans. In 1972, UNCF began broadcasting public service announcements highlighted by the slogan "A Mind Is a Terrible Thing to Waste," with the purpose of both educating the public about the organization and getting donations for the fund. Unchanged for almost four decades, the slogan has reached generations of people who have been encouraged to help African Americans get a college education.

UNCF makes it possible for more than sixty thousand African American students to attend college every year. It does this through grants, scholarships, and internship programs. UNCF plays a large role in closing the educational attainment gap between African American and white students.

and 2009 hit already cash-strapped HBCUs particularly hard, as donations dwindled. In response, the administration of President Barack Obama (1961–) pushed for a doubling of the funds set aside in the Department of Education budget for HBCUs, raising the allotment from $10.4 million to $20.6 million.

◆ SUPREME COURT'S *GREEN V. COUNTY SCHOOL BOARD OF KENT COUNTY* DECISION (1968)

Green v. County School Board of Kent County was the most important school desegregation case to follow 1955's *Brown II*. The 1954 U.S. Supreme Court decision in *Brown v. Board of Education of Topeka, Kansas* ordered that public schools be desegregated. In the so-called *Brown II* decision of 1955, the Court responded to complaints from school districts about the difficulties posed by immediate integration, and ruled that integration must be carried out "with all deliberate speed." In *Green*, the Supreme Court declared that school districts' freedom-of-choice plans did not meet the Court's standards for racially balanced schools. The Court established criteria to determine whether a school's desegregation plan was acceptable. Those criteria included the ratios of black-to-white students and faculty and equal access to facilities, transportation, and extracurricular activities. The Court's decision, written by Justice William Brennan and excerpted here, accelerated the pace of school desegregation. The percentage of African American students attending integrated schools in the South jumped from thirty-two percent in the 1968–1969 school year to seventy-nine percent in 1970–1971. The decision also sparked the controversial plan to bus students between school districts in order to achieve racial integration—plans that proved extremely unpopular with African American and white parents alike.

••••••••••••••••••••••••••••

The pattern of separate "white" and "Negro" schools in the New Kent County school system established under **compulsion** of state laws is precisely the pattern of segregation to which *Brown I* and *Brown II* were particularly addressed, and which *Brown I* declared unconstitutionally denied Negro school children equal protection of the laws. Racial identification of the system's schools was complete, extending not just to the composition of student bodies at the two schools but to every facet of school operations—faculty, staff, transportation, extracurricular activities, and facilities. In short, the State, acting through the local school board and school officials, organized and operated a dual system, part "white" and part "Negro."

It was such dual systems that 14 years ago *Brown I* held unconstitutional and a year later *Brown II* held must be abolished; school boards operating such school systems were required by *Brown II* "to effectuate a transition to a racially nondiscriminatory school system." . . . It is of course true that for the time immediately after *Brown II* the concern was with making an initial break in a long-established pattern of excluding Negro children from schools attended by white children. The

Compulsion

State of being forced

Plaintiffs

Those lodging a legal complaint

Effectuate

Cause to happen

Fourteenth Amendment

An 1868 amendment to the U.S. Constitution that granted full legal protection and citizenship to African Americans

Articulated

Explained

principal focus was on obtaining for those Negro children courageous enough to break with tradition a place in the "white" schools . . . . Under *Brown II* that immediate goal was only the first step, however. The transition to a **unitary**, nonracial system of public education was and is the ultimate end to be brought about; it was because of the "complexities arising from the transition to a system of public education freed of racial discrimination" that we provided for "all deliberate speed" in the implementation of the principles of *Brown I*. . . . Thus we recognized the task would necessarily involve solution of "varied local school problems." . . . In referring to the "personal interest of the **plaintiffs** in admission to public schools as soon as practicable on a nondiscriminatory basis," we also noted that "to **effectuate** this interest may call for elimination of a variety of obstacles in making the transition . . . ." Yet we emphasized that the constitutional rights of Negro children required school officials to bear the burden of establishing that additional time to carry out the ruling in an effective manner "is necessary in the public interest and is consistent with good faith compliance at the earliest practicable date." . . .

It is against this background that 13 years after *Brown II* commanded the abolition of dual systems we must measure the effectiveness of respondent School Board's "freedom-of-choice" plan to achieve that end. The School Board contends that it has fully discharged its obligation by adopting a plan by which every student, regardless of race, may "freely" choose the school he will attend. The Board attempts to cast the issue in its broadest form by arguing that its "freedom-of-choice" plan may be faulted only by reading the **Fourteenth Amendment** as universally requiring "compulsory integration," a reading it insists the wording of the Amendment will not support. But that argument ignores the thrust of *Brown II*. In the light of the command of that case, what is involved here is the question whether the Board has achieved the "racially nondiscriminatory school system" *Brown II* held must be effectuated in order to remedy the established unconstitutional deficiencies of its segregated system. In the context of the state-imposed segregated pattern of long standing, the fact that in 1965 the Board opened the doors of the former "white" school to Negro children and of the "Negro" school to white children merely begins, not ends, our inquiry whether the Board has taken steps adequate to abolish its dual, segregated system. *Brown II* was a call for the dismantling of well-entrenched dual systems tempered by an awareness that complex and multifaceted problems would arise which would require time and flexibility for a successful resolution. School boards such as the respondent then operating state-compelled dual systems were nevertheless clearly charged with the affirmative duty to take whatever steps might be necessary to convert to a unitary system in which racial discrimination would be eliminated root and branch. . . . The constitutional rights of Negro school children **articulated** in *Brown I* permit no less than this; and it was to this end that *Brown II* commanded school boards to bend their efforts. . . .

Although the general experience under "freedom of choice" to date has been such as to indicate its ineffectiveness as a tool of desegregation, there may well be instances in which it can serve as an effective device. Where it offers real promise of aiding a desegregation program to effectuate conversion of a state-imposed dual system to a unitary, nonracial system there might be no objection to allowing such a device to prove itself in operation. On the other hand, if there are reasonably available other ways, such for illustration as zoning, promising speedier and more effective conversion to a unitary, nonracial school system, "freedom of choice" must be held unacceptable.

The New Kent School Board's "freedom-of-choice" plan cannot be accepted as a sufficient step to "effectuate a transition" to a unitary system. In three years of operation not a single white child has chosen to attend Watkins school and although 115 Negro children enrolled in New Kent school in 1967 (up from 35 in 1965 and 111 in 1966) 85 percent of the Negro children in the system still attend the all-Negro Watkins school. In other words, the school system remains a dual system. Rather than further the dismantling of the dual system, the plan has operated simply to burden children and their parents with a responsibility which *Brown II* placed squarely on the School Board. The Board must be required to formulate a new plan and, in light of other courses which appear open to the Board, such as zoning, fashion steps which promise realistically to convert promptly to a system without a "white" school and a "Negro" school, but just schools.

◈ THE NO CHILD LEFT BEHIND ACT STATEMENT OF PURPOSE (2001)

The No Child Left Behind Act was spearheaded by President George W. Bush's administration. It was created to decrease the achievement gap

President George W. Bush speaks on the No Child Left Behind Act with students from a New York City public school in 2007. The act aimed to help minority students struggling in inner-city schools. *Paul J. Richards/ AFP/Getty Images*

between minority and non-minority students and between economically and non-economically disadvantaged students. The act received support from both Democrats and Republicans. Its effect was to significantly increase the federal government's involvement in education reform. The following excerpt from the act's statement of purpose lists twelve goals the act hoped to achieve.

· ·

The purpose of this title is to ensure that all children have a fair, equal, and significant opportunity to obtain a high-quality education and reach, at a minimum, **proficiency** on challenging State academic achievement standards and state academic assessments.

Proficiency
Competence

This purpose can be accomplished by—

(1) ensuring that high-quality academic assessments, accountability systems, teacher preparation and training, curriculum, and instructional materials are aligned with challenging State academic standards so that students, teachers, parents, and administrators can measure progress against common expectations for student academic achievement;

(2) meeting the educational needs of low-achieving children in our Nation's highest-poverty schools, limited English proficient children, migratory children, children with disabilities, Indian children, neglected or delinquent children, and young children in need of reading assistance;

(3) closing the achievement gap between high- and low-performing children, especially the achievement gaps between minority and non-minority students, and between disadvantaged children and their more advantaged peers;

(4) holding schools, local educational agencies, and States accountable for improving the academic achievement of all students, and identifying and turning around low-performing schools that have failed to provide a high-quality education to their students, while providing alternatives to students in such schools to enable the students to receive a high-quality education;

(5) distributing and targeting resources sufficiently to make a difference to local educational agencies and schools where needs are greatest;

(6) improving and strengthening accountability, teaching, and learning by using State assessment systems designed to ensure that students are meeting challenging State academic achievement and content standards and increasing achievement overall, but especially for the disadvantaged;

(7) providing greater decision-making authority and flexibility to schools and teachers in exchange for greater responsibility for student performance;

(8) providing children an enriched and accelerated educational program, including the use of schoolwide programs or additional services that increase the amount and quality of instructional time;

(9) promoting schoolwide reform and ensuring the access of children to effective, scientifically based instructional strategies and challenging academic content;

(10) significantly elevating the quality of instruction by providing staff in participating schools with substantial opportunities for professional development;

(11) coordinating services under all parts of this title with each other, with other educational services, and, to the extent feasible, with other agencies providing services to youth, children, and families; and

(12) affording parents substantial and meaningful opportunities to participate in the education of their children.

◈ IMPACT OF THE NO CHILD LEFT BEHIND ACT (2004)

This excerpt of the 2004 report *Closing the Achievement Gap: The Impact of Standards-Based Education Reform on Student Performance* from the U.S. Commission on Civil Rights examines the civil rights implications of the No Child Left Behind Act (NCLB). It also examines how the NCLB affected and addressed the gap in racial achievement. The report contains findings from two states, Maryland and Virginia. Based on those findings, the U.S. Commission on Civil Rights created guidelines for other states on the racial impact of NCLB and how to increase student achievement.

• •

The gap in educational achievement between white students and African American and Hispanic students has been well documented and is large and persistent. An average African American or Hispanic elementary, middle, or high school student currently achieves at about the same level as the average white student in the lowest **quartile** of white achievement. In reading, for example, the average African American 17-year-old performs at the same level as white 13-year-olds. The achievement gap has persisted for decades and has grave consequences for graduating from high school, earning secondary degrees, and earning a living. The gaps actually narrowed in the 1970s and '80s, but beginning in the late '80s, progress stalled and the remaining achievement gap differences remained large. Some performance gaps among students appear before children enter kindergarten and persist into adulthood. . . .

The bulk of the research literature concludes that high-poverty schools and those with higher numbers of African American and Hispanic students have higher rates of unlicensed teachers, higher student absenteeism, lower rates of parental involvement, higher rates of violence, and generally fewer resources. The Commission finds,

Quartile
One part of data from a large set of numbers that has been divided into four parts

LEP

Limited English
proficiency

Imperative

Necessary

Remediation

Acts designed to
improve or fix

therefore, that poverty, race, and ethnicity play significant roles in student achievement and that No Child Left Behind (NCLB) has substantial civil rights implications for minority and poor students, as well as **LEP** students and students with disabilities. One of the many concerns is the attachment of high stakes to students based on performance on assessments. While NCLB does not require the attachment of individual high stakes to any tests, states are beginning to attach high stakes such as retention in grade or failure to graduate in response to NCLB's requirements to show increased student academic performance in all student subgroups and create accountability at all levels. Therefore, the Commission also finds that it is **imperative** for standards-based education reform to give sufficient resources and support to provide effective **remediation** to failing students and failing schools....

The Commission further finds that highly qualified teachers in high-minority and high-poverty schools have positive results on student performance. Increased teacher pay will attract more qualified teachers to teaching as a career, better classroom resources will provide needed learning tools and opportunities for the students most at risk of underachieving, and appropriate accommodations for LEP students and students with disabilities will help to ensure that tests accurately reflect the performance of these students. We also find that funding to implement the required data collection and information sharing provision of NCLB is essential if parents are to make informed choices about the education of their children. Finally, we find that early and effective remediation programs for low-performing schools and students will help ensure that minority and low-income students are not disproportionately affected by increased dropout and retention rates.

Research and Activity Ideas

1. In 1972, the United Negro College Fund (UNCF) began broadcasting public service announcements with the slogan "A Mind Is a Terrible Thing to Waste." The commercials were designed to both educate the public about the organization and solicit financial support for the fund. The slogan has remained unchanged for several decades. It has reached generations of people who have been encouraged to help African Americans achieve their goal of receiving a college education. Using the Internet, locate some of the commercials that have been produced by the UNCF. Do you believe these ad campaigns are effective in helping the UNCF provide higher educational opportunities for African Americans? Pretend you have been selected to create one of these public service advertising commercials, including a new slogan for UNCF. Working in groups of three, create a storyboard, complete with dialogue, outlining your commercial, to present to the class. Be prepared to explain your new slogan and justify why you believe it represents the mission of UNCF.

2. Assume the role of the chairperson of an African American studies program in a college or university. As head of the program, you are in charge of hiring competent instructors to enrich the school's program and teach courses relevant to today's African American students. With this in mind, investigate the teaching methods of well-known—and often controversial—educators Michael Eric Dyson, Marva Collins, and Angela Davis. Decide what courses you want each of these instructors to teach in the upcoming semester. Write a syllabus (a summary of a course of study) for each class.

3. Read the article "Some Notes on Language..." by Ronald Kephart (http://www.unf.edu/~rkephart/Writings/Essay_on_Language.htm). Based on Kephart's assessment of language, would you classify Ebonics as a language, or should it be categorized as dialect, slang, or vernacular instead? What are some examples of Ebonics in mainstream society today?

4. With your classmates, list the advantages and disadvantages of neighborhood schools. Neighborhood schools are attended by students who live in the surrounding area. Students who live in the same neighborhood are often members of the same race. Next, list the advantages and disadvantages of integrated schools. Integrated schools are legally obligated to have racial balance no matter where students live. After compiling your lists, consider the following questions. Why do you think parents would want to send their

children to a neighborhood school? Why would they want their children to attend an integrated school? Which type of school would you choose to attend? Write a letter to the editor of your local newspaper explaining what kind of school—neighborhood or integrated—you think is better for your community. Make sure you support your opinion with clear, logical reasons and specific examples.

5. Find the lyrics to the song "Lean on Me" by Bill Withers. Next, find the lyrics to the song "Rap Summary (Lean on Me)" by Big Daddy Kane. Write an essay comparing and contrasting the two sets of lyrics. As you write the essay, consider these questions. Why do you think Bill Withers's song was featured in the movie about principal Joe Clark titled *Lean on Me*? Compare Kane's lyrics to those by Withers. What specific issues does Kane address in his song? What do you think was his purpose in writing the song?

 For More Information
....

BOOKS

Clotfelter, Charles. *After "Brown": The Rise and Retreat of School Desegregation.* Princeton, NJ: Princeton University Press, 2006.

Formisano, Ronald. *Boston Against Busing: Race, Class, and Ethnicity in the 1960s and 1970s.* Chapel Hill, NC: University of North Carolina Press, 1991.

Gill, Brian, et al. *State Takeover, School Restructuring, Private Management, and Student Achievement in Philadelphia.* Arlington, Va.: RAND Corporation, 2007.

Merseth, Katherine K., et al. *Inside Urban Charter Schools: Promising Practices and Strategies in Five High-Performing Schools.* Cambridge, Mass.: Harvard Education Publishing, 2009.

PERIODICALS

"Boston's Busing Battle." *Time* (September 24, 1965): p. 92.

Hanley, Robert. "Disciplinarian for Juveniles Quits in Wake of Censure." *New York Times* (January 5, 2002): p. B5.

Kellogg, Alex. "Detroit Schools on the Brink." *Wall Street Journal* (July 21, 2009): p. A3.

Paulson, Amanda. "True Believer." *Christian Science Monitor* (September 10, 2002): p. 15.

Williams, Joshua. "The 'War on Education': the Negative Impact of the No Child Left Behind Act on Inner-City Public Schools, Students, and Teachers." *Journal of Gender, Race and Justice* (Spring 2008): p. 573.

WEB SITES

Clyburn, James E. "HBCUs: Institutions for Past, Present, & Future." *United States Congressman James E. Clyburn: Representing the 6th District of South Carolina.* http://clyburn.house.gov/statements/049218hbcus.html (accessed on April 10, 2009).

"Dialects." *CAL: Center for Applied Linguistics.* http://www.cal.org/topics/dialects/aae.html (accessed on October 29, 2009).

Dylan, Reggie. "Restructuring Inner-City Schools for the Global Marketplace: Locke High School and the Green Dot 'Solution.'" *Dissident Voice.* http://dissidentvoice.org/2008/09/restructuring-inner-city-schools-for-the-global-marketplace-locke-high-school-and-the-green-dot-%E2%80%9Csolution%E2%80%9D (accessed on April 13, 2009).

Historically Black Colleges and Universities (HBCUs). *HBCUConnect.* http://www.hbcuconnect.com (accessed on October 29, 2009).

National Council for Black Studies. http://www.ncbsonline.org/home (accessed on October 29, 2009).

"Status and Trends in the Education of Racial and Ethnic Minorities." *IES National Center for Education Statistics.* http://nces.ed.gov/pubs2007/minoritytrends/index.asp (access October 29, 2009).

The White House Initiative on Historically Black Colleges and Universities. *Ed.gov.* http://www.ed.gov/about/inits/list/whhbcu/edlite-index.html (accessed October 29, 2009).

Where to Learn More

BOOKS

Aaron, Hank. *I Had a Hammer: The Hank Aaron Story*. New York: HarperTorch, 1992.

Ali, Muhammad, and Hana Yasmeen Ali. *Soul of a Butterfly: Reflections on Life's Journey*. New York: Simon & Schuster, 2004.

Angelou, Maya. *The Complete Collected Poems of Maya Angelou*. New York: Random House, 1994.

Baraka, Amiri. *The LeRoi Jones/Amiri Baraka Reader*. New York: Basic Books, 1999.

Botham, Fay. *Almighty God Created the Races: Christianity, Interracial Marriage, and American Law*. Chapel Hill: University of North Carolina Press, 2009.

Cosby, Bill, and Alvin F. Poussaint. *Come on People: On the Path from Victims to Victors*. Nashville, Tenn.: Thomas Nelson, 2007.

Dyson, Michael Eric. *Is Bill Cosby Right? Or Has the Black Middle Class Lost Its Mind?* New York: Perseus Book Group, 2006.

Farley, Reynolds. *Detroit Divided*. New York: Russell Sage Foundation, 2002.

Gates, Henry Louis, Jr., and Cornel West. *The Future of the Race*. New York: Vintage, 1997.

Giovanni, Nikki. *The Collected Poetry of Nikki Giovanni: 1968–1998*. New York: Harper Perennial Modern Classic, 2007.

Hendrix, Janie, and John McDermott. *Jimi Hendrix: An Illustrated Experience*. New York: Atria, 2007.

Hoffer, Richard. *Something in the Air: American Passion and Defiance in the 1968 Mexico City Olympics*. New York: Free Press, 2009.

Horne, Jed. *Breach of Faith: Hurricane Katrina and the Near Death of a Great American City.* New York: Random House, 2006.

Jemison, Mae. *Find Where the Wind Goes: Moments from My Life.* New York: Scholastic, 2001.

Lemann, Nicholas. *The Promised Land: The Great Black Migration and How It Changed America.* New York: Vintage, 1992.

Levenson, Jacob. *The Secret Epidemic: The Story of AIDS and Black America.* New York: Pantheon, 2004.

Morrison, Toni. *What Moves at the Margin: Selected Nonfiction.* Jackson, Miss.: University of Mississippi Press, 2008.

Newton, Huey. *Revolutionary Suicide.* New York: Harcourt Brace Jovanovich, 1973.

Perry, Theresa. *The Real Ebonics Debate.* Boston: Beacon Press, 1998.

Sims, Yvonne. *Women of Blaxploitation: How the Black Action Film Heroine Changed American Popular Culture.* Jefferson, NC: McFarland & Co., 2006.

Story, Rosalyn M. *And So I Sing: African American Divas of Opera and Concert.* New York: Grand Central Publishing, 1990.

Terry, Wallace. *Bloods: Black Veterans of the Vietnam War: An Oral History.* New York: Ballantine, 1985.

WEB SITES

"African American Odyssey: The Civil Rights Era." *The Library of Congress.* http://memory.loc.gov/ammem/aaohtml/exhibit/aopart9.html (accessed on November 18, 2009).

"African American Studies Graduate School Programs." *GradSchools.com.* http://www.gradschools.com/Subject/African-American-Studies/11.html (accessed on November 18, 2009).

"Barack Obama's Road to the White House." *ABC News.* http://abcnews.go.com/Politics/fullpage?id=5197404 (accessed on November 18, 2009).

The Congressional Black Caucus. http://www.thecongressionalblackcaucus.com/ (accessed on November 18, 2009).

"Racial Profiling." *American Civil Liberties Union.* http://www.aclu.org/racial-justice/racial-profiling (accessed on November 18, 2009).

Tuskegee Airmen. http://www.tuskegeeairmen.org/ (accessed on November 18, 2009).

U.S. Public Health Service Syphilis Study at Tuskegee. *Centers for Disease Control and Prevention.* http://www.cdc.gov/tuskegee/timeline.htm (accessed on November 18, 2009).

Index

Boldface type indicates entries; *Italic* type indicates volume; (ill.) indicates illustrations.

A

Aaron, Hank, *4:* 631, 635, 667–69, 667 (ill.)
Abacha, Sani, *3:* 396
Abdul-Jabbar, Kareem, *4:* 663
abolitionist movement, *4:* 699
abortion
    public health officials and, *3:* 465
    Roe v. Wade (1973), *3:* 551
    teen pregnancy, *2:* 296
Absence (dance), *1:* 88, 89
absentee fathers, *2:* 295. *See also* single-mother families
academics (people). *See* college and university faculty; intellectuals
Academy Award winners
    acting, *1:* 150; *2:* 202, 231, 243, 245, 248, 248 (ill.)
    music, *2:* 241; *4:* 655, 674, 684
    student awards, *2:* 218
accountability, schools. *See* No Child Left Behind Act (2001)

ACT*1 Personnel Services, *1:* 151, 152–53, 170–71, 178
activism and reform (chapter)
    chronology, *1:* 2–4
    headline makers, *1:* 8–33
    overview, *1:* 5–7
    primary sources, *1:* 64–70
    topics in the news, *1:* 34–63
actors and actresses, *2:* 202, 203, 239, 248, 254
    Sean Combs, *1:* 150–51
    Bill Cosby, *2:* 202, 211–13, 212 (ill.), 243–44, 250, 252–53, 253 (ill.)
    Whoopi Goldberg, *2:* 245
    Eddie Murphy, *2:* 245
    musicians/rappers as, *2:* 203, 227–28, 242–43, 246, 254; *4:* 644
    Richard Pryor, *2:* 244–45
    Will Smith, *2:* 227–28, 227 (ill.), 242–43, 254
    Denzel Washington, *2:* 229–31, 230 (ill.)
    Oprah Winfrey, *1:* 162, 164
Adarand Constructors, Inc. v. Pena (1995), *1:* 169; *3:* 542, 543
Adkins, Rodney, *4:* 799

adoption, and teen pregnancy, 2: 296

adult contemporary music, 4: 673–74

aerospace engineers, 4: 771–74, 790, 791–92, 794, 798

Aeschylus, 1: 67

affirmative action. *See also DeFunis v. Odegaard* (1974); *Gratz v. Bollinger* (2003); *Grutter v. Bollinger* (2003); *Regents of the University of California v. Bakke* (1978); reverse discrimination
  backlash, 1: 34–35, 142, 168–70
  conservatives' opposition, 1: 31, 169; 3: 532–33, 534, 550, 564–67
  Executive Order 10925, 1: 34, 142, 166, 167
  Executive Order 11246, 1: 34, 166–67, 189–91; 3: 508
  overviews, 1: 6, 34–36, 141–42, 166–70, 181; 3: 507, 508, 540–44
  states cessation, 1: 169–70; 3: 508, 511

Afghanistan
  U.S. involvement, 2001–, 3: 425, 427; 4: 576
  video activism in society, 1: 53

Africa Action, 3: 414

Africa Channel, 2: 255, 256

African American businesses. *See* black businesses

African American Jews, 4: 700, 728, 730–32, 731 (ill.)

African American literature, study, 2: 333–34, 335–37. *See also* specific writers and genres

African American National Biography (reference work), 2: 337

African American studies. *See also* historically black colleges and universities
  achievements in, 2: 344–46
  critical works, 2: 323–24
  criticisms, 2: 344–45
  department expansions, 2: 333–34, 335, 344, 345–46

department formations, 1: 78; 2: 315–16, 323, 343–44, 344 (ill.)
  pioneers, 2: 322–23

African American Vernacular English, 2: 336, 352–54

African American voters. *See* black voters, influence

African art, 1: 100, 101; 2: 326

African dance, 1: 110–11

African diaspora, 2: 322; 4: 729

African Methodist Episcopal (AME) Church, 4: 715, 716, 717, 740–41

Africana: The Encyclopedia of the African and African American Experience, 2: 336

African-centered schools, 2: 351, 355

AfricanDNA, 2: 337

AfriCobra, 1: 119

afro hairstyle, 4: 665–67, 666 (ill.)

Afro-American studies. *See* African American studies

Afro-Caribbean Americans, 2: 303

afrocentricity, 2: 351

agronomists, 4: 793

AIDS epidemic. *See* HIV/AIDS epidemic

Ain't I a Woman: Looking Back (hooks), 2: 278–79

Air Force. *See* U.S. Air Force, personnel

Air Force Space Test Program's Advanced Research and Global Observation Satellite (ARGOS), 4: 770

Air Jordans (Nike), 4: 648, 649, 678

airline industry, 4: 788–90, 788 (ill.)

Akil, Mara Brock, 2: 205–6, 205 (ill.)

alarm systems, 4: 800

Alcindor, Lew, 4: 663

Alcorn, George E., 4: 791–92

Alexander, Clifford, 4: 577–80, 577 (ill.), 620–23

Alexander, Elizabeth, 1: 124–25; 4: 580

Algeria, 1: 17, 19, 39

Ali (film), 2: 228, 243

Ali, Muhammad, 4: 602–6, 603 (ill.), 631, 688, 688 (ill.)

Alito, Samuel, *3*: 512

All American Women: Lines That Divide, Ties That Bind (Cole), *2*: 321–22, 323–24

All God's Children Need Traveling Shoes (Angelou), *1*: 82

All in the Family (television program), *2*: 250

All Things Considered (radio program), *2*: 221

Allaire, Paul, *1*: 144

Alliance of Black Jews, *4*: 730

Alvin Ailey Dance Group, *1*: 111

Amalgamated Food Employees Union v. Logan Valley Plaza (1968), *3*: 523

ambassadors, *1*: 129; *3*: 396

AME Church. *See* African Methodist Episcopal (AME) Church

American Association for the Advancement of Science, *4*: 804

American Bandstand (television program), *2*: 210, 211

American Bar Association, *3*: 534, 550

American Civil Liberties Union (ACLU)
    death penalty reports, *3*: 559
    Loving v. Virginia case, *2*: 282, 293
    police brutality monitoring, *1*: 54

American Civil Rights Institute, *1*: 169

American Dance Asylum, *1*: 88–89

American Express, *1*: 145–48, 172

American Film Institute, *2*: 219, 244

American flag, in art, *1*: 119–20

American Institute for the Prevention of Blindness, *3*: 445–46

American Legacy (magazine), *2*: 203, 234

American Muslim Mission, *4*: 734

American Recovery and Reinvestment Act (2009), *1*: 186

American Urban Radio Networks, *2*: 236

America's Promise, *4*: 593 (ill.), 594

Ames Autogenic Feedback Training System, *4*: 796

Amistad (opera), *1*: 129–30

Amnesty International, *1*: 12

Anderson, Marian, *1*: 128–29

Anderson, Michael, *4*: 797

Angelou, Maya, *1*: 79, **80–83, 80** (ill.), 108, 110, 123–24, 124 (ill.), 128

animated television series, *2*: 212, 213, 243, 251; *4*: 644

The Answer (screenplay), *2*: 218

anthropologists, *2*: 321–23, 325–26

antimiscegenation laws, *2*: 280, 281, 282, 293, 304–6. *See also* interracial marriage; *Loving v. Virginia* (1967)

antisemitism, *1*: 46, 56, 125; *3*: 389, 414; *4*: 707, 708–9

antiwar protests/protesters
    Afghanistan and Iraq invasions (2001/2003), *4*: 576
    Iraq War, 2003–, *1*: 105
    Persian Gulf War, *4*: 613
    Vietnam War, *1*: 9, 16, 61–62; *2*: 345; *4*: 575, 584, 601–2, 601 (ill.), 700

AOL (America Online), *1*: 157, 159, 172 (ill.); *4*: 808

apartheid opponents
    Americans, *1*: 32–33; *2*: 332; *3*: 413, 532; *4*: 655, 663, 726
    Olympic Games policy, *4*: 663

Apollo 16 mission (1972), *4*: 767, 769–70, 791

Apollo Theater, *4*: 637, 643–44

apparel lines. *See* fashion lines

Appiah, Anthony, *2*: 344

Archer, Dennis, *2*: 361–62; *3*: 415–16

Are You Experienced? (The Jimi Hendrix Experience), *4*: 642

Arista Records, *1*: 149

Arkansas, health issues, *3*: 463–65

armed forces integration, *4*: 575, 582–83

Army. *See* U.S. Army

The Arsenio Hall Show (television program), *2*: 254

art and artists. *See* choreographers; dance and dancers; musicians; visual art and artists

Art Ensemble of Chicago, *1*: 117, 117 (ill.)

art teachers, *1*: 100

the arts (chapter)
  chronology, *1:* 76–77
  headline makers, *1:* 80–105
  overview, *1:* 78–79
  primary sources, *1:* 131–33
  topics in the news, *1:* 106–30
Asante, Molefi Kete, *2:* 344, 351
Ashe, Arthur, *4:* 633, 633 (ill.), 659
Asian American populations, *2:* 285
assassination attempts/plots
  Louis Farrakhan, *4:* 709
  Al Sharpton, *1:* 30–31
assassinations
  Robert F. Kennedy, *1:* 67; *2:* 214;
    4: 663
  Martin Luther King, Jr., *1:* 5, 38,
    42–44, 44 (ill.), 66–68; *2:* 327;
    3: 409–10; *4:* 612, 663, 715
  Malcolm X, *1:* 82, 106; *4:* 708, 734
Association for the Advancement of
  Creative Musicians (AACM), *1:* 116
Association of American Medical
  Colleges, *3:* 441
astronauts, *4:* 763–66, 763 (ill.),
  784–87, 785 (ill.), 790–91, 794–97,
  795 (ill.), 805–6, 815–18
astrophysicists, *4:* 767–71
athletes, *4:* 631, 632, 668, 686. *See
  also* specific athletes; specific sports
  academic study and perspectives,
    2: 330, 332–33
  political action, *2:* 330, 331–32;
    4: 602–6, 603 (ill.), 632,
    663–65, 690–91
Atlanta Franchise Development
  Company, *1:* 177
Atlanta, Georgia, *2:* 302, 303, 307 (ill.)
Atlantic Records, *4:* 660
attorneys general, *3:* 517–19
The Audacity of Hope (Obama), *3:* 398
Australian Olympic team, *4:* 663 (ill.), 664
autobiographical literature, *1:* 108
  Maya Angelou, *1:* 80, 81, 82, 83,
    108, 124
  Eldridge Cleaver, *1:* 14, 16–17
  Hannah Crafts, *2:* 337
  Malcolm X, *1:* 108; *3:* 388
  Barack Obama, *2:* 296; *3:* 397–98

*The Autobiography of Malcolm
  X, 1:* 108; *3:* 388
*The Autobiography of Miss Jane
  Pittman* (television movie), *2:* 252
automatic implantable defibrillator,
  3: 467, 469–70
automation, industry trends,
  4: 800–801
automotive industry, *1:* 142, 183–86,
  187, 188; *2:* 301, 301 (ill.)
Axis: Bold as Love (The Jimi Hendrix
  Experience), *4:* 642

B

Baby Phat clothing, *4:* 650, 651, 679
back-to-Africa movement, *4:* 700, 729
Bad Boy Records, *1:* 149, 151; *4:* 684
Bad Boy Worldwide Entertainment
  Group, *1:* 148, 149
Bad (Jackson), *4:* 646, 675
bailouts
  auto industry, *1:* 185
  financial sector, *1:* 148
Bakke, Allan, *1:* 35–36, 168, 191–94,
  191 (ill.); *3:* 540–41, 562 (ill.). *See
  also Regents of the University of
  California v. Bakke* (1978)
Baldwin, James
  associates, *1:* 83, 97
  as icon, *2:* 297
  study, *2:* 343
Balkans conflict, *4:* 593
Baltimore Afro-American (newspaper),
  2: 203, 232, 233
BAM. *See* black arts movement
Bambaataa, Afrika, *4:* 681
Band of Gypsies, *4:* 643
bank executives, *1:* 158–59, 171
Baptist Church, *4:* 741, 746–47
Baraka, Amiri, *1:* 56, 100, 106, 107,
  112–13, 113 (ill.), 123, 125
barbeque, *1:* 174, 175
Barker, Justin, *1:* 59
Barry, Marion, *1:* 55; *2:* 288, 288 (ill.);
  3: 410–11
baseball players, *4:* 668, 686

Hank Aaron, *4:* 631, 635, 667–69, 667 (ill.)

Barry Bonds, *4:* 631, 634–36, 634 (ill.)

Jackie Robinson, *4:* 633

Bashen, Janet Emerson, *4:* 811

basketball players, *4:* 631, 668

Magic Johnson, *3:* 484, 485

Michael Jordan, *4:* 648–50, 649 (ill.)

Olympic teams, *4:* 650, 663

player-coaches, *4:* 684

Basquiat, Jean-Michel, *1:* 79, 83–85, 84 (ill.), 121, 131–32

Bassett, Angela, *2:* 203

Bath, Patricia, *3:* 442–48

Battle, Kathleen, *1:* 129

Bazile, Leon M., *2:* 282, 304, 304 (ill.)

Beard, Jesse Ray, *1:* 59

Beastie Boys, *1:* 160; *4:* 684

The Beatles, *4:* 645

Beatty, Christine, *3:* 417

Beck, Glenn, *1:* 52

Beck, Sherman, *1:* 119

Belafonte, Harry, *2:* 239, 242, 244

Bell, Mychal, *1:* 59–60, 61

Beloved (Morrison), *1:* 95–96, 127, 133

Beltway Sniper investigation, 2002, *3:* 524, 525 (ill.), 526

Ben Yahweh, Yahweh, *4:* 730

Ben-Israel, Ben Ammi, *4:* 700, 731–32

Bennett College for Women, *2:* 325, 326, 366

Bernard, Robert O., *3:* 443

Berry, Halle, *1:* 150; *2:* 203, 248 (ill.)

Berry, Shawn Allen, *3:* 553–54

BET (Black Entertainment Television), *1:* 155–57, 160, 171; *2:* 203, 226, 255–56, 256 (ill.); *4:* 676

BET Tonight (television program), *2:* 226

Betancourt, George, *4:* 782

Bethune-Cookman University, *2:* 364

Biafra, *4:* 775

bias in media. *See* media portrayals, stereotypes

Bible, interpretations, *1:* 48

Biden, Jill, *3:* 426 (ill.)

Biden, Joe, *3:* 424, 426 (ill.), 519

Big Willie Style (Smith), *2:* 228

Bijani, Ladan and Laleh, *3:* 458

The Bill Cosby Show (television program), *2:* 212, 251. *See also The Cosby Show* (television program)

Binder, Patrick and Benjamin, *3:* 454, 457

Bing, Dave, *2:* 363; *3:* 417

bioethics commissions, *3:* 458, 495–96

The Birth of a Nation (film), *2:* 218

bishops, *4:* 701, 709–11, 709 (ill.), 715–17, 716 (ill.), 742 (ill.)

Bittker, Boris I., *1:* 50

The Black Aesthetic (Fuller), *1:* 107

Black Americans to Support Israel Committee (BASIC), *1:* 18

"Black Art" (Baraka), *1:* 107

black arts movement

dance scene, *1:* 110

drama scene, *1:* 112–15

Kwanzaa legacy, *1:* 111

overviews/literature, *1:* 78, 106–10, 123, 125, 126

visual art scene, *1:* 100, 118–21

Black Arts Repertory Theater/School (BARTS), *1:* 112–13

black arts workshops, *1:* 109, 113, 118

black businesses, *2:* 300. *See also* entrepreneurs

black arts movement, *1:* 78

government support requests/full employment, *1:* 64; *3:* 413

Operation Breadbasket support, *1:* 29, 44–45

Rainbow/PUSH Coalition support, *1:* 44, 47

Black Career Women (BCW), *1:* 142–43, 178–79, 180

Black Coaches Association, *4:* 685–86

"Black Cultural Nationalism" (Karenga), *1:* 107

Black Declaration of Independence and Bill of Rights (1972 Democratic National Convention), *3:* 413

Black Economic Development Conference, *1:* 49–50

Black Enterprise (magazine), *1:* 152, 158, 170, 171, 172, 176; *2:* 202, 213, 214–15, 234, 235

Black Entertainment Television (BET). *See* BET (Black Entertainment Television)

Black Feeling, Black Talk (Giovanni), *1:* 107, 109 (ill.), 123

Black, Gregory, *4:* 616

Black History Month, *2:* 316

Black House, *1:* 16, 114

Black, Keith L., *3:* 448–50, 448 (ill.)

Black Leadership Forum, *3:* 418–19, 418 (ill.)

black literary criticism, *1:* 78

black Muslims. *See* Ellison, Keith M.; Nation of Islam

black nationalist movement, *1:* 78; *4:* 632. *See also* separatism philosophy
    religion, *4:* 700, 729, 734, 738–39

Black Panther Party, *1:* 5, 36–42, 40 (ill.). *See also* Black Power movement
    founding, *1:* 38–39, 64
    members, *1:* 14, 16, 17, 20, 37, 38, 41–42, 114; *3:* 529, 532
    reparations support, *1:* 49, 64
    ten-point platform/program, *1:* 39, 64–66

Black Periodical Literature Project (Gates), *2:* 335, 336

The Black Population: 2000 (census brief), *2:* 306, 307 (ill.)

Black Power movement, *1:* 5–6, 37–38; *3:* 529. *See also* Black Panther Party
    academic arena, *2:* 343
    black arts movement influence, *1:* 106, 110, 114, 118
    pop culture influence, *4:* 632, 637, 687–88
    supporters, *1:* 14, 16
    symbolism and salute, *1:* 37 (ill.); *2:* 332; *4:* 662–65, 663 (ill.), 690–91
    theology, *1:* 48
    on Vietnam War, *1:* 65; *4:* 602
    women leaders, *1:* 18–19

Black Press of America, *2:* 233

black separatist movement. *See* separatism philosophy

black studies. *See* African American studies

Black Terror (Wesley), *1:* 114

Black Theology and Black Power (Cone), *1:* 48; *4:* 700, 704, 705, 736

black theology movement, *1:* 32, 48; *4:* 700, 704, 705–6, 735–39

black voters, influence, *3:* 383, 407–9, 411, 414

Black World (periodical), *1:* 108, 109; *2:* 234

Blackenstein (film), *2:* 241

blackplanet.com, *2:* 204, 238, 239; *4:* 802

Blacula (film), *2:* 241

Blair, Jayson, *2:* 206–7, 206 (ill.)

Blakey, Art, *1:* 91

blaxploitation films, *2:* 203, 239–41, 240 (ill.), 244, 245–46

Blayton, J. B., *2:* 202

Blazing Saddles (film), *2:* 244

Blier, Suzanne, *2:* 344

Blige, Mary J., *1:* 149

blindness, *3:* 444, 445–46; *4:* 653

Bling (Kennedy), *1:* 128

Blitzer, Wolf, *3:* 389

Blix, Hans, *4:* 618

blogs
    Pop+Politics, *2:* 204, 209, 238
    writers', *1:* 105

Blondie, *4:* 682

blood-brain barrier, *3:* 450, 457

blues artists, *4:* 640

The Bluest Eye (Morrison), *1:* 94–95, 97, 110, 126

Bluford, Guion "Guy," *4:* 763–66, 763 (ill.), 794, 795, 795 (ill.), 806

Board of Education of Oklahoma v. Dowell (1991), *2:* 352

Bobb, Robert, *2:* 362 (ill.), 363

body mass index (BMI), *3:* 487, 488

Bohannan, Paul James, *2:* 323

Bolden, Charles F., Jr., *4:* 795 (ill.), 797, 815–18

Bolden v. Mobile (1980), *3:* 539

Bonds, Barry, *4:* 631, **634–36, 634 (ill.),** 669

Bonds, Bobby, *4:* 634

The Bondwoman's Narrative (Crafts), *2:* 337

bone marrow transplants, *3:* 489–91

Bontemps, Arna, *2:* 322

Booker, Cory, *3:* 383

Boozer, Melvin, *1:* 61, 62

born-again Christians, *1:* 17–18

Boston Independent School District, *2:* 348–49

Boston, Massachusetts, schools, *2:* 348–50, 356

Bow Wow, *2:* 243

boxers, *4:* 602–6, 603 (ill.), 631, 688, 688 (ill.)

Boyz n the Hood (film), *2:* 243, 247

Bradford, Walter, *1:* 109

Bradley, Benjamin, *4:* 797

Bradley, Ed, *2:* 202, **207–8, 207 (ill.)**

brain tumors, *3:* 448, 449–50, 456

Brand, Myles, *4:* 685

Brawley, Benjamin, *2:* 343

Brawley, Tawana, *1:* 30

The Breakthrough: Politics and Race in the Age of Obama (Ifill), *2:* 216

breast cancer, *4:* 475, 476, 478–82

Brennan, William, *2:* 369–71

Brewer, Lawrence Russell, *3:* 553–54

Bring in 'da Noise, Bring in 'da Funk, 1: 79, 86, 87

Broadside Press, *1:* 108

Broadway shows and plays, *1:* 79, 86, 87, 104, 105, 114, 126, 150–51

Brodsky, Robert, *3:* 491

Brooke, Edward, *4:* 412

Brooks, Gwendolyn, *1:* 107; *2:* 277

Brooks, Mel, *2:* 244

Brooks, Pauline C., *1:* 179

Brown, Albert, *4:* 800

Brown, Claude, *1:* 108

Brown, Clifford, *1:* 90

Brown, Elaine, *1:* 42

Brown, James, *4:* 632, **636–38, 636 (ill.),** 660, 669–71

radio station ownership, *1:* 26; *2:* 236

"Say It Loud—I'm Black and I'm Proud" lyrics, *4:* 687–88

Sharpton relationship, *1:* 29

Brown, Janice Rogers, *3:* **510–12, 510 (ill.)**

Brown, Jill, *4:* 790

Brown, Marie Van Brittan, *4:* 800

Brown, Ron, *4:* 807, 807 (ill.)

Brown II (1955), *2:* 346, 369–71

Brown v. Board of Education of Topeka, Kansas (1954), *2:* 271, 315, 346, 369; *3:* 522

  influence, *Green v. School Board of New Kent County* (1968), *2:* 369–71

  influence, society, *1:* 21, 103, 180–81; *2:* 297–98

  NAACP, *3:* 522, 528

Bullins, Ed, *1:* 113–14

Bundy, McGeorge, *4:* 578

Burma, *1:* 53

Burning Down My Master's House: My Life at the New York Times (Blair), *2:* 207

Burns, Ursula, *1:* **144–45,** 172

Bush, George H. W., *4:* 593 (ill.)

  affirmative action policy, *1:* 36

  debates, *2:* 225

  education policy, *2:* 365

  foreign affairs staff, *3:* 401

  judicial nominations, *3:* 516, 524, 530, 534, 549–50, 552

  military policy, *3:* 393; *4:* 592, 612–13

Bush, George W.

  administration staff, *3:* 399, 401–2

  black voters and, *3:* 408

  civil rights policy, *3:* 389

  domestic program cuts, *1:* 24

  economic policy, *3:* 425

  education policy, *2:* 316–17, 338, 341–42, 354, 356, 360, 371–74, 371 (ill.)

  elections, *3:* 419

  hate crimes policy, *3:* 555

  health policy, *3:* 458, 491

Hurricane Katrina response, *1:* 7, 57, 58; *3:* 394
   Iraq War policy, *3:* 401–2, 422; *4:* 594, 595, 615, 616
   judicial nominees, *3:* 511–12
   NAACP and, *1:* 28
   September 11 attacks, *3:* 394; *4:* 594, 751, 752
business and industry (chapter)
   chronology, *1:* 138–40
   headline makers, *1:* 144–65
   overview, *1:* 141–43
   primary sources, *1:* 189–94
   topics in the news, *1:* 166–88
business periodicals. *See Black Enterprise* (magazine)
busing, *2:* 301, 347 (ill.)
   alternatives, *2:* 351, 352
   Supreme Court cases, *2:* 272, 315, 346–50, 352
Butler, Octavia, *1:* 85
Bynum, Juanita, *4:* 701, 702–4, 702 (ill.)
Byrd, James, Jr., *3:* 509, 553–54, 553 (ill.), 555
Byrne, Jane, *3:* 421

C

cable networks, *1:* 155–57, 165, 171; *2:* 203, 224–25, 226, 254–57. *See also* HBO (Home Box Office) programming
Cable News Network (CNN), *2:* 224–25
California Supreme Court, *3:* 510, 511
Callender, Clive, *3:* 450–54
Camp Lejeune, North Carolina, *4:* 607, 607 (ill.)
Campbell, Clive, *4:* 680–81
cancer rates, *3:* 475, 476, 478–82; *4:* 782
Cannon, Katie, *1:* 48; *4:* 739, 740
cardiac arrhythmia, *3:* 470
cardiologists, *3:* 467–71
Carrey, Jim, *2:* 254
Caribbean & African Restaurant Association (CARR), *1:* 177

Carlos, John, *2:* 332; *4:* 632, 663 (ill.), 664–65
Carlucci, Frank, *4:* 590–91, 592
Carmichael, Stokely, *1:* 5, 37–38, 41, 43
Carolina Peacemaker (newspaper), *2:* 203, 233
Carruthers, George R., *4:* 767–71, 791
Carson, Benjamin, *3:* 454–60, 457 (ill.), 460 (ill.)
Carson Scholars Fund, *3:* 459, 460
Carter, Jimmy
   affirmative action policy, *1:* 168–69
   Detroit funding, *3:* 415
   education policy, *2:* 365
   military appointments, *4:* 577 (ill.), 579, 591
   President's Summit for America's Future, *4:* 593
Carter, Mandy, *1:* 8–10, 8 (ill.), 61, 62–63; *4:* 745
cartoon programs. *See* animated television series
Casserly, Michael, *2:* 353
Castro, Fidel, *1:* 17
cataracts, *3:* 446–47
Catholic Church
   history and challenges, *4:* 742–44
   liberation theory, *4:* 706
   priests and bishops, *4:* 701, 709–11
   sexual abuse scandal, *4:* 701, 709, 710–11
Caver, Keith A., *1:* 173
Cedars-Sinai Medical Center, *3:* 450
cell phones, *4:* 802–3
Census Bureau information
   black population concentrations, *2:* 302, 306, 307 (ill.)
   Census 2000, *2:* 271, 284–85, 294, 298, 306, 307 (ill.)
   future predictions, *2:* 285
   health information, *3:* 477, 478
   history, *2:* 271, 284
   Internet access/use, *4:* 801–2
   wage gap, *1:* 182; *2:* 273, 284, 284 (ill.), 285; *3:* 477

Center for Creative Leadership, *1:* 173

CEOs. *See* executives

chain imagery, in art, *1:* 120, 120 (ill.)

Challenger space shuttle, *4:* 763, 764–65, 786, 794, 795, 806

Chalpin, Ed, *4:* 641, 642, 643

Chandler, Chas, *4:* 641, 642

Chandler, Dana, *1:* 119

Chappell, Emmett, *4:* 792

Chappelle, Dave, *2:* 256–57

Chappelle's Show (television program), *2:* 256–57

character education, *2:* 355, 356–57

charity giving. *See* philanthropy

Charlestown High (Boston, MA), *2:* 350

Charlotte Bobcats, *4:* 650

Charlotte Hornets, *1:* 155

charter schools, *2:* 354–58

administration, *2:* 340

African-centric, *2:* 351, 355

criticisms, *2:* 357–58

Chartwell Education Group, *2:* 342

Chavis, Benjamin, *1:* 10–14, 11 (ill.), 27, 55

chemists, *4:* 792–93, 799

Chenault, Kenneth I., *1:* 145–48, 146 (ill.), 172

Chernobyl disaster, 1986, *4:* 782

Cheyney University, *2:* 363

Chic, *4:* 672, 681

Chicago Bulls, *4:* 648, 649–50

Chicago Defender (newspaper), *2:* 203, 232, 233

"chick lit," *1:* 127–28

chicken and waffles, *1:* 176

Chideya, Farai, *2:* 203, 204, **208–9,** 238

children of divorce, *2:* 295

Children's Defense Fund, *1:* 21, 23–24

children's rights activists, *1:* 21, 23–24, 164

children's writers, *1:* 102, 104

Childress, Alice, *1:* 126

China, *1:* 39

Chisholm, Shirley, *1:* 47; *3:* **385–87,** 385 (ill.)

choreographers, *1:* 88–89

choreopoetry, *1:* 102–3, 104, 114

The Chris Rock Show (television program), *2:* 256, 257

Christian churches and faiths, *4:* 699–700, 735. *See also* black theology movement; specific Christian churches

Christian, John B., *4:* 792–93

chronologies

activism and reform, *1:* 2–4

the arts, *1:* 76–77

business and industry, *1:* 138–40, 142

communications and media, *2:* 200–201

demographics, *2:* 268–70

education, *2:* 312–14

government and politics, *3:* 380–82

health and medicine, *3:* 436–38

law and justice, *3:* 504–6

military, *4:* 572–74

popular culture, *4:* 628–30

religion, *4:* 696–98

science and technology, *4:* 758–60

Chrysler Corporation, *1:* 185, 188

Chuck D, *4:* 682

Church of God and Saints of Christ, *4:* 730

churches

changes, modern times, *4:* 746–47

history and leadership, *4:* 699, 700, 701, 725–28, 735

social activism examples, *4:* 701, 706, 712, 713, 715–16, 725, 734, 735

Citigroup, *1:* 157, 159

citizen activism, *1:* 53

city contracts and corruption, *3:* 415

City of Richmond v. J. A. Croson Co. (1989), *3:* 541–42, 543

Civil Aeronautics Administration (CAA), *4:* 581–82

Civil Rights Act of 1964, *1:* 34, 141, 166, 171, 191; *2:* 271, 297; *3:* 507, 544

Civil Rights Act of 1991, *3:* 507–8, 545–46

civil rights movement
    academic arena, *2:* 331–32
    activists and legacies, *1:* 5, 9,
        36–37, 42, 44–45, 56
    artists' involvement, *1:* 82–83, 105
    churches/religious arena, *4:* 699,
        700, 725, 735–39, 747
    economic outcomes, *1:* 141, 142,
        166, 171; *2:* 297–99
    gay rights struggle within,
        1: 61–62; *4:* 744–45
    journalism and, *2:* 232, 234
    legal cases, *1:* 12; *3:* 521, 522, 528
    military arena, *4:* 575, 610,
        611–12, 611 (ill.)
    political opposition, *1:* 9–10
    terrorist incidents, *1:* 19; *4:* 700
Civil Rights Restoration Act (1988),
    3: 507, 544–45
civil service jobs/contracts.
    See government contracts, and equal
    employment/affirmative action;
    government jobs
Clark, Joe, *2:* 318–21, 318 (ill.)
Clark, Joseph, *1:* 23
Clark, Patrice Washington, *4:* 788 (ill.)
The Clash, *4:* 682
class action lawsuits. *See* lawsuits
classical musicians, *1:* 89, 91. *See
    also* opera
Cleage, Albert, *4:* 700, 739
Cleaver, Eldridge, *1:* 14–18, 14 (ill.),
    41, 42
Cleopatra Jones (film), *2:* 241
clergy. *See* bishops; ministers; priests
Clergy and Laymen Concerned About
    Vietnam, *4:* 601 (ill.)
Clifford, Clark, *4:* 612
Clinton, Bill
    advisers, *1:* 11, 13
    affirmative action policy, *1:* 169
    ambassador and envoy
        appointments, *3:* 396; *4:* 726
    arts policy, *1:* 79, 83, 124, 124
        (ill.)
    black voters, relationships,
        3: 407–8

    child health and development
        policy, *1:* 24, 164
    crime policy, *3:* 418–19, 555
    education policy, *2:* 354
    energy policy, *4:* 781–82
    Guinier nomination, *1:* 169;
        3: 512, 514–15
    health policy, *3:* 460, 464, 465–66
    judicial appointments, *3:* 518
    military policy, *4:* 593, 598,
        620–23
    philanthropy, *2:* 325
    science and technology policy,
        4: 762, 803 (ill.), 807–8, 807
        (ill.)
    telecommunications policy,
        2: 204, 236–37, 260–61; *4:* 762,
        807–8, 807 (ill.)
    Tuskegee syphilis study apology,
        3: 473, 494–96, 494 (ill.)
    youth assistance programs,
        4: 593–94, 593 (ill.)
Clinton, George, *4:* 671, 672, 680
Clinton, Hillary Rodham
    child health and development
        policy, *1:* 24
    National Action Network
        involvement, *4:* 726 (ill.)
    2008 election campaign, *3:* 399,
        422–24
Clockers (film), *2:* 203
*Closing the Achievement Gap: The
    Impact of Standards-Based Education
    Reform on Student
    Performance* (report), *2:* 373–74
clothing lines. *See* fashion lines
Clyburn, James E., *3:* 418 (ill.)
CNN (Cable News Network),
    2: 224–25
coaches, *2:* 338–39; *4:* 631, 684–86,
    685 (ill.)
COBRA (Coalition of Black
    Revolutionary Artists), *1:* 119
cocaine (crack) epidemic, *2:* 286–87,
    286 (ill.), 289; *3:* 561
Cochran, Johnnie, *1:* 51
Cockrel, Ken, Jr., *3:* 417
Coffy (film), *2:* 241

Cohen, Bernard S., 2: 282

Cold War, 3: 400, 401

Cole, Johnnetta B., 2: 321–26, 322 (ill.)

Cole, Nat "King," 2: 202

Cole, Robert S., 4: 598

Coleman, Hurtis, 4: 607 (ill.)

Coleman, J. Marshall, 3: 405

Coleman, Milton, 4: 708

Coleman, Ornette, 1: 116

college and university faculty, 2: 293

    Shirley Chisholm, 3: 387

    Johnnetta B. Cole, 2: 321–26

    Harry Edwards, 2: 330, 331–33

    Roland G. Fryer, 2: 274–76

    Henry Louis Gates Jr., 2: 333–37

    Shirley Ann Jackson, 4: 781, 783, 783 (ill.)

    minority faculty recruitment, 2: 336, 344, 366–67; 3: 470–71

    Rod Paige, 2: 339

    Cornel West, 1: 31, 31 (ill.), 32–33

    Clifton R. Wharton Jr., 2: 345

college enrollment and graduation. See also African American studies; historically black colleges and universities

    gender differences, 2: 292

    history and demographic trends, 1: 182; 2: 273, 285, 293, 298; 3: 477

    medical schools, 3: 441, 467, 469

    military deferment, 4: 575, 600 (ill.), 601, 602, 604

colleges, segregation, 3: 521, 528

Collins, Bootsy, 4: 671

The Color Purple (Walker), 1: 104, 105, 126, 164; 2: 245

Coltrane, John, 1: 116

Columbia space shuttle, 4: 797

Columbus-Green, Carol, 1: 180

Colwell, Rita, 4: 809

Combs, Sean, 1: 148–51, 148 (ill.), 177

    fashion, 1: 148, 150, 151; 4: 679, 680

    production, 1: 148, 149; 4: 639

comedians, 2: 243–45. *See also* Cosby, Bill; Joyner, Tom

Comedy Central, 2: 256–57

Commandment Keepers, 4: 728

Commission for Racial Justice, 1: 12

The Commodores, 2: 216

communications and media (chapter)

    chronology, 4: 200–201

    headline makers, 4: 205–31

    overview, 4: 202–4

    primary sources, 4: 258–62

    topics in the news, 4: 232–57

communism, support and affiliation, 1: 17, 18–19, 19–20, 21, 39

The Communist Manifesto (Marx), 1: 20

Communist Parties (international), 1: 39

Communist Party members, 1: 18–19, 20, 21

community murals, 1: 118–19

community ophthalmology, 3: 442, 444–45

composers

    jazz, 1: 89, 92

    opera, 1: 129–30

computer graphics engineering, 4: 799, 811

computer scientists, 4: 775–77, 799, 809–11

computers in schools, 4: 762, 801, 808, 813–15, 813 (ill.). *See also* personal computers

condom distribution, and sex ed, 3: 464, 465

Condon, Bill, 2: 248

Cone, James H., 1: 32, 48; 4: 700, 704–6, 736–38, 739

Congress. *See* Congressional Black Caucus; House of Representatives; Senate

Congressional Black Caucus, 3: 411–14

    and Black Leadership Forum, 3: 418

    formation, 3: 383, 411–12

    on judicial nominations, 3: 514–15

    members, 1: 27; 3: 383, 387, 412

NAACP and, *1:* 25, 28
    welfare reform debate, *3:* 408, 413
conjoined twins, *3:* 454, 457, 457 (ill.),
    458, 459–60
Connerly, Wardell, *1:* 169–70
conscientious objector status, *4:* 604,
    605
consolidation, television/radio stations.
    See media ownership and diversity
Constitution of the United States,
    3: 390, 392, 428–30, 507, 528, 536,
    544
Continental Airlines, *4:* 788–89
continuity of medical care, *3:* 439, 498
contraception, and sex ed, *3:* 464–65
*Conversations: Straight Talk with
    America's Sister President* (Cole),
    2: 325
Conway, William, *4:* 767, 769
Conyers, John, *1:* 50–51, 60, 68; *3:* 383,
    419
Cook, Toni, *2:* 352
corneal transplants, *4:* 445, 446
Cornelius, Don, *2:* 210–11, 210 (ill.)
**Cosby, Bill, *2:* 202, 203, 211–13, 212
    (ill.)**, 243–44, 250, 251, 252–53, 253
    (ill.)
        social criticism, *2:* 213, 353
The Cosby Show (television program),
    2: 203, 211, 213, 252–53, 253 (ill.),
    254, 299
Council of Independent Black
    Institutions, *2:* 351, 351 (ill.)
Cowlings, Patricia, *4:* 793–94, 796
Cox, Billy, *4:* 641, 642, 643
crack cocaine epidemic, *2:* 286–87, 286
    (ill.), 289; *3:* 561
Crafts, Hannah, *2:* 337
Creative Construction Company, *1:* 117
credit card industry, *1:* 145–48
crime profiling, *3:* 556. *See also* racial
    profiling
crime rates
    decreases in, *2:* 290
    drug-related, *2:* 286–87
    gang-related, *2:* 289
criminal justice reforms, *3:* 561
Crocker, Frankie, *2:* 236

Crooklyn (film), *2:* 249
cross burning, *4:* 607 (ill.)
Crowdy, William Saunders, *4:* 730
Cuba, *1:* 17, 39
Cullen, Countee, *2:* 297
Curbeam, Robert L., Jr., *4:* 797
The CW (television network), *2:* 205–6

D

Daily Blossom, *1:* 179–80
dance and dancers, *1:* 78, 79, 81–82,
    86–87, 88–89, 110–12; *4:* 643, 645
Dance Theatre of Harlem, *1:* 78,
    110–12
Dandridge, Dorothy, *2:* 223, 239
Dangerous (Jackson), *4:* 646
**Darden, Christine, *4:* 761, 771–74,
    805**
Darfur, Sudan, *3:* 414
Dash, Julie, *2:* 249
**Davis, Angela, *1:* 18–21, 18 (ill.), 56;
    3: 529; *4:* 665**
Davis, Anthony, *1:* 129–30
Davis, Miles, *1:* 91, 92
Davis, Ossie, *2:* 239, 260
Davis, Sammy, Jr., *1:* 86–87
Days, Drew S., *3:* 513–14
Dean, Mark, *4:* 809–10
*Death of the Last Black Man in the
    Whole Entire World* (Parks), *1:* 98
death penalty, *3:* 554, 559
death rates, *3:* 439, 475, 493. *See
    also* disease rates and race
Death Row Records, *4:* 684
debates, political
    moderators, *2:* 216, 225
    2008 election, *3:* 423, 424 (ill.),
    426–27
Dee, Ruby, *2:* 239, 260
Def Comedy Jam, *1:* 160
Def Jam Recordings, *1:* 159–60, 171;
    4: 682
Def Poetry Jam, *1:* 160
Defense Race Relations Institute,
    4: 608–9
deferments, military, *4:* 575, 600 (ill.),
    601, 602, 603–4

DeFunis v. Odegaard (1974), *1:* 35, 168

Democratic Select Committee.
  See Congressional Black Caucus

demographic information, 2000
  Census, *2:* 271, 284–85, 294, 298,
  306, 307 (ill.)

demographics (chapter)
  chronology, *2:* 268–70
  headline makers, *2:* 274–83
  overview, *2:* 271–73
  primary sources, *2:* 304–7
  topics in the news, *2:* 284–303

demographics, religious affiliations,
  4: 701, 735, 742–43, 746–47

Denny, Reginald, *1:* 53; *3:* 548

Denver, Colorado, *2:* 347–48

desegregation in education. *See Brown
  v. Board of Education of Topeka,
  Kansas* (1954); busing; "freedom of
  choice" education plans; integration;
  *Swann v. Charlotte-Mecklenburg
  Board of Education* (1971)

designers. *See* fashion designers

Detroit, Michigan. *See also* automotive
  industry
    failing schools, state takeover,
      2: 360–63
    mayors, and city crises, *3:* 414–17
    Milliken v. Bradley (1974) (busing/
      desegregation case), *2:* 352
    riots, 1967, *2:* 327; *4:* 612

diabetes rates, *3:* 463, 476, 487

Diallo, Amadou, *3:* 509, 546, 548–49

Diary of a Mad Black Woman (Perry),
  1: 115

Diaz, Al, *1:* 84, 121, 131

diet, health issues, *3:* 480, 487

A Different World (television program),
  2: 253

Diff'rent Strokes (television program),
  2: 252

Diggs, Charles, *3:* 411, 413; *4:* 596

digital divide, *2:* 237–38, 238 (ill.),
  262; *4:* 761–62, 801–3
    federal technology support,
      historically black colleges,
      4: 808–9, 813–15, 813 (ill.)

Dime Savings Bank/Bancorp,
  1: 158–59, 171

Dinkins, David, *1:* 31, 158

directors. *See* film directors

disaster relief, *1:* 6–7

disco music, *4:* 632, 637, 671–72, 680
  lead-up to, *4:* 669–71
  sampling, *4:* 681

Discovery space shuttle, *4:* 763, 765,
  794, 795

discrimination in the military, *4:* 595,
  610–12

discrimination remedies.
  See affirmative action;
  discrimination in the military;
  employment discrimination

disease rates and race, *3:* 439–40, 471,
  475, 479–86, 487, 488, 492–93

disenfranchisement, *1:* 28; *3:* 507, 536,
  538, 539

disparate impact lawsuits, *1:* 36, 141

dissents, Supreme Court cases, *3:* 524
    Grutter v. Bollinger (2003),
      3: 564–67
    *Regents of the University of
      California v. Bakke* (1978),
      3: 562–64

District of Columbia. *See* Washington,
  D.C.

diversity, television, *1:* 27; *2:* 202;
  4: 579. *See also* BET (Black
  Entertainment Television); cable
  networks; media ownership and
  diversity

divorce, *2:* 294–95

DJ Jazzy Jeff & the Fresh Prince,
  2: 227, 242

DJs, radio. *See* radio personalities

DJs (turntable/hip-hop), *4:* 680–81

DMX, *2:* 243

Do the Right Thing (film), *2:* 203, 218,
  219, 246, 247
    Ebert review, *2:* 258–60
    poster, *2:* 259 (ill.)

Dobson, Tamara, *2:* 241

doctoral degrees, science, *1:* 183

doctors. *See* physicians; surgeons

documentaries, *2:* 219–20, 246, 249, 336–37

Dodd, Christopher, *1:* 24

Dolemite (film), *2:* 241

Donaldson, Jeff, *1:* 118, 119

Don't Believe the Hype: Fighting Cultural Misinformation About African-Americans (Chideya), *2:* 209

Douglass, Frederick, *1:* 108
    quotations, *3:* 567
    study, *2:* 343

Dove, Rita, *1:* 79, 124

Dowell, Denzil, *1:* 40

Dr. Dre, *4:* 683

draft
    Muhammad Ali's refusal, *4:* 602–6, 603 (ill.)
    new draft ideas, *4:* 615
    Vietnam War, *4:* 575, 579, 600–601, 600 (ill.), 602, 606, 608, 613–14

draft boards, *4:* 602

drama and dramatists, *1:* 78, 79, 97–98, 102–4, 112–16

Dream the Boldest Dreams: And Other Lessons of Life (Cole), *2:* 325

Dreamgirls (film), *2:* 243, 243 (ill.)

Dreams from My Father (Obama), *2:* 296; *3:* 397–98

"driving while black," *3:* 556–57

drop-outs, high school, *2:* 295, 359

drug crime, and profiling, *3:* 556

drug deaths, *1:* 85; *4:* 639, 643

drug sentencing, *2:* 287, 290, 291; *3:* 560–61

drug treatment programs, churches, *4:* 701, 712, 713

drug-addicted babies, *2:* 287

drugs, as community blight, *2:* 285–91, 358; *3:* 560–61

Du Bois, W. E. B.
    academic goals, *2:* 336
    study, *2:* 343

Dukakis, Michael, *1:* 46; *2:* 225

Duncan, Arne, *2:* 362

Dungy, Tony, *4:* 685 (ill.), 686

Dunye, Cheryl, *2:* 249

Dutchman (Baraka), *1:* 112

Dwight, Edward J., *4:* 790

Dylan, Bob, *4:* 641

Dyson, Michael Eric, *2:* 326–30, 327 (ill.)

E

Earls, Julian, *4:* 794

early assessment programs
    education, *2:* 291
    health, *3:* 464

Earth, Wind and Fire, *4:* 671

Eastside High School (Paterson, NJ), *2:* 318–20

Eazy-E, *4:* 683

Ebert, Roger, *2:* 258–60

Ebonics, *2:* 352–54

Ebony (magazine), *2:* 234, 234 (ill.), 235; *4:* 666

economic downturns
    anticipated census data, *2:* 285
    black vulnerability, *1:* 182, 187; *2:* 299–300
    effects on health coverage, *3:* 478
    effects on historically black colleges, *2:* 367–68
    effects on media, *2:* 232
    global, *1:* 143, 182, 185, 186–88
    2008 election issue, *3:* 425–26

economics, public school systems, *2:* 291, 316, 352, 358–59, 359 (ill.); *4:* 804

economists, *2:* 274–76

economy, evolution, *1:* 186–87; *4:* 800–801

Eda, Eugene, *1:* 118

Edelman, Marian Wright, *1:* 21–24, 22 (ill.)

editors. *See* journalists; magazine editors

education administrators, *2:* 338–42. *See also* college and university faculty

education, and health care quality, *3:* 477, 497, 498

education (chapter)
    chronology, *2:* 312–14
    headline makers, *2:* 318–42

overview, 2: 315–17
   primary sources, 2: 369–74
   topics in the news, 2: 343–68
education desegregation. *See Brown v.
Board of Education of Topeka,
Kansas* (1954); busing; integration;
Marshall, Thurgood; *Swann v.
Charlotte-Mecklenburg Board of
Education* (1971)
educational attainment. *See* college
enrollment and graduation; high
school graduation rates
educational opportunities. *See
also* college enrollment and
graduation; high school graduation
rates
   affirmative action and cases,
    1: 34–36, 142, 166, 181
   science and math divide,
    4: 761–62, 780–81
   through athletics, 2: 330–31
educational success, and gender,
2: 291, 292
educational test scores.
See standardized tests and scores
Edwards, Harry, 2: 330–33; 4: 663
Edwards, John, 3: 423
Edwards, Melvin, 1: 120–21, 120 (ill.)
EEOC. *See* Equal Employment
Opportunity Commission (EEOC)
ElBaradei, Mohamed, 4: 618
Elder, Lee, 4: 658, 658 (ill.)
Elders, Joycelyn, 3: 460–67, 461 (ill.),
467 (ill.)
elected officials, growth trends,
3: 383–84, 537
Electric Lady Studios, 4: 642
Electric Ladyland (The Jimi Hendrix
Experience), 4: 642
elementary multicultural education,
2: 316, 317
Ellington, E. David, 4: 810
Ellis, Clarence A., 4: 809
Ellison, Keith M., 3: 387–90, 388 (ill.)
embryonic stem cell research, 3: 491,
492
Emeagwali, Philip, 4: 775–77, 810
Eminem, 4: 684

Emmy Award winners
   documentaries, 2: 219–20, 249
   dramas, 2: 202, 212, 250
   journalism, 2: 208, 222
   miniseries, 2: 252
   talk shows, 2: 256
Emory University, 2: 325
employment agencies, 1: 151, 152–53,
170–71, 178
employment discrimination. *See
also* Civil Rights Act of 1964; Equal
Employment Opportunity
Commission (EEOC)
   airline industry, 4: 788–90
   claims processing software, 4: 811
   corporations investigations, 4: 579
   impact discrimination, 3: 545–46
   newspaper industry, 2: 203, 233
employment statistics
   affirmative action, 1: 34, 142, 166,
    181
   civil rights era and onward, 1: 141,
    142
   unemployment, 1: 186, 188;
    2: 285; 3: 477, 478, 559
Encarta Africana (reference work),
2: 336
Endeavor space shuttle, 4: 784, 786,
787, 797
endocrinologists, 3: 460, 463
engineers, 4: 761, 762, 771–74,
775–77, 792–93
Engler, John, 2: 361
entrepreneurs
   Sean Combs, 1: 148–51, 148 (ill.)
   foods businesses, 1: 173–77
   Earl G. Graves, Sr., 1: 170; 2: 203,
    213–15, 214 (ill.)
   growing ranks, 1: 141, 142–43,
    178, 179–80
   Janice Bryant Howroyd, 1: 151–53,
    151 (ill.), 170–71, 178
   Daymond John, 1: 153–55, 153 (ill.)
   David L. Steward, 1: 161–62
environmental racism and justice,
1: 11, 12–13; 3: 480–81
environmental safety, nuclear issues,
4: 481–83

Episcopal Church, *4:* 718, 719–20, 735, 741, 742, 742 (ill.)

Equal Credit Opportunity Law, *1:* 27

Equal Employment Opportunity Commission (EEOC)
  claims processing software, *4:* 811
  formation, *1:* 141, 166, 171
  policy questions, *1:* 168
  staff members, *3:* 516, 530, 533–34, 549, 551; *4:* 578–79

Esposito, Giancarlo, *2:* 260

Essence (magazine), *2:* 202, 228, 229, 234

The Ethical Dimensions of Marxist Thought (West), *1:* 32

Ethiopia, *4:* 699, 700

ethnic cleansing, *4:* 619

eugenics, *2:* 281

Eurocentricity, *2:* 351

European colonialism, *1:* 19

evangelists, *4:* 703–4, 712–14

Executive Order 9981 (armed forces integration), *4:* 575

Executive Order 10925 (affirmative action), *1:* 34, 142, 166, 167

Executive Order 11246 (affirmative action), *1:* 34, 166–67, 189–91; *3:* 508

executives. *See also* entrepreneurs
  Ursula Burns, *1:* 144–45
  Kenneth I. Chenault, *1:* 145–48, 146 (ill.), 172
  Sean Combs, *1:* 148–51, 148 (ill.)
  growing ranks, *1:* 141, 143, 170–73, 179–80
  Janice Bryant Howroyd, *1:* 151–53, 151 (ill.), 170–71
  Robert L. Johnson, *1:* 155–57, 155 (ill.), 171; *2:* 255
  Richard Parsons, *1:* 157–59, 157 (ill.), 172 (ill.)
  David L. Steward, *1:* 161–62, 171
  John W. Thompson, *4:* 811–12, 812 (ill.)
  Oprah Winfrey, *1:* 162–65, 163 (ill.), 171; *2:* 203

exiles, *1:* 17

eye doctors and diseases, *3:* 442–48, 469

F

Fab 5 Freddy, *4:* 683

fabric art, *1:* 99, 99 (ill.), 101–2, 120

factory jobs, *1:* 142, 183–85, 186, 187, 188; *2:* 301, 301 (ill.); *4:* 800–801

failing schools, takeovers, *2:* 358–63

Fair Housing Act (1968), *2:* 271

Falling Through the Net: A Survey of the "Have Nots" in Rural and Urban America (report), *2:* 237; *4:* 801, 814

family life, changes, *2:* 291–300, 294 (ill.), 298 (ill.), 299 (ill.)

Family Matters (television program), *2:* 254

The Famous Flames, *4:* 637

Fannie Mae, *1:* 171

Fanon, Frantz, *1:* 19, 39

Farmer, James, *3:* 386

Farrakhan, Louis, *4:* 706–9, 706 (ill.), 734–35
  Congressional Black Caucus and, *3:* 413–14
  Jesse Jackson and, *1:* 46, 55; *4:* 708–9
  Malcolm X and, *4:* 706, 707–8, 734
  Million Man March, *1:* 13, 54–56; *4:* 701, 706, 709, 735
  as political campaign issue, *1:* 46; *3:* 389; *4:* 708
  response, September 11, 2001 terrorist attacks, *4:* 750–53

far-UV camera/spectrograph, *4:* 767, 767 (ill.), 769–70, 771, 791

fashion
  black culture, *4:* 631, 676
  black power/pride, *4:* 632, 665–67, 666 (ill.)
  hip-hop culture, *4:* 677–80, 677 (ill.)
  shoes, *4:* 648, 649, 677, 678

fashion designers
  Sean Combs, *1:* 148, 148 (ill.), 150, 151; *4:* 679
  Daymond John, *1:* 153–55, 153 (ill.); *4:* 678–79
  Kimora Lee Simmons, *4:* 650–52, 651 (ill.), 679

fashion lines
Baby Phat, *4:* 650, 651, 679
FUBU, *1:* 153–55; *4:* 678–79
G-Unit, *4:* 680
Phat Farm, *1:* 160; *4:* 651, 678
Rocawear, *4:* 679 (ill.), 680
Sean John/Sean by Sean Combs,
1: 148, 150, 151; *4:* 679, 680
*Fat Albert and the Cosby
Kids* (television show), *2:* 212, 213,
243, 251
federal and state jobs. *See* government
jobs
federal appeals courts and judges,
3: 510, 511–12, 522–23, 534, 549,
550
Federal Bureau of Investigation (FBI)
Coleman Young investigation,
3: 415
Hank Aaron threat investigations,
4: 669
Black Panther Party investigation,
1: 16, 41–42
Martin Luther King investigation,
1: 61; *4:* 736–37
Nation of Islam investigation,
4: 734, 736
Federal Communications Commission
(FCC)
appointees, *4:* 808
cable television, *2:* 255
Telecommunications Act (1996)
and deregulation, *2:* 204,
236–37, 260–62
Telecommunications Act (1996)
and information access/
education, *4:* 806–8
federal contracts. *See* government
contracts, and equal employment/
affirmative action
Federal Emergency Management
Agency (FEMA), *1:* 58
Federal National Mortgage
Association, *1:* 171
feminist movement, *1:* 6; *4:* 739–40.
See also womanist movement
National Organization of Women,
1: 47; *3:* 387; *4:* 719

racial divide, *1:* 10, 47–48;
2: 278–79; *4:* 739, 740
visual artists, *1:* 100, 101
writers, *1:* 47, 48, 61, 103–4;
2: 276–80
feminist theology, *1:* 48; *4:* 715, 718,
719–20
*Feminist Theory: From Margin to
Center* (hooks), *2:* 279
Feminista (Kennedy), *1:* 128
Fences (Wilson), *1:* 116
Fermilab, *4:* 780
fiction writers. *See* drama and
dramatists; novelists; science fiction
writers
Fifteenth Amendment, *3:* 507, 536, 544
50 Cent, *4:* 680, 684, 684 (ill.)
film directors, *2:* 203, 245–50
Spike Lee, *2:* 203, 218–20, 218
(ill.), 246–47, 247 (ill.), 249
Gordon Parks Jr., *2:* 240–41
Gordon Parks Sr., *2:* 240–41
John Singleton, *2:* 203, 247, 250
Mario Van Peebles, *2:* 203, 247,
249–50
Melvin Van Peebles, *2:* 239–40
The Final Call (newspaper), *2:* 232
(ill.)
fire alarm systems, *4:* 800
First Amendment-related cases, *3:* 523,
554–55
"first generation rights," *2:* 315
First Great Migration, *1:* 183;
2: 271–72, 300–302, 306, 348
flag imagery in art, *1:* 119–20
Fledgling (Butler), *1:* 85
The Flip Wilson Show (television
program), *2:* 243, 251–52
flooding, Hurricane Katrina, *1:* 57–58,
57 (ill.)
Florida
populations, *2:* 302, 303
2000 presidential election, *1:* 28
Florida A&M, *2:* 367
Folami, Alika N., *2:* 260–62
folk art. *See* graffiti art; quilts
folklorists, *1:* 105
food traditions, *1:* 173–77

football players, *4:* 668
  academic aspects, *2:* 331, 338
  college stars, *3:* 403
  psychological aspects, *2:* 333
*For Colored Girls Who Have Considered
  Suicide/When the Rainbow Is
  Enuf* (Shange), *1:* 102 (ill.), 103–4,
  110, 114
forced busing. *See* busing
Ford, Gerald, *1:* 158
Ford Motor Co., *1:* 184, 185
Forde, Evan B., *4:* 792
foreclosures crisis, *2:* 300
Foreman, George, *4:* 605, 688, 688
  (ill.)
Forman, James, *1:* 49–50, 49 (ill.)
Fortune 500 executives, *1:* 144–45,
  145–48, 171–72; *2:* 345
"forty acres and a mule," *1:* 49, 50, 64
four-star admirals, *4:* 595, 595 (ill.),
  598
four-star generals, *4:* 576, 580–81, 581
  (ill.), 585–86
Fourteenth Amendment, *3:* 544
Foxx, Jamie, *2:* 248, 254
Foxx, Red, *2:* 243, 251
fragging, *4:* 608
France, *1:* 17; *4:* 662
Francisco, Maranda, *3:* 456
Franklin, Aretha, *4:* 638–39, 638 (ill.),
  660, 662, 665
Franklin, John Hope, *2:* 343
Frazier, Joe, *4:* 605
Frazier, Skipper Lee, *2:* 235
Free D.C. movement, *2:* 288
free jazz, *1:* 116–17, 118
free trade agreements, *1:* 187
"freedom of choice" education plans,
  2: 315, 346, 369–71
Freedom of Information Act (1966),
  4: 736
Freeman, Al, Jr., *2:* 239
Freeman, Morgan, *2:* 203, 248
Fresh Prince. *See* Smith, Will
The Fresh Prince of Bel-Air (television
  program), *2:* 227, 242, 254
Friedan, Betty, *2:* 279; *4:* 719
Frost, Robert, *1:* 124

Fryer, Roland G., *2:* 274–76, 274 (ill.)
FUBU clothing, *1:* 153–55; *4:* 678–79
Fudge, Ann, *1:* 172
full employment, desires/calls, *1:* 64;
  3: 413
Fuller, Charles, *1:* 115; *2:* 231
Fuller, Hoyt, *1:* 107, 109
fundraising
  education/colleges, *2:* 344,
    365–66, 368; *4:* 814
  election campaigns, *2:* 422
funk music, *4:* 632, 637, 669–71, 670
  (ill.)
Funkadelic, *4:* 670 (ill.), 671, 672
Funnye, Capers C., Jr., *4:* 730
Furious Five, *4:* 681, 681 (ill.)

G

Gaines, Ernest J., *2:* 252
Galatis, George, *4:* 782
The Game (television program),
  2: 205–6, 254
gang violence
  community blight, *2:* 289, 290
    (ill.), 358
  crime statistics, *2:* 289
  drug trade and, *2:* 286–87, 289
  movie portrayals, *2:* 219, 240, 248,
    249
gangsta rap, *4:* 682–83. *See also* hip-
  hop music
  cultural criticism, *2:* 329–30
  fashions, *4:* 678
  media consolidation and airplay,
    2: 261–62
Gantt, Harvey, *1:* 9–10
Garner, Margaret, *1:* 95–96
Garvey, Marcus, *4:* 700, 729
Gates, Bill, *4:* 813 (ill.)
Gates, Daryl, *1:* 54
Gates, Henry Louis, Jr., *2:* 333–37,
  334 (ill.), 344
  Cambridge police incident, 2009,
    3: 530
  collaborations, *1:* 33; *2:* 276, 336
*Gather Together in My
  Name* (Angelou), *1:* 81

gay and lesbian activists, *1:* 6, 8–10, 61–63; *4:* 744–45

gay and lesbian rights, *2:* 297
    Black Panthers support, *1:* 39, 62
    challenges, black churches, *4:* 744–47
    marriage rights, *2:* 283, 297
    overviews, *1:* 6, 61–63
    womanist support, *1:* 48–49; *4:* 740

gay couples/families, *2:* 291, 297

gay marriage debate, *4:* 745, 746

Gaye, Marvin, *4:* 660, 669

Gaynor, Gloria, *4:* 672

gays in the military, *1:* 63; *4:* 580, 620–23

gender, and educational success, *2:* 291, 292

genealogical research, *2:* 337

General Motors, *1:* 185, 188; *3:* 534

genetics studies, breast cancer, *3:* 481–82

genocide, *2:* 281; *3:* 414

gentrification, *2:* 348

geologists, *4:* 792

Germany, Holocaust, *1:* 49, 64

Gershwin, George, *1:* 128

Gesell Committee, *4:* 610–12, 610 (ill.)

Gesell, Gerhard, *4:* 610, 610 (ill.)

Ghost (film), *2:* 245

Gibbs, Edward, *4:* 789

Gibson, Kenneth, *3:* 383

Gifted Hands: The Ben Carson Story (Carson), *3:* 454–55, 459

Gillam, Isaac Thomas, IV, *4:* 794

Giovanni, Nikki, *1:* 107, 109 (ill.), 123, 125

Gipson, Mack, Jr., *4:* 792

Girlfriends (television program), *2:* 205, 254

Giuliani, Rudy, *1:* 158; *4:* 750

glaucoma, *3:* 444, 445

global economic downturns. *See* economic downturns

globalization, *1:* 186–87

Glover, Savion, *1:* 79, 86–87, 86 (ill.), 116

"Go Down, Moses" (spiritual), *4:* 748–49

Goetz, Bernhard, *1:* 29–30

Goldberg, Whoopi, *2:* 245

golfers, *4:* 631, 656–57, 656 (ill.), 658–59, 658 (ill.)

Golub, Harvey, *1:* 147

gonorrhea rates, *3:* 486

Good Times (television show), *2:* 203, 250–51, 299

Gooding, Cuba, Jr., *2:* 248

goodwill ambassadors, *1:* 129

Gorbachev, Mikhail, *3:* 401; *4:* 592

Gordon, Quinland, *4:* 735

Gordone, Charles, *1:* 78, 115

Gordy, Berry, *4:* 644, 653–54, 660

gospel music, *4:* 699–700, 748–49, 748 (ill.)

gospel singers, *4:* 702–4, 702 (ill.)

Gossett, Louis, Jr., *2:* 248

government and politics (chapter)
    chronology, *3:* 380–82
    headline makers, *3:* 385–406
    overview, *3:* 383–84
    primary sources, *3:* 428–32
    topics in the news, *3:* 407–27

government bailouts, *1:* 148, 185

government contracts, and equal employment/affirmative action
    Executive Orders, *1:* 34, 141–42, 166–67, 189–91; *3:* 508
    ruled unconstitutional, *3:* 541–42
    "set asides," *1:* 36, 168, 169, 169 (ill.)

government jobs. *See also* government contracts, and equal employment/ affirmative action
    affirmative action bans, state-level, *1:* 169–70; *3:* 508, 511
    U.S. attorneys, *3:* 518

governors
    elections history, *3:* 384
    L. Douglas Wilder, *3:* 404–6, 404 (ill.)

Grady (television program), *2:* 252

graffiti art, *1:* 79, 84, 84 (ill.), 85, 121–23, 122 (ill.), 131–32

Grammy Award winners

James Brown, *4:* 637, 660

Aretha Franklin, *4:* 638, 639

Michael Jackson, *4:* 643, 645, 675

Wynton Marsalis, *1:* 91

opera singers, *1:* 129

Stevie Wonder, *4:* 655

Grand Wizard Theodore, *4:* 681

Grandmaster Flash, *1:* 149; *4:* 681, 681 (ill.)

Granholm, Jennifer, *3:* 417

Grant, Jacquelyn, *1:* 48; *4:* 739, 740, 741

Gratz v. Bollinger (2003), *3:* 508, 543

Graves, Denyce, *1:* 129, 129 (ill.)

Graves, Earl G., Sr., *1:* 170; *2:* 202, 203, **213–15, 214 (ill.),** 234

Gray, F. Gary, *2:* 249

Gray, Fred, *3:* 510

Gray, William H., III, *4:* 813–15, 813 (ill.)

Great Migration, *1:* 183; *2:* 271–72, 300–302, 306, 348

Green, Al, *4:* 669

Green, Marlon D., *4:* 788–89

Green Party, *3:* 395

Green v. County School Board of New Kent County (1968), *2:* 346, 369–71

Greene, Ralph "Petey," *2:* 202, 235

Gregory, Frederick D., *4:* 794, 795, 795 (ill.)

Gregory, Wilton, *4:* 701, **709–11, 709 (ill.),** 743–44

Grey's Anatomy (television program), *2:* 222, 223, 254

Grier, David Alan, *2:* 254, 257

Grier, Pam, *2:* 240, 241; *4:* 665

Griffith, Michael, *1:* 30

Griggs v. Duke Power Co. (1971), *1:* 141

Grove City College v. Bell (1984), *3:* 545

Grutter, Barbara, *3:* 542 (ill.)

Grutter v. Bollinger (2003), *3:* 508, 535, 542 (ill.), 543, 564–67, 564 (ill.)

Guevara, Ernesto "Che," *1:* 39

Guinier, Lani, *1:* 169; *3:* **512–15, 512 (ill.)**

guitarists, *4:* 639–43, 640 (ill.), 673 (ill.), 674

Gulf War, 1991, *2:* 225; *4:* 592, 612–13, 612 (ill.)

G-Unit Clothing, *4:* 680

Gunn, Sakia, *1:* 63

Guy-Sheftall, Beverly, *2:* 325–26

H

hairstyles, *4:* 665–67, 666 (ill.), 678

Haiti, *3:* 414; *4:* 593

Haley, Alex, *1:* 108; *2:* 252

Hall, Arsenio, *2:* 254

Halley's Comet, *4:* 770

Hamer, Fannie Lou, *1:* 47

Hammons, David, *1:* 120, 121

Hancock, Herbie, *1:* 91; *4:* 672–73

Hannah, Marc, *4:* 799

hardcore rap, *4:* 682. *See also* gangsta rap; hip-hop music

Haring, Keith, *1:* 121, 122

Harlem Hospital, *3:* 444, 444 (ill.), 445

Harlem Renaissance, *1:* 78, 105, 106, 125

Harpo Productions, Inc., *1:* 164, 171

Harris, Barbara, *1:* 48; *4:* 742, 742 (ill.)

Harris, Bernard A., *4:* 797, 806 (ill.)

Harris, Betty, *4:* 792–93

Harvard Law Review, *3:* 398

Harvard Law School faculty, *3:* 513, 515, 529–30

Harvard University and faculty

African American studies dept., *1:* 33; *2:* 333, 336, 344

Roland G. Fryer, *2:* 274, 275–76

Henry Louis Gates Jr., *2:* 333, 335, 336, 344

Cornel West, *1:* 32, 33; *2:* 336, 344

hat designers, *1:* 150, 153–54

Hatcher, Richard, *3:* 383

hate crimes, *3:* 509, 553–55, 553 (ill.)

busing- and integration-related, *2:* 349, 350

James Byrd Jr. murder, *3:* 509, 553–54, 553 (ill.)

cross burning, *4:* 607 (ill.)

homosexuality-related, *1:* 63

Jena Six case, 2006, *1:* 59–61
laws, *3:* 553, 554–55
political activism, *1:* 30, 63
Supreme Court on, *3:* 554–55
Hawkins, La-Van, *1:* 177
Hawkins, Yusuf, *1:* 30–31
Hayes, Elvin, *4:* 663
Hayes, Isaac, *2:* 241
HBCUs. *See* historically black colleges
and universities
HBO (Home Box Office) programming,
2: 219–20, 223, 249, 255, 256
Head Start program, *2:* 291
cuts to, *1:* 24
founders, *1:* 21, 23, 24
Health and Equity and Accountability
Act (2009 bill), *3:* 441
health and medicine (chapter)
chronology, *3:* 436–38
headline makers, *3:* 442–71
overview, *3:* 439–41
primary sources, *3:* 494–99
topics in the news, *3:* 472–93
health care equality. *See also* disease
rates and race
advocates, *1:* 21, 23; *3:* 444–46,
460, 467–68, 471, 492–93
economists' studies, *2:* 275
history and disparities, *3:* 439–41,
474–78, 496–99
2008 election issue, *3:* 425
health care reform, *3:* 493, 496–99
health insurance, *3:* 476, 477 (ill.),
478, 480, 493, 498
health literacy, *3:* 477, 497, 498
heart disease
obesity risks, *3:* 487, 488
rates and demographics, *3:* 439,
476
research, *3:* 467, 468, 471
The Heart of a Woman (Angelou), *1:* 82
heart surgery, *3:* 467, 469–70
Heavy D, *1:* 150
Hebrew Israelites, *4:* 730–32
Heller, Jean, *3:* 472
Helms, Jesse
campaigns against, *1:* 8, 9–10;
4: 745

Martin Luther King holiday
opposition, *3:* 420
Hemsley, Sherman, *2:* 250, 251 (ill.)
Henderson, Felicia D., *2:* 205
Henderson, Napoleon, *1:* 119
Hendricks, Barbara, *1:* 129
Hendricks, Jon, *1:* 120
Hendrix, Jimi, *4:* **639–43, 640** (ill.),
660, 662, 665
Herbert, F. Edward, *4:* 608
*A Hero Ain't Nothin' But a
Sandwich* (Childress), *1:* 126
Herskovits, Melville Jean, *2:* 322–23
Heyward, DuBose, *1:* 128
Higgenbotham, Joan E., *4:* 797
high school graduation rates
drop-outs, *2:* 295, 359
history and demographic trends,
2: 273, 285, 298
school inequalities' effects, *2:* 359
Higher Education Act (1965), *2:* 364
Hill, Anita, *3:* **515–17, 515** (ill.), 530,
534, 549, 551–53
Hill, Walter Andrew, *4:* 793
Hines, Gregory, *1:* 86–87, 116
hip-hop culture
clothing lines, *1:* 148, 150,
153–55, 160; *4:* 677, 678–80
fashion, *4:* 677–80, 677 (ill.)
graffiti art, *1:* 121–22
television, *1:* 160
hip-hop music. *See also* specific artists
artists as actors, *2:* 203, 227–28,
242–43, 246, 254
industry figures, *1:* 148–51,
159–60, 171
media consolidation's effects,
2: 260–62
pioneers and history, *1:* 149, 159;
4: 631, 680–84
Hip-Hop Summit/Action Network,
1: 14, 160; *3:* 407 (ill.)
Hirschkop, Phillip J., *2:* 282
Hispanic American populations,
2: 285, 294; *3:* 474–75
historians, *2:* 326, 328–30
historical drama, *1:* 98

Index

historically black colleges and
universities, *2:* 322, 363–68
challenges, *2:* 365–68
faculty and administrators, *2:* 293,
321–22, 324–26, 324 (ill.),
366–67; *4:* 803–4
funding aid, *2:* 217–18, 365–66,
367–68; *4:* 814
graduates and earning power,
1: 182; *2:* 364
health information technology,
3: 441
history, *2:* 363–64, 365, 366
medical schools, *3:* 443, 450, 451,
452
science education, *4:* 803–4,
808–9
Supreme Court cases, *3:* 535
technology support/digital divide,
4: 808–9, 813–15, 813 (ill.)
*HIStory: Past, Present, and Future Book
I* (Jackson), *4:* 647–48
Hitler, Adolf, *2:* 281
HIV/AIDS epidemic
activism, *1:* 62; *4:* 633
art relating to, *1:* 88, 89
black community conspiracy
theories, *3:* 474
black community, rates, *1:* 6;
3: 440, 475, 482–86, 558–59
church involvement in combating,
4: 706, 716, 717, 724
deaths from, *4:* 633
history, *3:* 482
prevention, *3:* 464, 474
prison populations, *3:* 558–59
Rainbow/PUSH concern, *1:* 47
Holder, Eric, *3:* **517–19, 517 (ill.)**
Holliday, George, *1:* 52, 53; *3:* 547
Hollywood Shuffle (film), *2:* 246–47
Holocaust, *1:* 49, 64; *2:* 281
home ownership rates
economic downturns, *2:* 299–300
single women, *2:* 295
home rule, Washington D.C., *2:* 288;
3: 409, 410
home security, *4:* 800
homophobia

activism to fight, *1:* 8, 9, 10,
62–63; *4:* 745
in black community, *2:* 297;
3: 486; *4:* 744, 745, 746
homosexual rights. *See* gay and lesbian
activists; gay and lesbian rights
Honsou, Djimon, *4:* 651, 652
Hooker, John Lee, *4:* 640
hooks, bell, *1:* **33;** *2:* **276–80, 277 (ill.)**
Hoover, J. Edgar, *1:* 41; *3:* 410;
4: 736–37
Hopwood v. Texas (1996), *3:* 542–43
hormone replacement therapy, *3:* 481
Horne, Lena, *2:* 242
Hoskins, Michele, *1:* 176
hospital desegregation, *3:* 439
House of Judah, *4:* 728
House of Representatives. *See
also* Congressional Black Caucus
Shirley Chisholm, *3:* 385, 385
(ill.), 386–87
John Conyers, *1:* 50–51, 60, 68;
3: 383, 419
Keith Ellison, *3:* 387, 388 (ill.),
389–90
growth trends, black elected
officials, *3:* 383, 538
Barbara Jordan, *3:* 390–92, 390
(ill.)
Judiciary Committee, *3:* 383, 390,
390 (ill.), 392, 428–30
John Lewis, *3:* 539 (ill.)
Cynthia McKinney, *3:* 392–95,
393 (ill.)
Kweisi Mfume, *1:* 25, 25 (ill.),
26–27; *3:* 413–14
Adam Clayton Powell Jr., *1:* 29, 61
Charles Rangel, *3:* 383, 413, 428;
4: 615
Edolphus Towns, *4:* 808, 809
J. C. Watts Jr., *3:* 402–4, 402 (ill.)
Ways and Means Committee,
3: 383, 497
House Party (film), *2:* 243, 246, 247
House Resolution 40 (reparations),
1: 50–51, 68–70
housing crisis, *2:* 300
housing fairness legislation, *2:* 271

Houston, Charles, 3: 521, 522

Houston (TX) Independent School District, 2: 339–41

Houston, Whitney, 4: 674

How Stella Got Her Groove Back (McMillan), 1: 127 (ill.), 128

Howard University, 2: 364, 364 (ill.), 367

    hospital and medical school, 3: 443, 450, 451, 452

    science camps, 4: 806 (ill.)

Howell, Leonard, 4: 729

Howroyd, Janice Bryant, 1: 151–53, 151 (ill.), 170–71

Hudlin, Warrington, 2: 246

Hudson, Herb, 1: 176

Hudson, Jennifer, 2: 243, 243 (ill.), 248

human medical experimentation, 3: 472–74

Humphrey, Hubert, 1: 167–68

Hunter, Frank O. D., 4: 582

The Huntley-Brinkley Report (television program), 2: 215

Hurricane Katrina, 2005, 1: 56–59, 57 (ill.)

    celebrity relief efforts, 1: 93

    criticisms of federal response, 1: 6–7, 58; 3: 394

    documentaries, 2: 219–20, 249

Hurston, Zora Neale, 1: 125

    adaptations, 1: 98

    rediscovery, 1: 104, 105

Hussein, Saddam, 3: 401; 4: 576, 592, 618–20

Hutton, Bobby, 1: 17, 41–42

I

I Know Why the Caged Bird Sings (Angelou), 1: 80, 81, 83, 110, 124

I Spy (television program), 2: 202, 212, 250

IBM, 4: 799, 809–10

Ice Cube, 2: 203, 243; 4: 683

Ice T, 2: 203, 243

Ifill, Gwen, 2: 203, 215–16, 215 (ill.), 233

Igbo Nigerians, 4: 775

I'm Just a DJ but . . . It Makes Sense to Me (Joyner), 2: 218

Image Award winners, 2: 223, 226–27, 231, 330

Imani Temple, 4: 743, 744 (ill.)

immigration

    demographic trends, 2: 285, 303

    NAFTA and, 1: 187

impact discrimination, 3: 545–46

impeachment hearings, Richard M. Nixon, 3: 390, 390 (ill.), 391–92, 428–30

Imperceptible Mutabilities in the Third Kingdom (Parks), 1: 98

imprisonment rates. *See* prisoners

In Living Color (television program), 2: 254

In Search of Our Mothers' Gardens: Womanist Prose (Walker), 1: 47; 4: 740, 741

income inequalities, 1: 141, 142, 180–82, 187; 2: 273, 285

    and health care, 3: 476–77

    improvements, 2: 284, 284 (ill.)

Independence Day (film), 2: 228, 243

infant mortality rates, 3: 464, 475, 476, 478, 493, 563

information revolution, 4: 761–62, 800–801, 809–12

information technology industry, 1: 157, 159, 161–62, 171; 4: 776–77, 799, 809–12

Ink Newspaper, 2: 233

Inner City Foods Corporation, 1: 177

Inner Visions Worldwide, Inc., 4: 722

Inside Man (film), 2: 219, 231, 249

Inside Politics (television program), 2: 109

Institute for Journalism Education, 2: 220–21

institutional racism, 1: 34, 182; 2: 297; 4: 725. *See also* affirmative action; Civil Rights Act of 1964

insurance, health, 3: 476, 477 (ill.), 478, 480, 493, 498

integration

    demographic history, 2: 271–72

education, *2:* 272, 315, 346–52, 358; *3:* 543–44

military history, *4:* 575, 582–83, 587, 606, 610–11

intellectuals

Michael Eric Dyson, *2:* 326–30

Henry Louis Gates Jr., *2:* 333–37

bell hooks, *2:* 276–80

Cornell West, *1:* 31–33

internalized racism, *1:* 95

International Space Station, *4:* 766, 797, 817

International Women in Medicine Hall of Fame, *3:* 448

Internet. *See also* blogs; digital divide; information technology industry; Web sites

access and usage, *2:* 204, 237–38, 238 (ill.), 262; *4:* 761–62, 801–3, 814

mobile devices, *4:* 802–3

news sources/sites, *2:* 204, 209, 232, 233–34

technology lead-up, *4:* 775, 776–77, 801, 810

internment camps, *3:* 521

interracial marriage

divorce and politics, *1:* 106

growth trends, *2:* 291, 293–94, 294 (ill.), 300

Loving v. Virginia (1967), *2:* 271, 280, 280 (ill.), 281–82, 283, 293, 304–6

Obama family history, *3:* 397

state precedents, *1:* 105

television portrayals, *2:* 250

The Interruption of Everything (McMillan), *1:* 128

intravenous drug use, *3:* 484–85

Introducing Dorothy Dandridge (film), *2:* 223

inventors and inventions, *4:* 761, 797–800, 805

George E. Alcorn, *4:* 791–92

Patricia Bath, *3:* 442, 446–47

George R. Carruthers, *4:* 767, 769–70, 771, 791

Robert E. Shurney, *4:* 791

investments and investing, *2:* 300

Invincible (Jackson), *4:* 648

Iowa caucuses, 2008 election, *3:* 384, 423

Iran, elections and video activism, *1:* 53

Iran hostage crisis (1979–80), *4:* 591

Iran-Contra scandal, *4:* 591–92

Iraq War (1991). *See* Persian Gulf War, 1991

Iraq War (2003–)

Bush administration policy, *3:* 401–2; *4:* 576, 594, 616, 617–20

draft ideas, *4:* 615

opposition, African Americans, *4:* 576, 616

opposition, politicians, *3:* 389, 394, 402, 422

2008 election issue, *3:* 422, 425, 427

Irving, Julius "Dr. J," *1:* 177

Islam. *See* Nation of Islam; Sunni Islam

Isley Brothers, *4:* 641

Israel, *4:* 731–32

J

Jackson Five, *4:* 643–44, 665, 675

Jackson, Jesse, *1:* 44–47; *4:* 665

contemporaries and influence, *1:* 29, 31, 44–45, 55, 59–60

election campaigns, *1:* 46; *3:* 384, 387, 418; *4:* 708, 725–26

Louis Farrakhan and, *1:* 46, 55; *4:* 708–9

gay rights support, *4:* 745

Grutter v. Bollinger (2003) decision support, *3:* 564 (ill.)

as pastor, *4:* 700–701, 714, 726

Rainbow/PUSH Coalition, *1:* 44, 45–46, 46 (ill.), 47; *2:* 246

Jackson, Joe, *4:* 643

Jackson, Mahalia, *4:* 700

Jackson, Michael, *4:* **631–32, 643–48, 644 (ill.), 647 (ill.), 674–75**

acting career, *2:* 242; *4:* 644

MTV airplay, *4:* 645, 676, 683

political partnerships, *1:* 29

Jackson, Shirley Ann, *4:* 761, 778–84, 781 (ill.), 783 (ill.), 800, 805, 817

The Jacksons, *4:* 644

Jacoby, Sydney, *4:* 800

Jagger, Mick, *4:* 631

Jakes, T. D., *4:* 701, 703, 712–14, 712 (ill.)

jam bands, *1:* 118

Jamaica, *4:* 729

James, Daniel "Chappie," Jr., *4:* 576, 580–86, 581 (ill.), 585 (ill.)

James, LeBron, *4:* 631

James, Rick, *4:* 676

Japanese American internment, *3:* 521

Jarrell, Jae, *1:* 119

Jarrell, Wadsworth, *1:* 119

Jay-Z, *4:* 679 (ill.), 680

jazz, *1:* 79, 89–93, 116–18; *4:* 659

Jazz Messengers, *1:* 91

Jazz (Morrison), *1:* 96, 127, 133

jazz operas, *1:* 81, 92, 128

jazz poetry, *1:* 107, 123

The Jeffersons (television program), *2:* 250, 251 (ill.)

Jelly's Last Jam (Wolfe), *1:* 87, 116

Jemison, Mae, *4:* 761, 784–87, 785 (ill.), 797, 806

Jena Six case, 2006, *1:* 59–61, 60 (ill.)

Jesus Christ, *1:* 48; *4:* 700, 705, 730, 736, 737, 738 (ill.), 739, 751

Jet (magazine), *2:* 234, 235

Jeter, Mildred. *See* Loving, Mildred

Jews. *See also* antisemitism
  African American, *4:* 700, 728, 730–32, 731 (ill.)
  Old Testament, *4:* 728, 748–49

The Jimi Hendrix Experience, *4:* 641–42, 662

Jodeci, *1:* 149

Joe Turner's Come and Gone (Wilson), *1:* 79

Joe's Bed-Stuy Barbershop: We Cut Heads (Lee), *2:* 218, 246

John, Daymond, *1:* 153–55, 153 (ill.); *4:* 678–79

Johns Hopkins University

Martin Luther King Jr. Commemoration, *3:* 471

medical school admissions, *3:* 467, 468, 469

neurosurgery, *3:* 456, 457

Johnson, Hazel, *4:* 580, 586–88, 587 (ill.)

Johnson, John H., *2:* 234

Johnson, Katherine G., *4:* 791

Johnson, Lonnie G., *4:* 798–99, 798 (ill.)

Johnson, Lyndon B. *See also* Voting Rights Act (1965)
  affirmative action policy, *1:* 34, 166–68, 189–91; *3:* 508
  campaigning, *3:* 391
  civil rights policy, *1:* 141; *3:* 407, 536–37; *4:* 578
  Freedom of Information Act (1966), *4:* 736
  judicial nominations, *3:* 522–23, 527 (ill.), 528
  King assassination and, *1:* 43
  media policy, *2:* 232
  military policy, *4:* 600–601, 602, 816
  staff, *4:* 578
  Washington D.C. administration, *3:* 409

Johnson, Magic, *3:* 484, 485

Johnson, Michelle T., *1:* 173

Johnson Publishing Company, *2:* 234

Johnson, Robert L., *1:* 155–57, 155 (ill.), 171; *2:* 255

Johnson's Luncheonette, *1:* 174–75

Joint Chiefs of Staff, chairman position, *4:* 576, 588, 589 (ill.), 612

Jolson, Al, *4:* 631

Jones, Barbara B., *1:* 119

Jones, Bill T., *1:* 88–89, 88 (ill.)

Jones, Edward, *1:* 79

Jones, James Earl, *2:* 239

Jones, LeRoi. *See* Baraka, Amiri

Jones, Marion, *4:* 631

Jones, Quincy, *1:* 164; *4:* 644–45, 675

Jordan, Barbara, *2:* 297; *3:* 390–92, 390 (ill.)

Nixon impeachment hearings, *3:* 390, 390 (ill.), 391–92, 428–30

Jordan, **Michael,** *1:* 177; *4:* 631, **648–50, 649 (ill.),** 678

journalists, *2:* 202, 203. *See also* political journalism
    Jayson Blair, *2:* 206–7, 206 (ill.)
    Ed Bradley, *2:* 202, 207–8, 207 (ill.)
    Farai Chideya, *2:* 203, 204, 208–9
    Michael Eric Dyson, *2:* 328
    hiring trends, *2:* 232–33
    Gwen Ifill, *2:* 203, 215–16, 215 (ill.)
    Internet sites and activity, *2:* 204, 209, 238
    Robert C. Maynard, *2:* 220–21, 220 (ill.)
    Bernard Shaw, *2:* 224–25, 224 (ill.)
    Tavis Smiley, *2:* 225–27, 226 (ill.)

journalists' associations, *2:* 202, 220–21, 222, 233

journals. *See* periodicals

Joyner, **Tom,** *2:* **216–18, 217 (ill.)**

Judaism, *4:* 700, 728, 730–32

judges
    Janice Rogers Brown, *3:* 510–12, 510 (ill.)
    Eric Holder, *3:* 517 (ill.), 518
    Thurgood Marshall, *3:* 519–24, 520 (ill.)
    Constance Baker Motley, *3:* 526–28, 527 (ill.)
    Clarence Thomas, *3:* 531–35, 531 (ill.), 535 (ill.)

Juilliard School of Music, *1:* 91

Jungle Fever (film), *2:* 203, 219, 249

juries
    Amadou Diallo shooting case, *3:* 549
    call for similar racial backgrounds, *1:* 65
    employment discrimination cases, *3:* 546
    Jena Six case, *1:* 59
    Rodney King beating case, *1:* 52, 54; *3:* 509, 547–48

Just Give Me a Cool Drink of Water 'Fore I Die (Angelou), *1:* 123–24

juvenile detention centers, *2:* 321

juvenile diabetes, *3:* 463. *See also* diabetes rates

juvenile offenders, tried as adults, *1:* 59–60, 61

K

Karenga, Ron, *1:* 107, 111

Keating, Edward M., *1:* 15–16

Keith, Floyd, *4:* 685–86

Kemp, Herb, *1:* 173

Kennard, William E., *4:* 808

Kennedy, Adrienne, *1:* 114

Kennedy, Edward, *1:* 24

Kennedy, Erica, *1:* 128

Kennedy, Flo, *1:* 47

Kennedy, John F.
    affirmative action policy, *1:* 34, 142, 166, 167, 189
    arts policy, *1:* 124
    campaigning, *3:* 391
    civil rights policy, *1:* 141; *3:* 407; *4:* 578
    judicial nominations, *3:* 522
    religion, *4:* 743
    space program, *4:* 790, 817
    staff, *4:* 578

Kennedy, Megorah, *1:* 6, 62

Kennedy, Robert F.
    assassination, *1:* 67; *2:* 214; *4:* 663
    King assassination speech, *1:* 66–68
    Loving v. Virginia case, *2:* 282
    poverty issues, *1:* 23
    staff members, *2:* 214

Kent, Herb, *2:* 235

Kent State shootings, 1970, *2:* 345

Kerner Commission, *2:* 232

Kid 'n Play, *2:* 243, 246

kidney transplants, *3:* 440, 452, 453

Kidwell, Earl, Jr., *3:* 469

Kilpatrick, Kwame, *3:* 416–17, 416 (ill.)

Kindred (Butler), *1:* 85

King, B. B., *4:* 640

King, Bernice A., *4:* 714–15, 714 (ill.)
King, Coretta Scott, *1:* 48 (ill.); *3:* 419
  (ill.), 471; *4:* 715
King, Dexter, *3:* 419 (ill.)
King, Don, *1:* 29
King, John, *3:* 553–54
King, Martin Luther, III, *1:* 60; *4:* 613
King, Martin Luther, Jr.
  advisers, *1:* 61–62
  assassination, *1:* 5, 38, 42–44, 44
    (ill.), 66–68; *2:* 327; *3:* 409–10;
    4: 612, 663, 715
  civil rights movement leadership,
    1: 5, 9, 29, 36–37, 42, 44;
    4: 700, 706, 725, 738
  FBI surveillance, *1:* 61; *4:* 736–37
  holiday, *1:* 9; *3:* 413, 419–20, 419
    (ill.)
  as minister, *1:* 5; *4:* 699, 700
  nonviolent methods questioned,
    1: 5, 16, 37–38; *4:* 663–64, 700
  Poor People's Campaign, *1:* 23, 42;
    3: 443
  speeches, *1:* 42, 43; *2:* 327
  on Vietnam War, *4:* 575, 601 (ill.),
    602
"King of Rock" (Run-DMC), *4:* 682
King, Reatha Belle Clark, *4:* 793
King, Rodney
  beating, 1991, *3:* 546, 547–48, 547
    (ill.)
  post-incident and -riots
    commentaries, *1:* 33
  post-incident riots, *1:* 15, 53;
    3: 509, 548
  verdict reactions, *1:* 52–54
Knight, Gladys, *4:* 660
Knowles, Beyoncé, *2:* 243, 243 (ill.)
The Known World (Jones), *1:* 79
Koch, Ed, *1:* 30
Kool and the Gang, *4:* 671
Kool Herc (deejay), *4:* 680–81
Korean War veterans, *4:* 583, 587
KRS-One, *1:* 149
Ku Klux Klan, terrorism, *1:* 19; *4:* 607
  (ill.), 700
Kuwait. *See* Persian Gulf War, 1991
Kwanzaa, *1:* 111, 111 (ill.)

L

labor statistics. *See* employment
  statistics
"Ladies First" (Queen Latifah),
  4: 688–90
Lady Sings the Blues (film), *2:* 242
Laird, Melvin, *4:* 608
Lama, Omar, *1:* 119
Lanier, Bob, *4:* 663
laser surgery techniques/devices,
  3: 442, 446–47, 467, 470
LaShane, Joanna, *2:* 234 (ill.)
law and justice (chapter)
  chronology, *3:* 504–6
  headline makers, *3:* 510–35
  overview, *3:* 507–9
  primary sources, *3:* 562–67
  topics in the news, *3:* 536–61
Law, Bob, *2:* 236
Law Keepers, *4:* 728
Law of Return, Israel, *4:* 732
Law schools, and affirmative action.
  See Grutter v. Bollinger (2003)
Lawrence, Carolyn M., *1:* 119
Lawrence, Robert H., *4:* 790
Lawrence v. Texas (2003), *2:* 297
lawsuits
  affirmative action, *1:* 35–36
  desegregation, *1:* 11
  election injustices, *1:* 28
  employment discrimination,
    3: 545, 546; *4:* 788–89
  NAACP, *1:* 11, 25, 27, 28
  reparations, *1:* 51–52
  sports leadership diversity,
    4: 685–86
  television diversity, *1:* 27
  Tuskegee syphilis study, *3:* 473
lawyers
  Clifford Alexander, *4:* 579
  Lani Guinier, *3:* 512–15, 512 (ill.)
  Anita Hill, *3:* 515–17, 515 (ill.)
  Eric Holder, *3:* 517–19, 517 (ill.)
  Thurgood Marshall, *3:* 519, 520
    (ill.), 521–22
  Constance Baker Motley,
    3: 526–28, 527 (ill.)

Charles J. Ogletree Jr., *3:* 528–30, 529 (ill.)

Laying Down the Law (Clark), *2:* 321

Leading in Black and White: Working across the Racial Divide in Corporate America (Livers and Caver), *1:* 173

League for Spiritual Discovery, *1:* 8

Lean on Me (film), *2:* 318

Lear, Norman, *2:* 250, 251

Leary, Timothy, *1:* 8

Lee, Barbara, *3:* 414, 418 (ill.)

Lee, Don L. *See* Madhubuti, Haki

Lee, Spike, *2:* 203, **218–20, 218 (ill.),** 231, 246–47, 247 (ill.), 248, 249
  acting roles, *2:* 219, 259, 259 (ill.)
  Do the Right Thing movie review, *2:* 258–60

Leffall, LaSalle D., Jr., *3:* 443

legal errors, court cases, *1:* 12

legalization of drugs, *3:* 465, 466

legislative redistricting, *3:* 383, 391, 393, 394, 405, 411–12, 421

Lemmons, Kasi, *2:* 248, 249

lesbian activists. *See* gay and lesbian activists

Letton, James C., *4:* 799

Leventhal, Melvyn, *1:* 105

Levi, Edward H., *1:* 168

Levitt, Steven D., *2:* 276

Lewis, Charles, *3:* 410–11

Lewis, John, *3:* 539 (ill.)

Lewis, Margie, *1:* 179

Lewis-Kemp, Jacqueline, *1:* 180

liberation theology, *1:* 6, 48; *4:* 704, 706, 736–38. *See also* black theology movement

Liberia, *4:* 731

life coaches, *4:* 722

life expectancies, *3:* 439, 475, 563

Lil Wayne, *4:* 684

Lilith's Brood (Butler), *1:* 85

Lincoln, Abraham, *2:* 337

Lincoln Center Jazz Orchestra, *1:* 92, 157

Lincoln Review (journal), *3:* 533

Lingo (programming language), *4:* 811

linguistics and Ebonics, *2:* 352–54

LinkLine, *4:* 811

literacy tests (disenfranchisement), *3:* 536, 538

Little Bill series (book and television series), *2:* 213

Little, Cleavon, *2:* 244

Little Jezebel Plantation, *1:* 177

Little Richard, *4:* 641

Live at the Apollo (Brown), *4:* 637

Livers, Ancella B., *1:* 173

Livingston Award winners, *2:* 222

LL Cool J, *1:* 153, 154, 160

lobbyists, *3:* 404

local area networks, *1:* 161

Long Binh, Vietnam, *4:* 606–7

Lopez, Jennifer, *2:* 254

Lorde, Audre, *1:* 123

Los Angeles Police Department, *1:* 33, 52–53, 53–54; *3:* 547–48, 547 (ill.), 556 (ill.)

Los Angeles riots. *See* King, Rodney; Watts, Los Angeles riots, 1965

Lotus Press, *1:* 108

Louisiana Superdome, *1:* 58

Love, Monie, *4:* 689–90

Loving, Mildred, *2:* **280–83, 280 (ill.),** 293, 297, 304–5

Loving, Richard, *2:* 280, 280 (ill.), 281–83, 293, 304–5

Loving v. Virginia (1967), *2:* 271, 280, 280 (ill.), 281–82, 283, 293, 297, 304–6

LSAT scores, *3:* 565, 566

Ludacris, *2:* 243

Lynch Fragments series (Edwards), *1:* 120, 120 (ill.)

lynching, *1:* 50 (ill.), 59

M

Mabley, Jackie "Moms," *2:* 243

MacArthur Foundation genius grant recipients, *1:* 85, 98; *2:* 336

Mack, Craig, *1:* 149

Madea series (Perry), *1:* 115

Madhubuti, Haki, *1:* 107, 109

Madison, Joe, *2:* 237

magazine editors, *2:* 202, 228–29, 234

magazines. *See* periodicals

Magnificent Montague (DJ), 2: 235

Mahogany (film), 2: 242

Majette, Denise, 3: 394

Make, Vusumzi, 1: 82

Making Malcolm: The Myth and Meaning of Malcolm X (Dyson), 2: 329

malaria, 3: 489

Malcolm X

    assassination, 1: 82, 106; 4: 708, 734

    autobiography of, 1: 108; 3: 388

    cultural criticism, 2: 329

    Louis Farrakhan and, 4: 706, 707–8, 734

    operas about, 1: 129

    rap music and, 4: 682

    religion and separatism, 1: 39; 4: 700, 705, 706, 734, 736, 738

    study, 2: 329, 343

    supporters, 1: 15, 16

Malcolm X (film), 2: 203, 218, 219, 231, 249

mammograms, 3: 479 (ill.), 480

Management Technology Inc., 1: 179

manufacturing industry.

    See automotive industry; factory jobs

Marchbanks, Vance, 4: 794

Marines. *See* U.S. Marine Corps, personnel

Market Women: Black Women Entrepreneurs—Past, Present, and Future (Smith), 1: 173

Marley, Bob, 4: 729

marriage law. *See* gay marriage debate; *Loving v. Virginia* (1967)

Marsalis, Branford, 1: 90, 91

Marsalis, Ellis, 1: 90

Marsalis, Wynton, 1: 79, **89–93,** 90 (ill.), 117–18

Marshall, Thurgood, 3: **519–24,** 520 (ill.)

    dissent, *Regents of the University of California v. Bakke* (1978), 3: 562–64

    retirement and replacement, 3: 534, 549

Martin and Malcolm in America (Cone), 4: 706, 738

Martin Luther King Jr. Center for Nonviolent Social Change, 4: 715

Martin Luther King Jr. federal holiday, 1: 9; 3: 413, 419–20, 419 (ill.)

Marvin X, 1: 114

Marxist philosophy, 1: 19–20, 32, 39

masks, 1: 101

Massachusetts Institute of Technology (MIT), 4: 778–80

Massey, Walter E., 4: 804, 805

mass-market fiction, 1: 127–28

Master P, 2: 256

Masters Tournament, 4: 657, 658, 658 (ill.), 659

masturbation, 3: 466

math and science education, 4: 761–62, 771, 787, 803–6, 805 (ill.)

mathematicians, 4: 761, 775–77, 794

matriarchal families, 2: 291, 292, 296

Matthew Shepard and James Byrd Jr. Hate Crimes Prevention Act (2009), 3: 555

Mauffrey, J. P., 1: 60–61

Mayfield, Curtis, 2: 241; 4: 641

Maynard, Nancy, 2: 220–21, 233

Maynard, Robert C., 2: 203, **220–21,** 220 (ill.), 233

mayors

    Chicago: Harold Washington, 3: 420–21

    Detroit, and city crises, 3: 414–17

    election growth trends, 3: 383, 414

    Washington D.C.: Walter Washington and Marion Barry, 1: 55; 2: 288, 288 (ill.); 3: 409–11

    L. Douglas Wilder, 3: 406

Mays, Willie, 4: 634

Maytag Corporation, 1: 171–72

MC Hammer, 4: 678, 683

MC Lyte, 4: 683

McCain, John, 3: 399, 408–9, 424–27, 424 (ill.), 512; 4: 595

McCartney, Paul, 4: 655, 674

McCoy, Sid, 2: 235

McDaniel, Hattie, 2: 248

McGee, Art, 4: 810

McGovern, George, *3:* 385 (ill.), 386

McGwire, Mark, *4:* 635

McKenzie, Vashti Murphy, *1:* 48; *4:* 701, 715–17, 716 (ill.)

McKinney, Cynthia, *3:* 392–95, 393 (ill.)

McKinney, Gene, *4:* 609

McMillan, Terry, *1:* 127 (ill.), 128

McNair, Ronald E., *4:* 765, 786, 794, 795, 795 (ill.), 805–6

McNamara, Robert, *4:* 600–601, 610–11, 612

McPhail, Sharon, *3:* 416

MCs, *4:* 681

Medeski Martin & Wood, *1:* 118

media ownership and diversity, *1:* 27; *2:* 204, 232–33, 235, 236–37, 260–62

media portrayals, stereotypes
   film, *2:* 202, 203, 240, 241, 246, 248
   journalism, *2:* 209, 232, 233
   television, *2:* 203, 213, 250–51, 252, 255

medical care. *See* health care equality; minority health care reform

medical devices and technologies
   automatic implantable defibrillator, *3:* 467, 469–70
   Laserphaco Probe (cataract surgery), *3:* 442, 446–47
   telemedicine, *3:* 447 (ill.), 448

medical experimentation, humans, *3:* 472–74

medical schools, enrollment and graduation, *3:* 441, 467, 469

Medicare Act (1965), *3:* 439

Medicare services, *3:* 498

megachurches, *4:* 701, 712, 713, 747

Melvin, Leland D., *4:* 797

Men in Black (film), *2:* 228, 243

mentorship programs, *1:* 180; *2:* 229, 324, 355

A Mercy (Morrison), *1:* 97

Meredith v. Fair (1962), *3:* 528

Meridian (Walker), *1:* 110, 126

Merrill Lynch, *1:* 172

Mexico City Olympic Games, 1968, *2:* 330, 332; *4:* 663–65, 663 (ill.), 690–91

Mfume, Kweisi, *1:* 24–28, 25 (ill.); *3:* 413–14

The Michael Eric Dyson Show (radio program), *2:* 330

Michele Foods, *1:* 176

Michigan State University, *2:* 345

microprocessing, *4:* 776–77, 810

Microsoft, *4:* 813 (ill.)

middle class, *2:* 297–300, 298 (ill.)

Middle East conflict, *4:* 752

migration
   north-south, *2:* 272, 300, 302–3
   south-north, *1:* 183; *2:* 271–72, 300–302, 306, 348

Miles, Buddy, *4:* 643

militancy philosophies, *1:* 5, 15, 16, 37–39; *4:* 664, 734

military and homosexuality, *1:* 63; *4:* 580, 620–23

military and racial tensions, *4:* 575, 582, 601, 602, 606–9, 610, 614

military bases, *2:* 303; *4:* 582, 607

the military (chapter)
   chronology, *4:* 572–74
   headline makers, *4:* 577–99
   overview, *4:* 575–76
   primary sources, *4:* 617–23
   topics in the news, *4:* 600–616

military councils, *4:* 590, 607–8

military personnel, *4:* 575–76, 609–10, 614
   Clifford Alexander, *4:* 577–80, 577 (ill.)
   Daniel "Chappie" James Jr., *4:* 576, 580–86, 581 (ill.), 585 (ill.)
   Hazel Johnson, *4:* 580, 586–88, 587 (ill.)
   Colin Powell, *4:* 576, 588–95, 589 (ill.), 593 (ill.), 612–13
   J. Paul Reason, *4:* 576, 595–99

military recruitment, *4:* 600, 610, 612, 615–16, 816

Miller, Pepper, *1:* 173

Milliken II (1977), *2:* 352

Milliken v. Bradley (1974), 2: 352

Million Family March, 1: 11, 14, 56

Million Man March, 1: 55 (ill.)
    organization, 1: 11, 13, 54–56;
      3: 388, 389; 4: 701, 706, 709,
      735
    participants, 1: 33

Millions More March, 1: 11, 56; 4: 701,
    706, 709, 735

Milwaukee Braves, 4: 667–69

Mingus, Charles, 1: 116

ministers
    Juanita Bynum, 4: 701, 702–4, 702
      (ill.)
    Katie Cannon, 1: 48; 4: 739, 740
    Michael Eric Dyson, 2: 328
    Louis Farrakhan, 4: 707–9
    Jacquelyn Grant, 1: 48; 4: 739, 740
    history, 4: 699, 700–701, 735
    T. D. Jakes, 4: 701, 712–14
    Bernice A. King, 4: 714–15, 714
      (ill.)
    Martin Luther King Jr., 1: 5;
      4: 699, 700
    Vashti Murphy McKenzie, 4: 701,
      715–17, 716 (ill.)
    Al Sharpton, 1: 29; 4: 700–701,
      726–27
    J. C. Watts Jr., 3: 403
    Jeremiah Wright, 4: 701, 722–24,
      723 (ill.)

minority health care reform, 3: 493,
    496–99

Minority Organ Tissue Transplant
    Education Program (MOTTEP),
    3: 453

Minority Serving Institution Digital
    and Wireless Technology
    Opportunity Act (2003/2007),
    4: 808–9. *See also* National
    Telecommunications and
    Information Administration (NTIA)

Mirowski, Michel, 3: 470

miscegenation, 2: 280, 281, 283, 285,
    293, 301, 304, 305

Mitchell, Arthur, 1: 111–12

Mitchell, Mitch, 4: 641–42

Mitchell, Parren, 1: 169 (ill.)

Mitchell, Todd, 3: 555

mixed-race marriage. *See* interracial
    marriage

Mo' Better Blues (film), 2: 219, 231, 249

mobile Internet, 4: 802–3

Moeller, Dennis, 4: 809–10

Moesha (television program), 2: 205

Montague, Nathaniel, 2: 235

Monterey International Pop Festival
    (1967), 4: 642, 660, 661 (ill.), 662

Montgomery, Edward, 1: 186

Moody, Anne, 1: 108

Moore, Rudy Ray, 2: 241

Moose, Charles, 3: 524–26, 525 (ill.)

morale, military, 4: 601, 602, 607–8

"A More Perfect Union" (speech),
    4: 701, 728

Morehouse College, 2: 367

Morgan v. Hennigan (1972), 2: 348–49

Morial, Marc, 3: 418 (ill.)

Mormons, 1: 18; 4: 746

Morning Glory Ministries, 4: 703–4

Morrison, Toni, 1: 78–79, 93–97, 93
    (ill.), 110, 126–27
    collaborative writings, 1: 33
    education, 1: 94; 2: 364
    Nobel Prize, 1: 78–79, 93, 96, 127,
      132–33
    womanist writings, 1: 48

mortgage crisis, 2: 300

Mos Def, 2: 243

Moseley-Braun, Carol, 3: 395–96, 395
    (ill.)

Moses, Bob, 1: 22

Motley, Constance Baker, 3: 526–28,
    527 (ill.)

Motown Records, 4: 644, 653–54, 655,
    675

movie directors. *See* film directors

MTV
    color barrier and Michael Jackson,
      4: 645, 676, 683
    news, 2: 209
    Yo! MTV Raps, 2: 255; 4: 683

Muhammad, Chavis. *See* Chavis,
    Benjamin

Muhammad, Elijah, *1:* 5, 15, 16, 49;
 4: 700, 706, 707–8, 733, 734. *See
 also* Nation of Islam
Muhammad, John Allen, *3:* 526
Muhammad, Wallace D., *4:* 708, 734
Muhammad, Wallace Fard, *4:* 733
Mulcahy, Anne, *1:* 145
multicultural education. *See
 also* African American studies;
 historically black colleges and
 universities
   African-centered schools, *2:* 351,
   355
   introduction, *2:* 316
multimedia art, *1:* 101
murals, *1:* 118–19
Murphy, Eddie, *2:* 245
Murray, Anna Pauline, *1:* 47, 48;
 4: 701, **718–20,** 741–42
music producers
   Sean Combs, *1:* 148, 149; *4:* 639
   Quincy Jones, *4:* 644–45, 675
   Russell Simmons, *1:* 159–60
music videos, *1:* 150, 155; *2:* 255;
 4: 676, 683
musicians
   as actors, *2:* 203, 227–28, 242–43,
   246, 254; *4:* 644
   black influence, *4:* 631, 659–62
   James Brown, *4:* 636–38, 636 (ill.)
   Sean Combs, *1:* 148, 150, 151
   Aretha Franklin, *4:* 638–39, 638
   (ill.)
   Jimi Hendrix, *4:* 639–43, 640 (ill.),
   660, 662
   Michael Jackson, *4:* 643–48, 644
   (ill.), 674–75
   Wynton Marsalis, *1:* 79, 89–93, 90
   (ill.), 116–18
   pop music color barrier, *4:* 645,
   672–76
   Prince, *2:* 242; *4:* 673 (ill.), 674
   Will Smith, *2:* 227, 228
   Stevie Wonder, *4:* 653–56, 654
   (ill.)
Muslim American politicians,
 3: 387–90, 388 (ill.)
Mutual Black Network, *2:* 202, 235–36

My Grandfather's Son (Thomas),
 3: 531, 535, 552–53
My Lai Massacre (Vietnam War),
 4: 590
Myanmar, *1:* 53
Myers, Dwight, *1:* 150

N
NAACP. *See* National Association for
 the Advancement of Colored People
 (NAACP)
NAFTA (North American Free Trade
 Agreement), *1:* 187
Nagin, Ray, *1:* 57, 58
names, *2:* 271
NASA. *See* National Aeronautics and
 Space Administration (NASA)
Nation of Islam, *4:* 707, 708–9,
 733–35, 733 (ill.). *See
 also* Farrakhan, Louis
   *The Autobiography of Malcolm
   X, 1:* 108
   Congressional Black Caucus and,
   3: 413–14
   conversions, *1:* 13–14, 15
   Million Man March, *1:* 13, 54–56;
   3: 388, 389; *4:* 701, 709
   newspaper, *2:* 232 (ill.)
   recruitment, *1:* 5; *4:* 707
   separatist philosophy, *1:* 39, 49;
   4: 705, 734
   September 11, 2001 terrorist
   attacks response, *4:* 749–53
Nation of Yahweh, *4:* 730
National Action Network, *4:* 726 (ill.)
National Aeronautics and Space
 Administration (NASA), *4:* 763,
 764–66, 770, 773–74, 790–97,
 805–6, 815–18
National Assessment of Educational
 Progress (NAEP), *2:* 291
National Association for the
 Advancement of Colored People
 (NAACP)
   affirmative action, *1:* 169
   and Black Leadership Forum,
   3: 418

Clarence Thomas investigation and non-support, *3:* 530, 534, 550

executive directors/presidents, *1:* 11, 13, 24–25, 27–28

Image Award winners, *2:* 223, 226–27, 231, 330

Legal Defense Fund and legal support, *1:* 22–23; *3:* 514, 521, 522, 527–28

membership, *1:* 25

police brutality concern, *1:* 54

sports leadership, and diversity, *4:* 685

television/media criticism, and diversity, *1:* 27; *2:* 202, 239

volunteers, *1:* 21; *3:* 407 (ill.)

voter registration, *3:* 407 (ill.), 408

National Association of Black Journalists, *2:* 202, 222, 233, 328

National Bank of Arkansas, *3:* 466

National Basketball Association (NBA). *See also* basketball players

clothing, *1:* 154

coaches, *4:* 684, 686

players ratios, *4:* 668

team owners, *1:* 155; *4:* 650

National Black Catholic Clergy Caucus, *4:* 743

National Black Lesbian and Gay Leadership Forum, *1:* 10, 62; *4:* 745

National Black Network, *2:* 202, 235–36

National Black Women's Health Imperative, *3:* 475, 478, 492–93

National Body of the Black Men's and Women's Exchange, *1:* 62

National Book Award winners, *1:* 96, 126

National Child Protection Act (1993), *1:* 164

National Coalition of Black Lesbians and Gays, *1:* 62; *2:* 297

National Coalition of Blacks for Reparations in America (NCOBRA), *1:* 50

National Collegiate Athletic Association (NCAA), team leadership, *4:* 685–86

National Conference of Black Churchmen, *4:* 705. *See also* black theology movement

National Dental Association, *3:* 441

National Football League (NFL), *4:* 668, 686

National Guard

civil rights protests and, *4:* 611–12, 611 (ill.)

national disasters, deployments, *1:* 58

recruitment, *4:* 612

riots and, *1:* 43, 53; *3:* 409–10, 548

National Organization for Women (NOW), *1:* 47; *3:* 387; *4:* 719

National Political Congress of Black Women, *3:* 387

National Public Radio (NPR), journalists, *2:* 221–22, 226

National Rainbow Coalition, *1:* 44, 47. *See also* Rainbow/PUSH Coalition

National Science Foundation, *1:* 183; *4:* 762, 804, 809

national security advisors, *3:* 401; *4:* 576

National Security Council (NSC), *4:* 591–92

National Society for Black Engineers, *2:* 316

National Telecommunications and Information Administration (NTIA), *2:* 237; *4:* 801, 807, 813–15

National Urban League, *1:* 184

National Youth Gang Center, *2:* 289

National Youth Movement, *1:* 29

nationalism. *See* black nationalist movement

Native American populations, *2:* 294

Navy. *See* U.S. Navy

Naylor, Gloria, *1:* 126

NCLB. *See* No Child Left Behind Act (2001)

Neal, Larry, *1:* 107

needle drug use, *3:* 484–85

negative political campaigns, *1:* 26

Negro Airmen International, *4:* 789

Nelson, Willie, *1:* 93

NetNoir Online, *4:* 810–11

neurosurgeons, *3:* 448–50, 454–60

Neverland Ranch, *4:* 646, 648

The New Bill Cosby Show (television program), *2:* 251

New Black Panther Party, *1:* 42

New Great Migration, *2:* 272, 300, 302–3

New Hampshire primary, 2008 election, *3:* 423

New Orleans, Louisiana. *See* Hurricane Katrina, 2005

New York Age (newspaper), *2:* 220

New York Daily News (newspaper), *2:* 203, 233

New York Times (newspaper), *2:* 206, 207

Newman v. Piggy Park Enterprises (1968), *1:* 175

newspapers, black-owned/black-interest, *2:* 202, 203, 220–21, 232–34, 232 (ill.)

Newsweek (magazine), *2:* 209

Newton, Huey, *1:* 5, 14, 16, 39, 41, 42, 62, 64, 114; *4:* 664, 665
    documentaries, *2:* 249

Newton, Pamela, *3:* 490–91

Nicaragua, and Iran-Contra scandal, *4:* 591–92

Nigeria, *3:* 396, 451; *4:* 721–22, 775

Nike, *4:* 648, 649, 678

9/11 attacks. *See* September 11, 2001 terrorist attacks

1999 (Prince), *4:* 674

Nineteenth Amendment, *3:* 507

Nixon, Richard
    affirmative action policy, *1:* 168
    civil rights policy, *3:* 407
    Congressional Black Caucus and, *3:* 412–13
    domestic policy, *1:* 23; *2:* 350; *3:* 560
    impeachment hearings, *3:* 390, 390 (ill.), 391–92, 428–30
    judicial nominations, *3:* 523
    military policy, *4:* 606

Watergate scandal, *3:* 428, 429–30

No Child Left Behind Act (2001), *2:* 316–17, 338, 341–42, 356, 371 (ill.)
    reports, effects, *2:* 373–74
    and school takeovers, *2:* 360
    Statement of Purpose, *2:* 371–73

No Place to Be Somebody (Gordone), *1:* 78, 115

No Way Out (Puff Daddy & the Family), *1:* 150

Nobel Peace Prize nominees/winners, *1:* 10; *3:* 443

Nobel Prize winners, literature, *1:* 78–79, 93, 96, 127, 132–33; *2:* 335

non-integration. *See* separatism philosophy

nonviolent protest methods and philosophy, *1:* 5, 9, 36–37, 42

Norman, Jessye, *1:* 129

Norman, Peter, *4:* 663 (ill.), 664

Norris, Michele, *2:* 221–22, 221 (ill.), 233

North American Air Defense (NORAD), *4:* 585–86

North American Free Trade Agreement (NAFTA), *1:* 187

North Korea, *3:* 402

Northeast Utilities, *4:* 782–83

north-south migration, *2:* 272, 300, 302–3

Northwest Austin Municipal Utility District Number One v. Holder (2009), *3:* 539–40

Notorious B.I.G., *4:* 684

Nottage, Lynn, *1:* 116

novelists, *1:* 78–79, 94–97, 104–5, 126–28; *2:* 209, 335, 337

NPR (National Public Radio) journalists, *2:* 221–22, 226

NSC. *See* National Security Council (NSC)

nuclear accidents, *4:* 782

nuclear chemists, *4:* 792–93

nuclear disarmament, *1:* 21; *3:* 402

Nuclear Regulatory Commission (NRC), *4:* 781–83, 781 (ill.), 800

Nunn, Bill, *2:* 260

Nunn, Sam, *4:* 593
nurses, *4:* 586–88
Nutter, Michael, *3:* 383
NWA, *4:* 682–83

O

O, The Oprah Magazine, 1: 165;
  2: 234–35
Oakland Tribune (newspaper), *2:* 203,
  221, 233
Oakland Unified School District,
  2: 352–53, 354
Obama, Barack, *3:* 397–99, 397 (ill.)
  advisers, *1:* 159; *4:* 580
  auto industry and, *1:* 185, 186
  campaign support, *1:* 10; *3:* 422,
    423, 519; *4:* 595
  drug policy, *2:* 287, 291
  education, *3:* 397–98, 530
  education policy, *2:* 368; *4:* 762
  family, *2:* 296, 296 (ill.); *3:* 397,
    398
  hate crimes policy, *3:* 555
  health policy, *3:* 493
  inauguration poetry and music,
    1: 125; *4:* 580, 639
  media coverage, *2:* 216, 235;
    4: 667
  Million Man March, 1995, *1:* 55
  reparations opposition, *1:* 52
  science and technology policy,
    4: 762, 784, 815–16
  2008 presidential election, *3:* 384,
    397, 399, 408–9, 422–27, 424
    (ill.), 426 (ill.)
  victory, as precedent, *1:* 45, 143;
    2: 272–73; *3:* 384, 397, 399,
    422, 427
  victory speech, 2008 election,
    3: 427, 430–32
  Jeremiah Wright and, *4:* 701, 723
    (ill.), 724, 727–28, 727 (ill.)
Obama, Michelle, *3:* 398, 426 (ill.),
  530; *4:* 667
obesity
  in African Americans, *3:* 486–88,
    486 (ill.)
  and breast cancer, *3:* 480
Obie Award winners, *1:* 98, 104, 112;
  2: 231
oceanographers, *4:* 792
O'Connor, Carroll, *2:* 250
O'Connor, Sandra Day, *1:* 169; *3:* 512
O'Connor, Vince, *1:* 9
Off the Wall (Jackson), *4:* 645, 675
Office of Minority Health, *3:* 474, 476
officers, military, *4:* 576, 582, 601, 610,
  611. *See also* specific biographies
Ogletree, Charles J., Jr., *1:* 51; *3:*
  528–30, 529 (ill.), 556–57
Olds, Robin, *4:* 583, 584
Olympic Games, and activism, *2:* 330,
  332; *4:* 603, 632, 663–65, 663 (ill.),
  690–91
Olympic Project for Human Rights,
  2: 332; *4:* 664, 690–91
"On the Pulse of Morning" (Angelou),
  1: 79, 83, 124 (ill.)
O'Neal, Stanley, *1:* 172
open enrollment, colleges, *2:* 367
opera
  classical, *1:* 128–30, 129 (ill.)
  jazz, *1:* 81, 92, 128
Operation Breadbasket, *1:* 29, 44–45
Operation Desert Shield/Storm, *2:* 225;
  4: 592, 612–13, 612 (ill.)
Operation Restore Hope (Somalia),
  4: 613
ophthalmologists, *3:* 442–48, 469
The Oprah Winfrey Show, 1: 162,
  163–64; *2:* 203, 253–54
Oprah's Angel Network, *1:* 165
Oprah's Book Club, *1:* 96–97, 164
Oregon v. Mitchell (1970), *3:* 538
organ donation, attitudes, *4:* 452–53,
  494, 495–96
organ transplants, *3:* 440, 450–51,
  452–53
Organization of Black American
  Culture (OBAC), *1:* 109, 118–21
Oscar winners. *See* Academy Award
  winners
Our Nig (Wilson), *2:* 335
overviews
  activism and reform, *1:* 5–7

the arts, *1:* 78–79

business and industry, *1:* 141–43

communications and media, *2:* 202–4

demographics, *2:* 271–73

education, *2:* 315–17

government and politics, *3:* 383–84

health and medicine, *3:* 439–41

law and justice, *3:* 507–9

military, *4:* 575–76

popular culture, *4:* 631–32

religion, *4:* 699–701

science and technology, *4:* 761–62

Oxygen (cable channel), *1:* 165

P

P. Diddy. *See* Combs, Sean

Pagones, Steven, *1:* 30

Paige, Rod, 2: 338–42, 339 (ill.), 342 (ill.), 364

Palestine, *4:* 752

Palin, Sarah, *3:* 424–25

Pan African Resource Guide (online directory), *4:* 810

pan-African studies. *See* African American studies

pan-Africanism, *1:* 41, 116; *4:* 729

Parallax, *1:* 179

parallel processing, *4:* 776

pardons, *3:* 518

parenting. *See* family life, changes; single-mother families

Parents Involved in Community Schools v. Seattle School District No. 1 (2007), *3:* 543–44

Parker, Linda Bates, *1:* 178–79, 180

Parker, Patricia Sue, *1:* 173

Parks, Gordon, Jr., *2:* 240–41

Parks, Gordon, Sr., *2:* 240–41

Parks, Saundra, *1:* 179–80

Parks, Suzan-Lori, 1: 79, 97–98, 98 (ill.), 116

Parliament-Funkadelic, *4:* 670 (ill.), 671, 672

Parsons, Richard, 1: 157–59, 157 (ill.), 171, 172 (ill.)

particle physics, *4:* 779–80

pastors. *See* ministers; priests

Pataki, George, *4:* 750

patent laws, *4:* 797. *See also* inventors and inventions

Paterson, David, *3:* 384

Patrick Air Force Base, *4:* 608–9

Patrick, Deval, *3:* 384

Patternist series (Butler), *1:* 85

Paul, Clarence, *4:* 654

Payne Memorial African Methodist Episcopal Church (Baltimore), *4:* 715–16, 717

PBS (Public Broadcasting Service) documentary series, *2:* 336–37 news programs, *2:* 216, 226

Peabody Award winners, *2:* 208, 222

Peace and Freedom Party, *1:* 17, 39

peaceful protest methods and philosophy, *1:* 5, 9, 36–37, 42

Peete, Calvin, *4:* 658–59

Pelosi, Nancy, *3:* 387, 418 (ill.)

penicillin, *3:* 472–73

Pentecostal Church, *4:* 701, 712, 713, 741

People United to Save Humanity (PUSH), *1:* 44, 45–46, 46 (ill.), 47; *2:* 246

"The People's Flag Show" (art exhibit), *1:* 120

periodical literature, study, *2:* 335, 336

periodicals
black magazines, *1:* 156, 170, 171, 172; *2:* 202, 203, 213, 214–15, 228, 229, 232, 234–35
industry and economy, *2:* 232, 235
literary journals, *1:* 15–16, 108–9, 123
O, The Oprah Magazine, 1: 165; *2:* 234–35

Perry, Tyler, *1:* 115, 115 (ill.)

Persian Gulf War, 1991, *2:* 225; *4:* 592, 612–13, 612 (ill.)

Person, Waverly, *4:* 793

personal computers, *4:* 777, 799, 801, 802, 809–10. *See also* computers in schools

P-Funk, *4:* 670 (ill.), 671, 672

PGA championships, *4:* 656, 656 (ill.),
657, 658, 658 (ill.)

Phat Farm (clothing line), *1:* 160;
4: 651, 678

Philadelphia public schools, *2:* 363

"Philadelphia Sound," *4:* 669

Philadelphia Tribune (newspaper),
2: 233–34

philanthropy
Benjamin Carson, *3:* 459
Bill Clinton, *2:* 325
Bill Cosby, *2:* 213, 324
Earl G. Graves, Sr., *2:* 215
Michael Jackson, *4:* 645–46
Tom Joyner, *2:* 217–18
Tavis Smiley, *2:* 226
David L. Steward, *1:* 162
Denzel Washington, *2:* 231
Oprah Winfrey, *1:* 165; *2:* 325

Phish, *1:* 118

physicians, *3:* 439, 441, 498
Patricia Bath, *3:* 442–48
Keith L. Black, *3:* 448–50
Clive Callender, *3:* 450–54
Benjamin Carson, *3:* 454–60
Joycelyn Elders, *3:* 460–67
Levi Watkins Jr., *3:* 467–71

physicists, *4:* 778–84, 791–92, 793, 800

The Piano Lesson (Wilson), *1:* 116

Pickett, Wilson, *4:* 660

pilots. *See* airline industry; U.S. Air
Force, personnel

Pittsburgh Pirates, *4:* 634

plagiarism, *2:* 206–7

plays. *See* drama and dramatists

Plessy v. Ferguson (1896), *3:* 522,
566–67

poetry and poets, *1:* 79, 123–25
Maya Angelou, *1:* 80, 81, 83
black arts movement, *1:* 106–9,
123, 125
bell hooks, *2:* 277
Ntozake Shange, *1:* 103–4

Poitier, Sidney, *1:* 150; *2:* 202, 239,
244, 248

police brutality/violence, *3:* 508–9,
546–49

Amadou Diallo shooting, *3:* 509,
546, 548–49
Black Panthers opposition, *1:* 5,
14, 16, 39–41, 64, 65
Rodney King beating and trials,
1: 52–54; *3:* 509, 546, 547–48,
547 (ill.)
Sharpton/National Youth
Movement opposition, *1:* 29–30
voter registration, *1:* 23

police departments, reforms, *1:* 54;
3: 415, 526

police officers and chiefs, *3:* 524–26

political journalism, *2:* 203, 204, 208,
209, 215–16, 220, 224–25, 226

political literature. *See* protest
literature; protest theater

political prisoners, *1:* 12, 20

politicians. *See* elected officials, growth
trends; governors; House of
Representatives; mayors; presidential
candidates; presidential primary
candidates; secretaries of state;
Senate; Speakers of the House; state
legislators; specific politicians

politics of the oppressed, *1:* 19, 39. *See
also* liberation theology

poll taxes, *3:* 536

pollution, minority areas.
See environmental racism and justice

polygamy, *4:* 732

Poor People's Campaign, *1:* 23, 42;
3: 443

pop music, *4:* 631–32, 643, 645,
672–76. *See also* adult contemporary
music; disco music; funk music; hip-
hop music; soul music

Pope John Paul II, *4:* 711

popular culture, academic study,
2: 326, 328–30

popular culture blogs, *2:* 204, 209, 238

popular culture (chapter)
chronology, *4:* 628–30
headline makers, *4:* 633–57
overview, *4:* 631–32
primary sources, *4:* 687–91
topics in the news, *4:* 658–86

popular fiction, *1:* 127–28

population information. *See* Census
Bureau information; demographics;
migration
Porgy and Bess (Gershwin and
Heyward), *1:* 81, 128
"post-racial" era, *2:* 272–73; *3:* 384
Potter's House church, *4:* 701, 703,
712, 713
poverty
and health care disparities, *3:* 440,
474–78, 483–84, 497
imprisonment link, *2:* 290; *3:* 560
program advocacy, *1:* 23, 42;
3: 443
Powell, Adam Clayton, Jr., *1:* 29, 61
Powell, Colin, *4:* 588–95, 589 (ill.)
America's Promise, *4:* 593 (ill.),
594
Persian Gulf War, *4:* 592, 612–13,
612 (ill.)
as secretary of state, *3:* 384; *4:* 588,
594–95
WMDs presentation, United
Nations, *4:* 594, 617–20, 617
(ill.)
Powell, Lewis, *1:* 191–93
"Praise Song for the Day" (Alexander),
1: 125; *4:* 580
prenatal care, *3:* 464, 476, 493, 493
(ill.)
presidential candidates. *See*
also presidential primary candidates
Green Party (McKinney), *3:* 395
Barack Obama, *1:* 45; *3:* 384, 399,
408–9, 422–27, 424 (ill.);
4: 727–28
Peace and Freedom Party
(Cleaver), *1:* 17
presidential debates
journalism and moderation,
2: 216, 225
2008 election, *3:* 423, 424 (ill.),
426–27
presidential elections
2000, NAACP involvement, *1:* 28
2008, *3:* 408–9, 422–27
Presidential Medal of Arts recipients,
1: 83

Presidential Medal of Freedom
recipients, *1:* 24; *3:* 460, 460 (ill.);
4: 639
presidential pardons, *3:* 518
presidential primary candidates
Shirley Chisholm, *3:* 385, 386
Jesse Jackson, *1:* 46; *3:* 384, 387,
418; *4:* 708–9, 725–26
Carol Moseley-Braun, *3:* 396
Al Sharpton, *1:* 31; *4:* 726–27
L. Douglas Wilder, *3:* 406
President's Committee on Equal
Employment Opportunity. *See* Equal
Employment Opportunity
Commission (EEOC)
President's Council on Bioethics,
3: 458
President's National Commission on
AIDS Research, *3:* 485
Presley, Elvis, *4:* 631
Presley, Lisa Marie, *4:* 647
preventive health care, *3:* 439, 476–77,
480, 492–93
Price, Leontyne, *1:* 128
priests, *4:* 701, 709–11, 718–22, 741
primary candidates. *See* presidential
primary candidates
primary care physician relationships,
3: 439, 498
primary source documents
activism and reform, *1:* 64–70
the arts, *1:* 131–33
business and industry, *1:* 189–94
communications and media,
2: 258–62
demographics, *2:* 304–7
education, *2:* 369–74
government and politics,
3: 428–32
health and medicine, *3:* 494–99
law and justice, *3:* 562–67
military, *4:* 617–23
popular culture, *4:* 687–91
religion, *4:* 748–53
science and technology, *4:* 813–18
Prince, *2:* 242; *4:* 673 (ill.), 674
Prince George's County, Maryland,
2: 302

Prince-Bythewood, Gina, *2:* 205
Princeton University and faculty
    Toni Morrison, *1:* 96, 132
    Cornel West, *1:* 31, 32, 33
Prison Satellite Network, *4:* 713–14
prisoners
    advocates, *1:* 20, 47, 65
    death penalty, *3:* 554, 559
    literary portrayals, *1:* 14, 95–96
    prison experiences, *1:* 15, 17–18
    rates, black men, *1:* 182;
        2: 289–91, 359; *3:* 508, 557,
        558, 558 (ill.), 559, 560
    rates, black women, *2:* 290; *3:* 508
    sentencing, drug crimes, *2:* 287,
        290, 291; *3:* 560, 561
    wrongfully imprisoned, *1:* 10–11,
        11–12, 19
Privacy Act (1974), *4:* 736
Procter & Gamble, *4:* 799
producers. *See* music producers
Project 3000 by 2000, *3:* 441
Project 100,000 (Vietnam War),
    4: 600–601
Proposition 8 (California), *4:* 746
Proposition 209 (California),
    1: 169–70; *3:* 511
"prosperity gospel," *4:* 747
protest literature, *1:* 105, 107
protest theater, *1:* 113–14
Protestant theology, *4:* 699
protests, campus
    anti-busing, *2:* 349, 350
    anti-war, *2:* 345
    black studies needs, *2:* 343, 344
        (ill.)
protests, domestic
    civil rights, and violence/
        intimidation, *3:* 546; *4:* 611–12,
        611 (ill.)
    civil rights marches and sit-ins,
        1: 42, 61; *4:* 719
    gay rights, *1:* 9, 62; *4:* 745
    Persian Gulf War, *3:* 613
    Poor People's Campaign, *1:* 42;
        3: 443
    racial profiling, *3:* 556 (ill.)

Vietnam War, *2:* 345; *4:* 575,
    601–2, 601 (ill.)
protests, international stage, *2:* 330,
    332; *4:* 632, 663–65, 663 (ill.),
    690–91
Pryor, Richard, *2:* 244–45, 244 (ill.)
psychologists, *2:* 330–33
psychophysiology, *4:* 793, 796
Public Broadcasting Service. *See* PBS
    (Public Broadcasting Service)
public defenders, *3:* 528, 529
Public Enemy, *1:* 160; *4:* 682
public health education and programs,
    3: 464–65
public schools. *See Brown v. Board of
    Education of Topeka, Kansas* (1954);
    busing; school systems, and
    economics
publishing sources. *See also* periodicals
    black readership magazines,
        1: 158, 170, 171, 172; *2:* 202,
        203, 213, 214–15, 228, 229,
        234–35
    black readership/ownership,
        newspapers, *2:* 202, 203,
        220–21, 232–34, 232 (ill.)
    magazine presses, *2:* 234
    poetry presses, *1:* 108, 123
Puff Daddy. *See* Combs, Sean
Pulitzer Prize winners
    drama, *1:* 78, 79, 97, 115, 116
    fiction, *1:* 79, 93, 96, 105, 127
    music, *1:* 92
    poetry, *1:* 124; *2:* 277
Purple Rain (film and soundtrack
    album), *2:* 242; *4:* 674
PUSH Coalition, *1:* 44, 45–46, 46 (ill.),
    47; *2:* 246

Q

Qaddafi, Muammar al-, *4:* 584
Qaeda, al-, *4:* 576, 749
Queen Latifah, *2:* 243; *4:* 683, 688–90
quilts, *1:* 99, 99 (ill.), 101–2, 120
quotas. *See also* affirmative action
    "set asides" examples, *1:* 36, 168,
        169, 191; *3:* 540–41, 562

Supreme Court cases, *1:* 35–36,
191; *3:* 508, 540–41, 562
Qur'an, *3:* 389; *4:* 751

R

Race, Gender, and Leadership (Parker),
1: 173
race riots. *See* riots
Racial Integrity Act (Virginia, 1924),
2: 281, 282
racial profiling, *3:* 509, 525, 526,
556–58
racial violence, Vietnam War/era,
4: 606–9, 614
racially-motivated crimes. *See* hate
crimes
radio comedies, *2:* 202, 211–12
Radio One, *2:* 237, 239
radio ownership, networks, and
stations, *1:* 26; *2:* 202, 204, 235,
236–37, 260–62
radio personalities, *2:* 202, 235, 236,
236 (ill.), 237
Ed Bradley, *2:* 208
Tom Joyner, *2:* 216–18, 217 (ill.)
Kweisi Mfume, *1:* 26
Michele Norris, *2:* 221–22, 221
(ill.)
Tavis Smiley, *2:* 225–27, 226 (ill.)
Rainbow/PUSH Coalition, *1:* 44, 46, 46
(ill.), 47
Raines, Franklin, *1:* 171
Raleigh, North Carolina, *2:* 302
Ramparts (magazine), *1:* 15–16
Rangel, Charles, *3:* 383, 413, 428;
4: 615
rap. *See* gangsta rap; hip-hop culture;
hip-hop music
Rap City (television program), *2:* 255
rape
Eldridge Cleaver crime, *1:* 15
Maya Angelou experience, *1:* 81
Tawana Brawley trial, *1:* 30
"Rapper's Delight" (Sugarhill Gang),
4: 681
Rapping with Petey Greene (radio
show), *2:* 202, 235

Rashad, Phylicia, *1:* 150–51; *2:* 213,
252, 253 (ill.)
Rastafarianism, *4:* 699, 700, 729, 729
(ill.)
Ray, James Earl, *1:* 43
Reagan Democrats, *4:* 591
Reagan, Ronald
affirmative action policy, *1:* 36,
169; *3:* 534
civil rights policy, *3:* 407
conservative staff, *3:* 533
critics, *1:* 46
education policy, *2:* 318, 320, 365
foreign policy, *4:* 592
judicial appointments, *3:* 518
Martin Luther King holiday,
3: 419 (ill.), 420
military policy, *4:* 591–92
President's Summit for America's
Future, *4:* 593
supporters, *1:* 18
war on drugs, *2:* 287; *3:* 560
Reason, J. Paul, *4:* 576, **595–99,** 595
(ill.)
recessions. *See* economic downturns
Reconstruction era, *4:* 699
record label originators, *1:* 149, 151,
159–60, 171; *4:* 644, 653–54, 660,
681
Recovery for Auto Communities and
Workers, *1:* 186
recruitment, military, *4:* 600, 610, 612,
615–16, 816
Red Guard, *1:* 39
Redding, Noel, *4:* 641–42
Redding, Otis, *4:* 660–62, 661 (ill.)
redistricting, political, *3:* 383, 391, 393,
394, 405, 411–12, 421
Redman, John, *2:* 337
Reed, Ishmael, *1:* 109–10
reference works, African American
history/culture, *2:* 336–37; *4:* 810
*Reflecting Black: African-American
Cultural Criticism* (Dyson),
2: 328–29
reform and activism. *See* activism and
reform (chapter)

Regents of the University of California v. Bakke (1978), *1:* 35–36, 168; *3:* 508, 540–41, 543
    dissenting opinion, *3:* 562–64
    majority opinion, *1:* 191–94
religion (chapter)
    chronology, *4:* 696–98
    headline makers, *4:* 702–24
    overview, *4:* 699–701
    primary sources, *4:* 748–53
    topics in the news, *4:* 725–47
Render, Frank, II, *4:* 607
reparations
    Black Panthers support, *1:* 49, 64
    overviews, *1:* 6, 49–52, 68
    Resolution 40, *1:* 50–51, 68–70
Reparations Coordinating Committee, *1:* 51–52
Reserve Officer Training Corps (ROTC), *4:* 589
Resolution 1441 (United Nations), *4:* 618, 620
restaurants and owners, *1:* 150, 173–77, 174 (ill.), 180
reverse discrimination, *1:* 34–36, 35 (ill.), 142, 168, 169; *3:* 540–41
Revolutionary Association of the Women of Afghanistan (RAWA), *1:* 53
Rhimes, Shonda, *2:* 222–23, 222 (ill.), 254
Riccardi, Michael, *1:* 30–31
Ricci v. DiStefano (2009), *1:* 36
Rice, Condoleezza, *3:* 384, 399–402, 400 (ill.); *4:* 594
Rich, Marc, *3:* 518–19
Rich, Matty, *2:* 247
Richards, Ann, *3:* 392
Richie, Lionel, *2:* 216; *4:* 646, 674
Rickover, Hyman, *4:* 596–97
Ride, Sally K., *4:* 794
right to fair trial, *1:* 65; *3:* 528, 547, 549. *See also* juries; prisoners
Ringgold, Faith, *1:* 78, 99–102, 99 (ill.), 120
riots, *2:* 272, 302
    busing- and integration-related, *2:* 349

Detroit, 1967, *2:* 327; *4:* 612
newspaper coverage/controversies, *2:* 232
post-King assassination, 1968, *1:* 5, 17, 43; *3:* 409–10; *4:* 612
post-Rodney King beating, Los Angeles, 1992, *1:* 15, 33, 53; *3:* 509, 548
Watts, Los Angeles, 1965, *1:* 14–15, 82; *2:* 235; *4:* 612
Wilmington Ten case, *1:* 10–11, 11–12
Robert C. Maynard Institute for Journalism Education, *2:* 220–21
Robert Wood Johnson Minority Faculty Development Program, *3:* 470–71
Robinson, Bill "Bojangles," *1:* 86, 87
Robinson, Frank, *4:* 684–85
Robinson, Jackie, *4:* 633
Robinson, Smokey, *4:* 660
Robinson, T. J., *1:* 180
Rocawear (clothing line), *4:* 679 (ill.), 680
Rock and Roll Hall of Fame inductees, *4:* 637, 639, 655
Rock, Chris, *2:* 256
Rockefeller, Nelson, *1:* 157–58
rocketry, *4:* 768
Roe v. Wade (1973), *3:* 551
Roman Catholicism. *See* Catholic Church
Rooney, Dan, *4:* 686
Roosevelt, Franklin D., *4:* 582
Roots (miniseries), *2:* 252
Roscoe's House of Chicken 'n Waffles, *1:* 176
Ross, Diana, *2:* 242; *4:* 644, 665
ROTC (Reserve Officer Training Corps), *4:* 589
Roundtree, Richard, *2:* 240, 240 (ill.), 241
Rowe, Debbie, *4:* 647
Rubin, Rick, *1:* 159
Ruined (Nottage), *1:* 116
Rumsfeld, Donald, *4:* 594
Run-DMC, *1:* 149, 153, 159, 160; *4:* 677, 677 (ill.), 682

RuPaul, *2:* 297
Rush Artist Management, *1:* 159
Rush, Bobby L., *4:* 807–8
Russell, Bill, *4:* 684
Russell Simmons Music, *1:* 160
Rustin, Bayard, *1:* 9, 61–62
Ruth, Babe, *4:* 631, 667 (ill.), 668–69

S

Salt-N-Pepa, *1:* 153; *4:* 683
same-sex marriage debate, *4:* 745, 746
sampling, *4:* 681–82
San Antonio Express-
News (newspaper), *2:* 207
San Antonio Independent School District
v. Rodriguez (1973), *3:* 524
San Francisco Giants, *4:* 634–35
San Francisco State College, *2:* 343,
344 (ill.)
Sanchez, Sonia, *1:* 107, 114
Sanford and Son (television show),
2: 203, 243, 251, 299
Satel, Sally, *3:* 496–99
Saturday Night Live (television
program), *2:* 245
savings, personal, *2:* 300
"Say It Loud—I'm Black and I'm
Proud" (Brown), *4:* 632, 637,
687–88, 687 (ill.)
school choice
African-centered schools, *2:* 351
charter schools, *2:* 354, 357 (ill.)
unhelpful for desegregation,
2: 315, 346, 369–71
School Daze (film), *2:* 219, 246
school desegregation. *See Brown v.*
Board of Education of Topeka,
Kansas (1954); busing; integration;
Marshall, Thurgood; *Swann v.*
Charlotte-Mecklenburg Board of
Education (1971)
school systems, and economics, *2:* 291,
316, 352, 358–59, 359 (ill.); *4:* 804
school takeovers, *2:* 358–63
school violence
anti-integration-related, *2:* 348–50
charter schools, *2:* 356

Eastside High School, and Joe
Clark, *2:* 319
urban schools, *2:* 358
school voucher plans, *2:* 341, 351
Schweitzer, Albert, *3:* 443
Science and Engineering Apprentice
Program (SEAP), *4:* 771
science and math education, *4:* 761–62,
771, 787, 803–6, 805 (ill.)
science and technology (chapter)
chronology, *4:* 758–60
headline makers, *4:* 763–87
overview, *4:* 761–62
primary sources, *4:* 813–18
topics in the news, *4:* 788–812
science degrees, *1:* 183; *2:* 316; *4:* 771
science fiction writers, *1:* 85
scientists, *4:* 761, 803–4, 805–6. *See*
also astrophysicists; chemists;
computer scientists; engineers;
inventors and inventions;
mathematicians; physicists
Scott, Bobby, *3:* 418 (ill.)
Scott, Roland, *3:* 440
Scott, Tony, *2:* 248
Scowcroft, Brent, *3:* 401
screenwriters, *2:* 218–19, 223, 244
Seale, Bobby, *1:* 5, 14, 16, 39, 41, 42,
64; *4:* 664
Sean John/Sean by Sean Combs
(fashion lines), *1:* 148, 150, 151;
4: 679, 680
search engines, *2:* 238
"second generation rights," *2:* 315–16
Second Great Migration, *1:* 183;
2: 301
Second Morrill Land Grant Act (1890),
2: 363
secondary education, and multicultural
awareness, *2:* 316, 317. *See also* high
school graduation rates
secretaries of state, *3:* 384, 399, 400
(ill.), 402; *4:* 588, 594–95, 617
security systems, *4:* 800
segregation. *See also Brown v. Board of*
Education of Topeka, Kansas (1954);
Supreme Court
colleges examples, *3:* 521, 528

military, *4:* 582, 610–11
political platforms, *1:* 9
Selassie, Haile, *4:* 700, 729
self-defense, *1:* 5, 16, 30, 37, 39–41, 64, 65, 106. *See also* Black Panther Party
self-help books, *4:* 722
self-improvement, *1:* 106
Selfridge Field air base, *4:* 582
Selig, Bud, *4:* 635
Senate
    Judiciary Committee, confirmations and hearings, *3:* 515 (ill.), 516, 522, 523, 530, 534–35, 550 (ill.), 551–52
    Carol Moseley-Braun, *3:* 395–96
    Barack Obama, *3:* 398–99, 422
sentencing, drug crimes
    laws/policies, *2:* 287, 290, 291; *3:* 560, 561
    prison populations, *2:* 289–90; *3:* 560, 561
"separate but equal" precedent, *3:* 522; *4:* 582
separatism philosophy, *1:* 5–6, 32, 39, 49, 78
    black arts movement, *1:* 106, 107, 111
    religions, *1:* 32, 48, 49; *4:* 699, 700, 705, 707, 729, 734, 739
September 11, 2001 terrorist attacks, *4:* 576
    American Express assistance, *1:* 147
    Bush administration opinions, *3:* 401
    Cynthia McKinney commentary, *3:* 394
    Jeremiah Wright commentary, *4:* 727
    Nation of Islam response, *4:* 749–53
    reportage, *2:* 208, 222
"set asides" (quotas), *1:* 36, 168, 169, 169 (ill.), 191; *3:* 540–41, 562
Set It Off (film), *2:* 249
settlements for slavery. *See* reparations
sex educators, *3:* 464–65

sexual abuse scandal, Catholic Church, *4:* 701, 709, 710–11
sexual harassment
    Clarence Thomas confirmation hearings, *3:* 515–17, 530, 534, 549, 551, 552
    military cases, *4:* 598, 609
sexually transmitted diseases, *3:* 440, 464, 485–86. *See also* HIV/AIDS epidemic; Tuskegee syphilis study
Shabazz, Quibilah, *4:* 709
Shaft (film), *2:* 240–41, 240 (ill.), 249
Shakur, Tupac, *2:* 329; *4:* 684
Shalala, Donna, *4:* 495–96
Shange, Ntozake, *1:* 102–4, 102 (ill.), 110, 114
Sharpton, Al, *1:* 28–31, 28 (ill.); *4:* 726
    Amadou Diallo case, *3:* 548–49
    Jena Six case, *1:* 59–60, 60 (ill.)
    as pastor, *4:* 700–701, 714, 746
Shaw, Bernard, *2:* 224–25, 224 (ill.)
Shaw, Herman, *3:* 495, 496
Sheldon, Lou, *1:* 10; *4:* 745
Shepard, Matthew, *3:* 555
Sheridan Broadcasting Network. *See* Mutual Black Network
Sherman, William Tecumseh, *1:* 49
She's Gotta Have It (film), *2:* 203, 218, 219, 246
Shurney, Robert E., *4:* 791
sickle cell anemia, *3:* 440–41, 488–89, 489 (ill.)
    awareness, *3:* 490
    cure hopes and research, *3:* 489–92
Sickle Cell Anemia Control Act (1972), *3:* 440
The Signifying Monkey: Towards a Theory of Afro-American Literature (Gates), *2:* 336
Silent Gesture (Smith), *4:* 690–91
Silicon Graphics Incorporated, *4:* 799
Silver Streak (film), *2:* 244
Simmons, Kimora Lee, *1:* 160; *4:* 650–52, 651 (ill.), 679
Simmons Jewelry Co., *1:* 160
Simmons, Russell, *1:* 14, 159–60, 159 (ill.), 171; *4:* 651, 652, 678

Simpson, Delmar, *4:* 609

Sims, Naomi, *1:* 178

Singin' and Swingin' and Gettin' Merry Like Christmas (Angelou), *1:* 82

single-mother families, *2:* 291, 292, 295, 296; *3:* 559–60

single-parent families, *2:* 294–95

Singleton, John, *2:* 203, 247, 248, 250

sitcoms, *2:* 203, 250–51, 252–53, 254. *See also* specific sitcoms

Sixteenth Street Baptist Church bombing, 1963, *1:* 19; *4:* 700

60 Minutes (television program), *2:* 207, 208

slang, *2:* 336

slavery, *1:* 38, 68–69; *3:* 546. *See also* reparations

    affirmative action relevance, *3:* 562–63

    census data, *2:* 271, 284

    economic effects on blacks, *1:* 141, 180

    inventions, *4:* 797

    literary themes and portrayals, *1:* 95–96, 97, 98, 125, 127

    outlawed, *3:* 544

    related foods/recipes, *1:* 174, 176

    religion, *4:* 699, 728, 748

    study, *1:* 51, 68, 69–70

Sly & the Family Stone, *4:* 662, 670

Smalls, Biggie, *1:* 149, 150

The Smiley Report (radio program), *2:* 226

Smiley, Tavis, *2:* **225–27,** 226 (ill.)

Smith, Bev, *2:* 237

Smith, Cheryl A., *1:* 173

Smith, Lovie, *4:* 685 (ill.), 686

Smith, Nick, *4:* 808–9

Smith, Tommie, *2:* 332; *4:* 632, 663 (ill.), 664–65, 690–91

Smith, Will, *2:* 203, **227–28,** 227 (ill.), 242–43, 254; *4:* 678

Snipes, Wesley, *1:* 177

social criticism

    Bill Cosby, *2:* 213, 353

    Michael Eric Dyson, *2:* 328–30

social gospel movement, *4:* 699

social networking sites, *2:* 204, 238, 239; *4:* 802

social theorists, *2:* 274, 275–76, 276–80

A Soldier's Play (Fuller), *1:* 115; *2:* 231

Soledad Brothers, *1:* 20–21

Somalia, *4:* 593, 613

"Somebody Blew Up America" (Baraka), *1:* 125

Song of Solomon (Morrison), *1:* 95, 96–97, 126–27, 133

sonic boom research, *4:* 771, 773–74

Sotomayor, Sonia, *1:* 36

soul food, *1:* 174–75, 177

soul music, *4:* 632, 636–37, 638–39, 641, 660–62, 669

Soul on Ice (Cleaver), *1:* 14, 16–17

Soul Train (television program), *2:* 209–10

South African apartheid

    American opponents, *1:* 32–33; *2:* 332; *3:* 413, 532; *4:* 655, 663, 726

    Olympic Games and, *4:* 663

South Boston High School, *2:* 349, 349 (ill.)

South Carolina v. Katzenbach (1966), *3:* 537

South Central (television program), *2:* 205

Southern Christian Leadership Conference (SCLC), *1:* 5, 42

    and Black Leadership Forum, *3:* 418

    members, *1:* 29, 44–45, 82

south-north migration, *1:* 183; *2:* 271–72, 300–302, 306, 348

Soviet Union, *3:* 401; *4:* 662–63

Soyinka, Wole, *2:* 335

space exploration. *See* astronauts; astrophysicists; National Aeronautics and Space Administration (NASA)

space photography, *4:* 767, 767 (ill.), 769–70, 771, 791

Speakers of the House, *3:* 387

special education, *2:* 340–41

special effects engineering, *4:* 799

Spelman College, *2:* 324, 364
   National Women's Health
      Imperative, *3:* 492
   presidents, *2:* 321–22, 324–26,
      324 (ill.)
spinning (records), *4:* 680–81
spirituals, *4:* 748–49, 748 (ill.)
sports and activism, *2:* 330–33;
   4: 602–6, 603 (ill.), 632, 663–65,
   663 (ill.), 690–91
sports management and owners,
   1: 155; *4:* 631, 650. *See also* coaches
sportswear. *See* fashion lines
St. Louis American (newspaper),
   2: 233–34
Stallings, George, *4:* 743, 744 (ill.)
Stand! (Sly & the Family Stone), *4:* 662
Standard English Proficiency (SEP)
   program, *2:* 353
standardized tests and scores
   charter schools, *2:* 355
   college entrance, historically black
      colleges, *2:* 367
   improvement plans/proposals,
      2: 352–53
   as learning/accountability
      measure, *2:* 340, 341
   racial achievement gap, *2:* 291,
      316
stand-up comedians, *2:* 212, 244, 244
   (ill.), 245
Stanley v. Georgia (1969), *3:* 523
state and federal jobs. *See* government
   contracts, and equal employment/
   affirmative action; government jobs
state legislators, *3:* 384
   Shirley Chisholm, *3:* 386
   Keith Ellison, *3:* 389
   Barbara Jordan, *3:* 391
   Carol Moseley-Braun, *3:* 395
   Constance Baker Motley, *3:* 526,
      528
   Barack Obama, *3:* 398, 422
   Harold Washington, *3:* 420
   J. C. Watts Jr., *3:* 403
   L. Douglas Wilder, *3:* 405
state takeovers, failing schools,
   2: 358–63

State University of New York, *2:* 345
Stax Records, *4:* 660
STDs. *See* sexually transmitted diseases
Stein-Evers, Michelle, *4:* 730
stem cell research, *3:* 491–92
stereotypes
   gender and education, *2:* 292
   gender and sexuality, *2:* 297
   racial profiling, *3:* 509, 557–58
stereotypes, media portrayals
   film, *2:* 202, 203, 240, 241, 246,
      248
   journalism, *2:* 209, 232, 233
   television, *2:* 203, 213, 250–51,
      252, 255
steroid use, *4:* 631, 634, 635
Stevens, Lisa, *4:* 792 (ill.), 793
Stevens, Nelson, *1:* 119
Steward, David L., *1:* **161–62,** 171
Still Here (dance), *1:* 89
stockades, military, *4:* 606–7
Stokes, Carl, *3:* 383
Stone, Sly, *2:* 202, 235; *4:* 662, 670
story quilts, *1:* 99, 99 (ill.), 101–2, 120
Straight Out of Brooklyn (film), *2:* 247
stroke rates and risks, *3:* 475, 476, 487,
   488, 492
student activism, *2:* 331–32, 343–44,
   344 (ill.), 345
student athletes, *2:* 330–31
Student Nonviolent Coordinating
   Committee (SNCC), *1:* 5
   members, *1:* 20, 22, 37; *2:* 288
   and reparations, *1:* 49–50
Students for a Democratic Society
   (SDS), *1:* 39
style. *See* fashion
subatomic particle research, *4:* 779–80
subprime mortgage crisis, *2:* 300
suburban life. *See* urban vs. suburban
   life
Sudan, *3:* 414
Sugarhill Gang, *4:* 681
Sugarhill Records, *4:* 681
Sula (Morrison), *1:* 95, 97
Summer, Donna, *4:* 672
Summers, Larry, *1:* 33
Sun Belt populations, *2:* 302–3

Sun Ra, *1:* 113, 116

Sunni Islam, *4:* 708, 735

Super Fly (film), *2:* 241

Super Soaker water gun, *4:* 798–99

supercomputing, *4:* 776–77, 810

superconductors, *4:* 779

superdelegates, *3:* 424

supersonic research, *4:* 771, 773–74

Supreme Court

    affirmative action, cases, *1:* 6, 35–36, 168, 169, 170 (ill.), 191–94; *3:* 508, 535, 540–44, 562–67

    African American justices, *3:* 519–24, 520 (ill.), 531–35, 531 (ill.), 535 (ill.)

    busing/integration, cases and influence, *2:* 272, 315, 346–50, 352

    Civil Rights Acts and, *3:* 544, 545–46

    confirmation hearings, *1:* 36; *3:* 515–17, 515 (ill.), 530, 534–35, 549–53, 550 (ill.)

    desegregation, cases (business), *1:* 175

    desegregation, cases (education), *1:* 180–81; *2:* 271, 315, 346, 369–71; *3:* 522, 528

    employment discrimination, cases, *1:* 141

    First Amendment-related cases, *3:* 523, 555

    Fourteenth Amendment coverage ruling, *3:* 544

    hate crimes laws, *3:* 509

    historically black colleges and universities cases, *3:* 535

    homosexuality, cases, *2:* 297

    interracial marriage constitutionality, cases, *2:* 271, 280, 280 (ill.), 282, 283, 293, 297, 304–6

    redistricting decisions, *3:* 394

    voting rights cases, *3:* 537, 538, 539–40

surgeons

    eye surgery, *3:* 442, 445, 446–48

    heart surgery, *3:* 467, 469–70

    neurosurgery, *3:* 448–50, 454–60

surgeons general, *3:* 460, 465–66

surveillance. *See* Federal Bureau of Investigation (FBI)

Swann v. Charlotte-Mecklenburg Board of Education (1971), *2:* 272, 315, 346–47, 347 (ill.)

Sweet Sweetback's Baadasssss Song (film), *2:* 239–40

Sykes, Wanda, *2:* 257, 364

Sylvia's Restaurant, *1:* 174–75, 174 (ill.)

Symantec Corporation, *4:* 811–12, 812 (ill.)

syndicated radio programs, *2:* 217

syphilis rates, *3:* 486. *See also* Tuskegee syphilis study

syrup, *1:* 176

T

T. D. Jakes Ministries, *4:* 713–14

tagging. *See* graffiti art

takeovers, failing schools, *2:* 358–63

talk shows

    radio, *1:* 26; *2:* 202, 235, 237, 330

    television, *1:* 162, 163–64; *2:* 202, 203, 215, 226, 253–54, 256

TALKERS (magazine), *2:* 237

Tamayo-Mendez, Arnaldo, *4:* 764, 791

tap dancers, *1:* 86–87

Tapping the Power Within (Vanzant), *4:* 722

Tavis Smiley Foundation, *2:* 226

Tavis Smiley (television program), *2:* 226

taxes

    busing costs, *2:* 350

    prison system usage, *2:* 291

    schools support, *2:* 357; *3:* 524; *4:* 804

    2008 election issue, *3:* 425

Taylor, Susan L., *2:* 202, **228–29**, **228 (ill.)**, 234

Teachers Insurance and Annuity Association-College Retirement Equities Fund (TIAA-CREF), *1:* 171

technology and society, *4:* 762,
800–803. *See also* digital divide;
information technology industry
teen pregnancy
blacks vs. non-blacks, *2:* 291, 295;
3: 440
economic struggles, *2:* 295–96
medical providers' observations/
care, *3:* 463–64
prevention, *1:* 23, 24; *3:* 440
Telecommunications Act (1996)
deregulation and media
consolidation, *2:* 204, 236–37,
260–62
information access and education,
4: 762, 806–8
telemedicine, *3:* 447 (ill.), 448
television journalists, *2:* 202, 207–8,
209, 216, 222, 224–25
television networks, diversity issues,
1: 27; *2:* 202; *4:* 579. *See also* BET
(Black Entertainment Television);
cable networks; media ownership
and diversity
television programs, *2:* 203, 250–54,
256–57. *See also* specific programs
television writers, *2:* 205–6, 222–23,
253
Temple University, *2:* 344
tennis players, *4:* 631, 633, 633 (ill.),
652–53, 652 (ill.), 658, 659
Tereshkova, Valentina, *4:* 791
terrorism. *See also* September 11, 2001
terrorist attacks
civil liberties issues and, *3:* 389
domestic incidents, anti-civil
rights movement, *1:* 19; *4:* 700
Iraq fears and accusations, *4:* 576,
594, 617–20
test scores, educational.
See standardized tests and scores
Texas, Lawrence v. (2003), *2:* 297
Texas State University, *2:* 339
textile arts, *1:* 99, 99 (ill.), 101–2, 120
theoretical physicists, *4:* 778–84, 800
Theus, Lucius D., *4:* 608
*Think Big: Unleashing Your Potential for
Excellence* (Carson), *3:* 459

Third World Press, *1:* 108
third-party presidential candidates,
1: 17; *3:* 395
Thirteenth Amendment, *3:* 544
Thomas and Beulah (Dove), *1:* 124
Thomas, Clarence, 3, 524, **531–35,
531 (ill.), 535 (ill.)**
affirmative action opposition,
1: 31; *3:* 532–33, 534, 550,
564–67
confirmation hearings and Anita
Hill, *3:* 515–17, 515 (ill.), 530,
534–35, 549–53, 550 (ill.)
dissent, *Grutter v.
Bollinger* (2003), *3:* 564–67
NAACP investigation, *3:* 530, 534,
550
Thomas, Rufus, *2:* 236 (ill.)
Thomas-Richardson, Valerie L., *4:* 794
Thompson, John Henry, *4:* 811
Thompson, John W., *4:* 811–12, 812
(ill.)
Thriller (Jackson), *4:* 645, 675, 676
TIAA-CREF (Teachers Insurance and
Annuity Association-College
Retirement Equities Fund), *1:* 171
Till, Emmett, *1:* 15
Time Warner, *1:* 157, 158–59, 172
(ill.); *4:* 808
timelines. *See* chronologies
Toche, Jean, *1:* 120
Tolan, Robbie, *3:* 557
Tom Joyner Foundation, *2:* 217–18
The Tom Joyner Morning Show (radio
program), *2:* 216, 217, 226
The Tom Joyner Show (television
program), *2:* 218
Tommy Boy Records, *4:* 682
The Tonight Show (television program),
2: 212
Tony Award winners, *1:* 89, 150–51
Topdog/Underdog (Parks), *1:* 98, 116
Touré, Askia M., *1:* 107
"Toward a Black Aesthetic" (Fuller),
1: 107
Townes, Jeffrey, *2:* 227
Towns, Edolphus, *4:* 808, 809
Townsend, Robert, *2:* 246

traditional foods, and restaurants, *1:* 173–77

traditional jazz, *1:* 79, 91, 117–18

Traditional Values Coalition, *1:* 10; *4:* 745

Transportation Auditing Services, *1:* 161

Transportation Business Services, *1:* 161

transportation challenges, *1:* 187–88

Travis Air Force Base, *4:* 607

A Tribe Called Quest, *4:* 683

Trinity United Church of Christ, *4:* 701, 722, 724, 727, 727 (ill.), 728, 745

Truman, Harry, *4:* 575

Truth, Sojourner, *1:* 49

turntable spinning, *4:* 680–81

Tuskegee Airmen, *4:* 582–83, 789

Tuskegee Institute, *3:* 472, 495; *4:* 581

Tuskegee syphilis study, *3:* 472–74, 494

    apology, *3:* 473, 494–96, 494 (ill.)

TV One, *2:* 255, 256

2 Live Crew, *2:* 336; *4:* 683

Tyson, Neil deGrasse, *4:* 805

U

ultraviolet astrophysics, *4:* 767, 767 (ill.), 768–69, 770, 791

unemployment rates, *1:* 186, 188; *2:* 285; *3:* 477

    ex-convicts, *3:* 559

United Airlines, *4:* 790

United Black Students for Action (USBA), *2:* 331–32

United Church of Christ, *4:* 701, 722

United Nations, *1:* 25

    Security Council presentation, Colin Powell, *4:* 594, 617–20, 617 (ill.)

    Universal Declaration of Human Rights, *2:* 315

United Negro College Fund, *2:* 368

    digital divide testimony, *4:* 813–15

historically black colleges and universities support, *2:* 366; *4:* 813–15

    Michael Jackson giving, *4:* 646

    students, *4:* 814, 815

Unity Fellowship Church Movement, *1:* 62

Universal Declaration of Human Rights (1948), *2:* 315

universities. *See* college and university faculty; college enrollment and graduation; colleges, segregation

University of California, affirmative action case (*Bakke*), *1:* 35–36, 168, 191–94; *3:* 508, 540–41, 543, 563–64

University of Michigan, affirmative action cases (*Grutter; Gratz*), *1:* 35 (ill.); *3:* 508, 535, 542 (ill.), 543, 564–67, 564 (ill.)

University of Mississippi, desegregation cases, *3:* 528

University of Texas, affirmative action cases, *3:* 542–43

University of Washington, affirmative action cases, *1:* 35, 168

Unseld, Wes, *4:* 663

Uptown Records, *1:* 149, 150

urban contemporary radio, *2:* 236

urban decay, *2:* 272, 348, 358, 360

urban fashion. *See* fashion lines

urban vs. suburban life

    blacks transition to suburbs, *2:* 301

    census data, *2:* 284–85

    job locations and transportation, *1:* 187–88; *2:* 272

    school choice and busing, *2:* 352

    school systems, economic differences, *2:* 316, 352, 358–59, 359 (ill.); *4:* 804

    white flight, *1:* 43–44; *2:* 239, 272, 348, 352

U.S. Air Force, personnel, *4:* 580, 581 (ill.), 582–86, 585 (ill.), 608, 614, 615, 763–64, 788, 790, 794

U.S. Army, *4:* 614

    integration, *4:* 575

officials, *4:* 577, 579–80, 588, 589–92, 589 (ill.), 620–23

U.S. attorneys, *3:* 518, 522–23

U.S. Commission on Civil Rights, reports, *2:* 373–74

U.S. Conference of Catholic Bishops, *4:* 709, 711, 743–44

U.S. Constitution, *3:* 390, 392, 428–30, 507, 536, 544

U.S. Department of Education, officials, *2:* 338, 339 (ill.), 341–42, 342 (ill.), 362

U.S. Marine Corps, personnel, *4:* 614–15, 816

U.S. Navy, personnel, *4:* 576, 595–99, 595 (ill.), 614, 615

U.S. Nuclear Regulatory Commission (NRC), *4:* 781–83, 781 (ill.), 800

U.S. Postal Service, *1:* 187

U.S. Public Health Service, *3:* 472, 494

U.S. v. Fordice (1992), *3:* 535

V

vaccination rates, *3:* 446, 464, 475

Van Peebles, Mario, *2:* 203, 239, 247, 248, 249–50

Van Peebles, Melvin, *2:* 239–40

Vanilla Ice, *4:* 683

Vanzant, Iyanla, *4:* 720–22, 720 (ill.)

The Venus Hottentot (Alexander), *1:* 124–25

Viacom, *1:* 155, 157; *2:* 226, 255; *4:* 808

Vick, Michael, *2:* 333; *3:* 519

video activism, *1:* 53

video game inventors, *4:* 799

videotape evidence, *1:* 52–53; *3:* 547, 547 (ill.)

Vietnam, *1:* 39; *2:* 208

Vietnam War, *4:* 600
   draft, and black participation ratios, *4:* 575, 600–602, 600 (ill.), 606, 608, 613–14
   draft refusals, *4:* 602–6, 603 (ill.)
   military personnel/veterans, *1:* 63; *4:* 583–84, 590, 602, 763–64
   politicians' stances, *3:* 386, 413

protests and protesters, *1:* 9, 16, 61–62; *2:* 345; *4:* 575, 584, 601–2, 601 (ill.), 700

racial violence, *4:* 606–9, 614

reporters, *2:* 208

violence in schools. *See* school violence

Virginia, Loving v. (1967), *2:* 271, 280, 280 (ill.), 281–82, 283, 293, 297, 304–6

Virginia Tech University, *1:* 125

visual art and artists, *1:* 78, 79, 83–85, 99–102, 118–23, 131–32

voter intimidation, *3:* 507, 536, 538

voter registration workers
   Black Leadership Forum, *3:* 418, 419
   legal support, *1:* 22–23
   Rainbow/PUSH Coalition, *1:* 47

voters. *See* black voters, influence

Voting Rights Act (1965), *3:* 383, 407, 411, 507, 536–40
   legal challenges, *3:* 537, 538–40
   voting increases, *3:* 537–38, 537 (ill.)

voting rights, practical history, *3:* 507, 536–40, 537 (ill.)

vouchers, education, *2:* 341, 351

W

wage gap, *1:* 141, 142, 180–82, 187; *2:* 273, 285
   and health care, *3:* 476–77, 497
   improvements, *2:* 284, 284 (ill.)

Waiting to Exhale (McMillan), *1:* 128

Walker, Alice
   life and career, *1:* 78, **104–5,** 126, 164
   womanism, *1:* 47, 48, 61, 126; *4:* 740, 740 (ill.), 741

Walker, Bill, *1:* 118, 119

Walker, Jimmy, *2:* 250–51

Walker, T. Bone, *4:* 640

Wall of Respect, *1:* 118–19

war on drugs, *2:* 287; *3:* 560–61

war on terror, *3:* 394

War Resisters League, *1:* 9, 61–62

Ward, Anita, *4:* 672

Ward, Lloyd, *1:* 171–72

Ware, Lincoln, *2:* 237

Warhol, Andy, *1:* 85

Warren Court, *3:* 523

Warren, Earl, *2:* 304–6; *3:* 523, 538

Washington, D.C.
  Beltway Sniper case, 2002, *3:* 524, 525 (ill.), 526
  D.C. Circuit Court, *3:* 510, 511–12, 534, 549
  King assassination and, *1:* 43–44; *3:* 409–10
  mayors, *2:* 288; *3:* 409–11
  populations, *2:* 302
  voting rights and self-government history, *2:* 288; *3:* 409, 410

Washington, Denzel, *1:* 177; *2:* 203, 219, **229–31, 230 (ill.),** 248, 248 (ill.)

Washington, Harold, *3:* 420–21

Washington Post (newspaper), *2:* 216, 220, 221–22

Washington, Robin, *4:* 730

Washington, Walter, *1:* 43; *3:* 409–10, 409 (ill.)

Washington Week (television program), *2:* 216

Washington Wizards, *4:* 650

Watergate scandal, *3:* 428, 429–30

Waters, Maxine, *1:* 160

Waters, Muddy, *4:* 640

Watkins, Levi, Jr., *3:* 467–71

Watkins, Perry, *1:* 61, 63

Watts, J. C., Jr., *3:* **402–4, 402 (ill.)**

Watts, Los Angeles riots, 1965, *1:* 14–15, 82; *2:* 235; *4:* 612

Wayans, Keenen Ivory, *2:* 254

We a BaddDDD People (Sanchez), *1:* 107

"We Are the World" (song), *4:* 646

weapons of mass destruction (WMDs), *2:* 402; *4:* 576, 594, 616, 617–20

Web sites, *2:* 238–39; *4:* 811
  Black Career Women, *1:* 180
  Black Enterprise, *2:* 215
  NetNoir, *4:* 810–11
  social networking, *2:* 204, 238, 239; *4:* 802

TheRoot.com, *2:* 337
  360hiphop.com, *1:* 160
  Oprah Winfrey, *1:* 164; *2:* 203

Webster (television program), *2:* 252

Weeks, Thomas, III, *4:* 704

Weinberger, Caspar, *4:* 590, 591

welfare reform, *3:* 408, 413, 418, 478

Wesley, Richard, *1:* 114

West Africa, disease links
  breast cancer, *3:* 481–82
  sickle cell anemia, *3:* 489

West, Cornel, *1:* **31–33, 31 (ill.)**
  collaborations, *1:* 33; *2:* 336, 344

West, Kanye, *4:* 684

Wharton, Clifton R., Jr., *1:* 171; *2:* 345

What's Black about It? Insights to Increase Your Share of a Changing African-American Market (Miller and Kemp), *1:* 173

What's Happening!! (television program), *2:* 252

Wheatley, Phillis, *1:* 125

Wheelus Air Force Base (Libya), *4:* 584, 585 (ill.)

When the Levees Broke: A Requiem in Four Acts (Lee documentary), *2:* 219–20, 249

Whitaker, Forest, *2:* 248

White, Barry, *4:* 669, 680

white flight, *1:* 43–44; *2:* 239, 272, 348, 352

White, Jaleel, *2:* 254

white supremacist crime and terrorism, *1:* 19; *3:* 554; *4:* 607 (ill.), 700

Wilder, Gene, *2:* 244

Wilder, L. Douglas, *3:* 384, **404–6, 404 (ill.)**

Williams, Delores, *1:* 48; *4:* 739, 740, 741

Williams, Gerald, *1:* 119

Williams, Lindsey, *1:* 177

Williams, Robert F., *1:* 39

Williams, Robert L., *2:* 352

Williams, Serena, *4:* 631, **652–53, 652 (ill.),** 659

Williams, Venus, *4:* 631, **652–53, 652 (ill.),** 659

Williams, Willie, *1:* 54

Williamson, Fred, *2:* 240

Wilmington Ten, *1:* 10–11, 11–12

Wilson, August, *1:* 79, 116

Wilson, Flip, *2:* 243, 251–52

Wilson, Harriet E., *2:* 335

Wilson, Pete, *1:* 169–70; *3:* 510

Wilson, William Julius, *2:* 344

Wimbledon Championships, *4:* 633, 652 (ill.), 653, 659

Winfrey, Oprah, *1:* **162–65,** 163 (ill.), 171, 180; *2:* 292

    artist championing, *1:* 83, 96–97, 164

    O, The Oprah Magazine, *1:* 165; *2:* 234–35

    The Oprah Winfrey Show, *1:* 162, 163–64; *2:* 203, 253–54

    wealth, *1:* 164, 165; *2:* 292

Wisconsin v. Mitchell (1993), *3:* 555

The Wiz (film), *2:* 242; *4:* 644

Wolfe, George, *1:* 87, 116

Woman, Thou Art Loosed (Jakes), *4:* 712, 713

womanist movement, *1:* 47–49; *4:* 740 (ill.)

    activists, *1:* 8, 10

    central texts, *1:* 126; *4:* 741

    political lead-up, *1:* 6, 48; *4:* 704

    religious arena/womanist theology, *1:* 48; *4:* 700, 704, 715, 718, 739–42

women filmmakers, *2:* 249

women in business. *See also* entrepreneurs; executives

    Black Career Women (BCW), *1:* 142–43, 178–79, 180

    increasing entrepreneurship, *1:* 142–43, 178, 179–80

women military personnel, *4:* 580, 586–88, 614–15

The Women of Brewster Place (Naylor), *1:* 126

women presidential candidates, *3:* 385, 386, 395, 396

women religious leaders, *1:* 48; *4:* 701, 702–4, 714–22, 739–42

women writers, *1:* 78–79, 125–28; *2:* 335. *See also* children's writers; drama and dramatists; novelists; poetry and poets; specific writers

women's health issues, *3:* 475, 478, 481, 492–93

Wonder, Stevie, *2:* 236; *4:* **653–56,** 654 (ill.), 674

The Wonders of the African World (documentary miniseries), *2:* 336–37

Woods, Sylvia, *1:* 174–75, 174 (ill.), 177

Woods, Tiger, *4:* 631, **656–57,** 656 (ill.), 659

Woodstock Festival (1969), *4:* 642

Working While Black: The Black Person's Guide to Success in the White Workplace (Johnson), *1:* 173

workplace discrimination. *See* employment discrimination

workshops, arts, *1:* 109, 113, 118

workshops, business, *1:* 178–79

World Community of Al-Islam in the West, *4:* 708, 734

World War II

    Holocaust, *1:* 49, 64; *2:* 281

    troops integration, *4:* 575

    Tuskegee Airmen, *4:* 582–83, 789

World Wide Technology, *1:* 161–62, 171

Wright, Jeremiah, *4:* 701, **722–24,** 723 (ill.), 727–28, 727 (ill.), 745

writers. *See* autobiographical literature; children's writers; drama and dramatists; journalists; novelists; poetry and poets; science fiction writers; screenwriters; social theorists; television writers

writing workshops, *1:* 109

X

X (opera), *1:* 129

Xenogenesis trilogy (Butler), *1:* 85

Xerox Corporation, *1:* 144–45, 172; *4:* 809

x-ray spectrometer, *4:* 791–92

Index

Y

Yo! MTV Raps (television program), 2: 255; 4: 683
Yoruba priests, 4: 720, 721–22
Young & Rubicam Brands, 1: 172
Young, Coleman, 3: 414–15
Young, Larry, 2: 237
Young, Otis B., Jr., 4: 789
Young, Perry H., 4: 788

Z

Zami: A New Spelling of My Name (Lorde), 1: 123
Zane, Arnie, 1: 88–89
zoologists, 4: 792 (ill.), 793
Zumwalt, Elmo, 4: 608